Elie Wiesel and the Art of Storytelling

Edited by Rosemary Horowitz

McFarland & Company, Inc., Publishers

Jefferson, North Carolina, and London

LIBRARY OF CONGRESS CATALOGUING-IN-PUBLICATION DATA

Elie Wiesel and the art of storytelling / edited by Rosemary
    Horowitz.
        p.   cm.
    Includes bibliographical references and index.

    ISBN-13: 978-0-7864-2869-4
    (softcover : 50# alkaline paper) ∞

    1. Wiesel, Elie, 1928–   — Technique.   2. Storytelling in
literature.   I. Horowitz, Rosemary.
PQ2683.I32Z658   2006
813'.54 — dc22   2006028087

British Library cataloguing data are available

Cover art ©2006 Image Zoo Illustrations

Manufactured in the United States of America

*McFarland & Company, Inc., Publishers
    Box 611, Jefferson, North Carolina 28640
    www.mcfarlandpub.com*

Table of Contents

Preface   1

Introduction   3

Mosaics and Mirrors: Wiesel, American Autobiographies,
   and the Shaping of a Storied Subject
    Zoe Trodd   15

Creative Ambiguity in Wiesel's Storytelling
    Rosemary Horowitz   38

Elie Wiesel: Telling Stories of Children and Loss
    Katherine Lagrandeur   57

The Storyteller and His Quarrel with God
    Alan L. Berger   71

Wrestling with Oblivion: Wiesel's Autobiographical
   Storytelling as Midrash
    Deborah Lee Ames   90

The *Maggid* of Sighet: Jewish Contexts for Wiesel's Storytelling
    David Patterson   102

Laughter and the Limits of Holocaust Storytelling:
   Wiesel's *The Gates of the Forest*
    Jacqueline Bussie   123

Transfiguration
    Graham B. Walker, Jr.   156

The Artist as Witness, Prophet, and Encourager
    Carole J. Lambert   182

Shaliach Tzibor: Wiesel as Storyteller of His People
    Caren S. Neile   197

Teaching Beyond the Text: Examining and Acting On
  the Moral Aspects of *Night*
    Elaine O'Quinn   212

Afterword: *Night*— the Memoir — a Promise Fulfilled
    Miriam Klein Kassenoff   226

About the Contributors   231
Index   235

Preface

On October 14, 1986, the Nobel Committee named Elie Wiesel as the recipient of that year's Peace Prize. The press release announcing the award notes that:

> Wiesel is a messenger to mankind; his message is one of peace, atonement and human dignity. His belief that the forces fighting evil in the world can be victorious is a hard-won belief. His message is based on his own personal experience of total humiliation and of the utter contempt for humanity shown in Hitler's death camps. The message is in the form of a testimony, repeated and deepened through the works of a great author.

The repetition of "message" underscores the committee's position that Wiesel's beliefs about peace and justice permeate his substantial *oeuvre*. By contrast, Wiesel calls himself simply a teller of stories. Given that, it was not surprising that his Nobel lecture, entitled *Hope, Despair and Memory*, delivered on December 11, 1986, begins with a story. He starts the lecture by recounting an episode between the Hasidic master Baal-Shem-Tov and his servant, each of whom as a punishment lost the ability to pray. When pressed by his master to recall anything, the servant says that he remembers only the letters of the Hebrew alphabet. So, the two men begin to recite the letters, in effect, turning the alphabet into a prayer. Their passionate recitation was enough to restore the master's memory and undo the punishment. Wiesel explains that the story demonstrates the power of prayer, as well as the importance of memory. Wiesel continues the lecture by delving more deeply into the role of memory in contemporary affairs. At the end of his speech, Wiesel again mentions the Baal-Shem-Tov in order to re-emphasize that the need to remember is as great as ever. By connecting Hasidic and modern concerns, Wiesel reminds the audience that memory provides hope for all people. It is this ability to draw from religious, folk, and secular sources for diverse audiences that makes Wiesel a master storyteller. This collection of essays is about that mastery.

The authors of the essays in this collection discuss Wiesel as a storyteller by examining his texts from a variety of perspectives. Some of these writers focus on the religious influences on Wiesel's writing; others on the secular influences; and still others on the transformative effects of his stories on teachers and students. Taken as a whole, the essays cover a wide range of Wiesel's books. For those readers primarily familiar with *Night*, this collection will serve as an introduction to the breadth of Wiesel's writing. For those readers already familiar with his writings, this collection will yield new insights about his works. The ultimate goal is to deepen the appreciation of Wiesel's storytelling for all readers.

Introduction

Storytelling is a quintessential human activity. Yet, where people tell stories; the ways people tell stories; the purposes served by stories; and the values, attitudes, and beliefs toward stories vary across communities. Historical, economic, class, social, religious, gender, and other factors also affect stories and storytelling. Without a doubt, storytelling is a complex, fascinating phenomenon. There are many ways to explore that complexity. One way is to study the work of a master storyteller. Taking that approach, this volume looks closely at the works of Elie Wiesel, who is considered by many to be such a storyteller. Wiesel's mastery comes from his ability to adapt religious, folk, and secular texts and experiences for various audiences using a variety of genres. Combined with that is his ability to elevate storytelling to an ethical level. For him, storytelling is a form of activism. Elie Wiesel is the embodiment of Walter Benjamin's definition of an ideal storyteller. To Benjamin, the storyteller

> has counsel — not for a few situations, as the proverb does, but for many, like the sage.... His gift is the ability to relate his life; his distinction, to be able to tell his entire life. The storyteller: he is the man who could let the wick of his life be consumed completely by the gentle flame of his story. This is the basis of the incomparable aura of the storyteller, in Leslov as in Hauff, in Poe as in Stevenson. The storyteller is the figure in which the righteous man encounters himself.[1]

Like the writers on Benjamin's list, Wiesel draws on his life's experiences and uses them to teach his readers and listeners. He also uses them to promote a standard of conduct. To understand Wiesel's genius, though, it is first necessary to identify the sources of his storytelling in order to provide a context from which to more deeply appreciate his work.

An Overview of Jewish Storytelling

In her research, Barbara Kirshenblatt-Gimlett finds that for Eastern European Jewry "stories are important and storytelling is frequent in this culture."[2] She also finds that Eastern European Jews view storytelling as a cultural inclination. As she writes: "The Aggadah, the stories (and other non-legalistic materials) in the Talmudic-Midrashic literature, and the fame of ancient saints and sages as narrators are often cited as evidence of the antiquity of the Jewish penchant for narration."[3] This coupling of writing and speaking suggests that Eastern European Jews believe their oral and written storytelling practices are interrelated.

Along with the Scriptures and the Midrash, the rabbinical commentary on the scriptures, and the Talmud and the Aggadah, the commentary on the Torah, the works specifically noted by Kirshenblatt-Gimlett, there are other Jewish religious texts. These include the Zohar, the kabbalistic commentary on the Torah, as well as the collections of hasidic tales. This body of sacred works contains a treasure of stories. In addition to these religious texts, there are the folk texts, including lore, legends, proverbs, and tales. Although the religious and folk texts have extremely different purposes, they are each comprised of stories and are also sources for stories. Modern Jewish literature may also be added to this mix.

Since Jewish storytelling has its religious, folk, and secular aspects, its storytellers have varying degrees of religiosity. Some practitioners emphasize the religious traditions; others the folk ones. Examples of present-day storytellers with different approaches to their practice are Peninnah Schram and Yitzhak Buxbaum.

Peninnah Schram is the founder and director of the Jewish Storytelling Center, a program offered by the 92nd Street Y in New York City. She offers storytelling workshops and tells stories in Jewish and non–Jewish settings to Jewish and non–Jewish audiences. Religious and folk sources are foundational to her work. For example, in *Jewish Stories One Generation Tells Another*, she recalls that her father's "biblical, Talmudic, and midrashic tales" along with her mother's "folktales, teaching tales and proverbs" are the sources for her storytelling.[4] She tells stories because she loves them and because they "are what link Jews to their heritage, to the memory of those who came before them, to their past and to their future. Stories are the legacies of my parents and the treasure that I transmit to my children."[5] Given this goal of intergenerational legacy, her emphasis is on the folk aspects of storytelling, especially, the transmission of culture.

By contrast, Yitzhak Buxbaum is an authorized *maggid*, a religious storyteller, who is inspired by the Lubavicher form of hasidism. In *Storytelling and Spirituality in Judaism,* he writes that unlike other Jews, as a rule, hasidim "vigorously encouraged storytelling, moving it from the periphery to the center of Judaism. Rebbes praised it as a *mitzvah* (divine commandment) and a spiritual practice; they reflected on it deeply and taught about its significance."[6] He notes that historically the hasidim made storytelling equal to the study of Torah or prayer by raising storytelling to a religious activity. Like Schram, Buxbaum performs in a variety of settings for a variety of audiences, but with another aim. As a hasid, he uses stories to praise, teach, inspire, comfort, and proselytize. Storytelling, for Buxbaum, is a deeply spiritual endeavor. He believes that the current interest in storytelling "can contribute considerably to the current renewal of Judaism in America."[7] Buxbaum highlights the spiritual nature of storytelling, with the hopes that American Jewry will grow more interested in religious life.

Although Schram and Buxbaum are each Jewish storytellers, they have different purposes and backgrounds. As noted, Schram emphasizes the transmission of culture; Buxbaum emphasizes the transmission of spirituality. Regardless, each is a member of the contemporary Jewish storytelling movement. However, for some, this movement, which combines Jewish religious and folk storytelling under the category of Jewish storytelling, has its problems. While acknowledging with interest, the revival in Jewish storytelling, David Roskies, for instance, points out that the Jewish stories told to audiences at storytelling festivals and community centers have little "in common with the practice of Jewish men studying sacred texts out loud."[8] Moreover as Roskies notes, as a rule, observant Jews do not value stories or storytelling. He points out that modern Jewish storytelling and its literature developed as a response to the breakdown of traditional life and the ideas of the Enlightenment in the mid–nineteenth century. As he describes it, the storytellers of that period adapted folk and traditional storytelling for their audiences who were unfamiliar with religious practices. For those audiences, the stories functioned as a "surrogate for faith."[9] Contemporary storytelling may serve a similar role.

Just like Schram and Buxbaum, Wiesel tells stories in Jewish and non–Jewish settings to Jewish and non–Jewish audiences. And, like them, he draws on multiple sources. This use of religious traditions in secular settings for secular purposes has a precedent. Listing Elie Wiesel specifically, Howard Schwartz notes in *Reimagining the Bible* that modern Jewish authors often mine traditional sources. Moreover, as Schwartz writes:

> The methods by which modern Jewish authors are inspired by and make use of traditional sources are diverse. In terms of the amount of ancient material incorporated into the modern work, this ranges from mere illusions and echoes of the source material to the actual incorporation of the source into an expanded retelling. The retelling itself may range from the reverent to the ironic, and in some cases may be literal and in others a radical reworking.[10]

The point is that religious sources have been used by modern Jewish writers for narrative purposes for over one hundred years. Elie Wiesel's particular method of blending the religious, folk, and secular sources makes him an exceptional storyteller. In other words, as Robert McAfee Brown writes, Wiesel is a storyteller to humanity.

An Overview of Wiesel's Storytelling

At a minimum, Elie Wiesel's storytelling repertoire includes the Scriptures, the Talmud, the Midrash, the Aggadah, hasidic texts, Jewish oral traditions, Yiddish language, Yiddish literature, and postwar secular texts. The Jewish sacred texts were Wiesel's first books. As a child, he studied them in *heder*, elementary religious school. *Heder* education focused on the study of religion and was a rigorous style of teaching. Unhappy at first, Wiesel remembers his early school years:

> With time, however, study became a true adventure for me. My teacher, the Batizer rebbe, a sweet old man with a snow-white beard that devoured his face, pointed to the twenty-two holy letters of the Hebrew alphabet and said: "Here children are the beginning and the end of things. Thousands upon thousands of works have been written and will be written with these letters. Look at them and study them with love, for they will be your links to life. And to eternity."[11]

With their knowledge of the Hebrew alphabet, the children could study the Torah, the prophets, the Talmud, the commentaries, and other works.

Although Wiesel also attended a secular elementary school and a high school, where he studied subjects, such as history and geography, he always preferred the "holy books," as he says.

Along with his religious and secular education, Wiesel received a hasidic one from his grandfather. Describing what he learned from his grandfather, Wiesel writes:

> It is to him I owe everything I have written on Hasidic literature. The enchanting tales of Rebbe Nahman of Bratslav, the parables of the Rebbe of Kotzk, the sayings of the Rebbe of Rizhin, and the witticisms of the Rebbe of Ropshitz; he knew them all, and he taught me to savor them.[12]

The hasidic style of storytelling and the hasidic value of storytelling play a large role in Wiesel's style. He publishes interpretations of tales told by and about hasidic masters and gives lectures on the hasidic masters. In his speeches, he draws on their oral traditions. He repeats the tales because he believes that their messages are still relevant. For Wiesel, the lives of the hasidic masters contain lessons about hope, despair, joy, madness, friendship, and other human feelings and actions.

Yiddish language and literature also mark Wiesel's style. He writes about his love of the language:

> I need Yiddish to laugh and cry, to celebrate and express regret, to delve into my memories anew. Is there a better language for evoking the past, with all its horror? Without Yiddish the literature of the Holocaust would have no soul. I know that had I not written my first account in Yiddish, I would have written no others.[13]

This "first account" refers to *Un di Velt Hot Geshvign* [*And the World Was Silent*], which is Wiesel's initial recollection of his Holocaust experiences, published in 1956 in Buenos Aires. The Jewish publishing industry in Argentina was particularly vibrant at that time, and Mark Turkow, one of the prominent writers and publishers of the time, was very interested in Yiddish works, especially those about Polish Jewry.[14] His series *Dos Poylishe Yidntum* published over 100 Yiddish books from 1946 to 1954.[15] *Un di Velt Hot Geshvign* was the 117th volume in the series.[16] Its French language version, entitled *La Nuit,* published in 1958, and later translated into English as *Night* in 1960, positioned Wiesel for his life's work.

Although Wiesel speaks Yiddish, his childhood education did not include the literature. He started studying Yiddish literature in Paris after his Yiddish translation of a Hebrew newspaper article was criticized by his editor. He recalls that criticism:

> That was not surprising, since I was wholly ignorant of Yiddish grammar and its vast, rich literature. I had not read — except for a few fragments — the works of Peretz, Sholem Aleichem, or Mendele. The names Leivick and Makish, Bergelson and Der Nister, Glatstein and Manger, were still unfamiliar to me. I had a lot to learn.[17]

Since the Yiddish writers listed are secular, they were not part of the *heder* curriculum, with its focus on religious works. In addition to studying Yiddish literature, Wiesel studied French philosophy and literature in Paris. About those studies, he writes:

> I was intrigued and stimulated by the intellectual and artistic ferment of Paris. Still working on my education, I was an insatiable patron of the library. Never have I read so much. I devoured the works of Malraux, Mauriac, Paul Valery, George Bernanos, Ignazio Silone, and Roger Martin du Gard. I read everything by Camus ... and Sartre....[18]

Given this roster of authors, Jack Kolbert concludes that Wiesel was clearly influenced by French Existentialism. Kolbert also notes that Wiesel seems to have adopted some of the writing techniques of the French New Novelists, who experimented with the flow of time in their novels.

Like Kolbert, other scholars have studied Wiesel's writing. There are excellent works focusing on Wiesel as a literary figure. Examples include Ellen Fine's *Legacy of Night: The Literary Universe of Elie Wiesel,* Simon Sibelman's *Silence in the Works of Elie Wiesel,* and Colin Davis's *Elie Wiesel's Secretive Texts*.[19] There are also important works concentrating on Wiesel as a theological figure. These include Michael Berenbaum's *A Vision of the Void: Theological Reflections on the Works of Elie Wiesel* and Robert McAfee Brown's *Elie Wiesel: Messenger to All Humanity*.[20]

However, despite the importance of these literary and theological analyses, none emphasizes Wiesel as a storyteller. This is surprising, because Wiesel regularly calls himself a storyteller. Without question, the storyteller is Wiesel's self-proclaimed role. For instance, in *Souls on Fire*, he writes that he is not an historian or philosopher. Instead he notes that "the only role that suits him is the one, less presumptuous though more limited, of storyteller who transmits what was given to him, as faithfully as possible."[21] In *Messengers of God*, he writes about himself in a similar manner: "And so, faithful to his promise, the storyteller does nothing but tell the tale: he transmits what he has received, he returns what was entrusted to him. His story does not begin with his own; it is fitted into the memory that is the living tradition of his people."[22] In book after book, he regularly claims the role of storyteller. Moreover, a number of his publications are retellings of biblical, talmudic, or hasidic legends. These include *Souls on Fire: Portraits and Legends of Hasidic Masters*; *Messengers of God: Biblical Portraits and Legends*; *Four Hasidic Masters and Their Struggle Against Melancholy*; *Somewhere a Master: Further Hasidic Portraits and Legends*; and *Sages and Dreamers: Biblical, Talmudic, and Hasidic Portraits and Legends*. In addition, many of Wiesel's speeches and essays include legends.

Despite Wiesel's many references to himself as a storyteller and the volumes of published legends, critics generally overlook that aspect of his writing. One exception is David Booth, who has studied the writings of Elie Wiesel and Sholem Aleichem, perhaps two of the best-known Jewish storytellers. Booth concludes that each author felt that the traditional religious rituals and liturgies did not offer meaning and so each turned "to storytelling as a way of finding that meaning in the modern world."[23] Booth goes on to say that the hasidic belief in storytelling is the basis for each writer's work. However, Booth makes the point that unlike Sholem Aleichem who uses storytelling in a secular way, Wiesel does make overt religious references.[24] Despite that difference, Booth argues that for each writer, storytelling is not a religious act. For Sholem Aleichem, storytelling was primarily secular. To Booth, just like to Roskies, Wiesel uses traditional Jewish storytelling sources, but not the traditional lifestyle, to interest people in Judaism.

For the contributors to this volume that is not an issue. As a group, they consider Wiesel a masterful storyteller, in part, because he culls multiple sources in an effort to reach diverse audiences. That is the mark of his talent. Some of the authors in this volume argue for his genius by discussing the secular aspects of his stories; others by discussing the religious aspects. The moral dimension of his stories adds to his esteem.

The first three chapters look at Wiesel as a literary storyteller. In *Mosaics and Mirrors: Wiesel, American Autobiographies, and the Shaping of a Storied Subject*, Zoe Trodd, explores Wiesel as storyteller in light of his ideas about the self-as-subject and the self-in-exile, the importance of retelling and remembering while retaining one's own story as an intact and sacred realm, the relationship between the narrator of *Night* and several of his other survivor-characters, the different endings of *Night*, and the example of Moshe's failed storytelling in the opening of *Night*. She explores the ways in which American autobiographers reconstruct the self and revisit the past in order to move toward the future, in an open loop of dialogic encounter — gazing upon the self in the mirror, and feeling the gaze of a young child upon their faces.

The question of how to act in the face of ambiguity underlies many of Wiesel's novels. What is clear from Wiesel's refusal to provide answers in his novels is that he wants to use the disparity between our expectations as readers and his theme of uncertainty to jolt us from complacency into action. His goal is transmission, not resolution. Using examples from a range of Wiesel's fiction, *Creative Ambiguity in Wiesel's Storytelling* looks at Wiesel's writing techniques — the framing devices, the embedding of stories, the unreliability of narrators, and the sequencing of events — to discuss how the ambiguity in the storytelling structure parallels the theme of ambiguity in the stories.

In *Elie Wiesel: Telling Stories of Children and Loss,* Katherine Lagrandeur explores the question of how to articulate the loss of one million Jewish children during the Second World War, and the loss of innocence of those children who survived the war or who were the children of survivors. Lagrandeur suggests that Wiesel's decision to discuss the plight of children during and after the *Shoah* through storytelling is the only way to try to create what Lawrence Langer calls a "language of the inconsolable." She points out that Wiesel remains mindful of Rabbi Greenberg's contention that "No statement, theological or otherwise, should be made that would not be credible in the presence of burning children." Considering this, she argues that Wiesel's use of storytelling becomes a way to create a space where we may sit quietly and ponder the loss of life and the loss of innocence among the children of the *Shoah*. At the same time, he questions storytelling itself and the necessity and the impossibility of articulating such an overwhelming loss.

Another group of authors in this collection looks at religious elements of Wiesel's stories. In *The Storyteller and His Quarrel with God*, Alan Berger considers the ways that for Wiesel storytelling is a form of praying. Berger observes that Wiesel's life is a commentary on his work. Consequently, his writings tell a tale and bear theological significance. This chapter treats Wiesel's narrative interrogation of God by examining his classic memoir

Night, Ani Ma'amin, The Trial of God, and his two-volume autobiography. Wiesel's writings provide a riveting and eloquent witness to the tension between the believer that he was and the survivor that he is. Storytelling makes this tension a basis for Jewish identity.

In *Wrestling with Oblivion: Wiesel's Autobiographical Storytelling as Midrash,* Deborah Lee Ames asserts that Wiesel's autobiographical storytelling surpasses memoir because he writes in a midrashic manner. She shows how one Biblical story becomes Wiesel's own story and the Jewish people's story — the *akeda,* or the binding of Isaac — to demonstrate the ways in which Wiesel's storytelling is midrashic. His tales are important because so few people survived the Holocaust; the compelling nature of his storytelling and the depth of his reflective nature cause him to be the primary voice of the survivor. His authorial presence emerges from his style of writing — his midrashic, terse, and haunting stories involving God and humanity — and in the *testimonio* — his need to bear witness. Wiesel participates in a Jewish storytelling tradition in the divine mode: God is the author of creation, and the storyteller mirrors that creativity.

In *The Maggid of Sighet: Jewish Contexts for Wiesel's Storytelling,* David Patterson situates Wiesel's work within a distinctively aggadic tradition by examining some of the ways in which Wiesel draws on that tradition in his tales. Patterson holds that figures, images, and motifs from the Midrash, Kabbalah, and Aggadah hover between the words and float in the margins of every line that Wiesel writes. They are what make him a Jewish writer. To approach him as anything else would amount to more than failing to understand him. Moreover, it would be to a betrayal of the murdered Jews whose muted outcry also abides between the words and the margins.

Jacqueline Bussie's *Laughter and the Limits of Holocaust Storytelling: Wiesel's Gates of the Forest* proposes that Wiesel sustains the inexpressibility of the world-shattering, language-rupturing experience of the Holocaust through hasidic storytelling — particularly Bratzlavian storytelling, a tradition that incorporates paradox and *ab intra* acknowledges the limits of human understanding and language and the incorporation of the trope of laughter into his hasidic stories. Once contextualized, the otherwise incomprehensible laughter within Wiesel's hasidic tales emerges as testimony to the limitations of Holocaust storytelling. *Gates of the Forest* and the laughter found in its pages begs to come into dialogue with the thought and life of the greatest hasidic storyteller, Rebbe Nachman of Bratzlav.

In *Transfiguration*, Graham Walker examines the ways in which Wiesel's fiction identifies commonly held mythological structures and how his work critiques these from within his semiotic world. It shows how Wiesel's work interacts with and critiques the traditional hero as portrayed in the monomyth found in Joseph Campbell and Lord Ragland and how Wiesel's critique of mythological structures effectively challenges the mythological structures that buttress the politics of the victim-executioner cycle. The conclusion is that Wiesel has articulated a fundamental narrative quality of experience upon which new community may be built in the wake of seemingly ontological tragedy.

In *The Artist as Witness, Prophet, and Encourager*, Carole Lambert uses novels, speeches, memoirs, lecture notes, as well as published and personal interviews, to discuss the purpose and power of Wiesel's storytelling. She identifies six functions of Wiesel's storytelling. She notes that storytelling allows Wiesel to be a witness, to be a voice in the wilderness, to transmit a heritage, to communicate autobiographical experience, to challenge God, and to touch readers. Her chapter emphasizes his fictional storytelling power in three of those areas: the storyteller as witness to a Jewish past that risks being forgotten; the storyteller as prophet in the post–Holocaust era; and the storyteller as encourager of his readers.

In *Shaliach Tzibor: Wiesel as Storyteller of His People*, Caren Neile uses *A Beggar in Jerusalem*, *The Gates of the Forest*, *The Oath*, *The Testament*, *and The Town Beyond the Wall* to explore Wiesel's role as a messenger. She demonstrates that while the theme of memory permeating Wiesel's writing suggests that he upholds more of Jewish tradition than he eschews, his work also reflects the desire expressed in the introduction to *Legends of Our Time*: not to be attached to the name of his grandfather. This tension between tradition and innovation in Wiesel's work is at the heart of his storytelling. That is to say, at the same time that stories or traditions are transmitted among generations and honored for their connection to the past, they are also updated, revised, and personalized by everyone who comes into contact with them.

Given that Elie Wiesel's storytelling is a form of activism, the collection ends by focusing on the transformative nature of storytelling. In *Teaching Beyond the Text: Examining and Acting on the Moral Aspects of Night*, O'Quinn highlights storytelling in the classroom. She notes that many high school English teachers believe that their role in teaching literature is to make certain that students can name themes, unveil symbolism, and analyze stories. However, as she points out, texts such as *Night* require the teacher do much more than that. Wiesel's narrative opens the door to existential questions of evil and faith that invite students to examine their own beliefs about the world. By personally grappling with such questions, students discover their connectedness with others. It is not a cognitive study of Wiesel's story as text that makes people better human beings, but an affective confrontation of his experience, painful to the point of unreal, that allows the possibilities of more humane world. Stories must be felt and not just understood if they are to operate as transformative touchstones in our lives.

And finally, from her special perspective as a Holocaust survivor and educator, Miriam Klein Kassenoff offers a personal account of the role of Wiesel, the man and the writer, in her classroom, as well as in her life. In the words of her students, she finds evidence that Elie Wiesel's powerful storytelling memoir transforms their lives. She also hopes that other educators who have been already transformed by his work are carrying on his message. In turn, they will affect the lives of their students who will go on to transform others.

Notes

1. Walter Benjamin, "The Storyteller," in *Illuminations: Essays and Reflections*, ed. Hannah Arendt and trans. Harry Zohn (New York: Schocken Books, 1968), 108–109.
2. Barbara Kirshenblatt-Gimlett, "The Concept and Varieties of Narrative Performance in Eastern European Jewish Culture," in *Explorations in the Ethnography of Speaking*, Second edition, eds. Richard Bauman and Joel Sherzer (Cambridge, England: Cambridge University Press, 1989), 283.
3. Ibid., 283.
4. Peninnah Schram, *Jewish Stories One Generation Tells Another* (Northvale, N.J.: Jason Aronson, Inc., 1987), xxv.
5. Ibid., xxxiii.
6. Yitzhak Buxbaum, *Storytelling and Spirituality in Judaism* (Northvale, N.J.: Jason Aronson, Inc., 1994), 7.
7. Ibid., xvii.
8. David G. Roskies, "The Story's the Thing," in *What Is Jewish Literature?* ed. Hana Wirth-Nesher (Philadelphia: Jewish Publication Society, 1994), 121.
9. Ibid., 123.
10. Howard Schwartz, *Reimagining the Bible: The Storytelling of the Rabbis* (New York: Oxford University Press, 1998), 191.
11. Elie Wiesel, *All Rivers Run to the Sea*, trans. Marion Wiesel (New York: Alfred A. Knopf, 1997), 10.

12. Ibid., 42.

13. Ibid., 292.

14. Robert Weisbrot, The *Jews of Argentina: From the Inquisition to Perón*, with the research assistance of Robert Murciano (Philadelphia: Jewish Publication Society of America, 1979), 108–109.

15. See Jan Schwarz, "A Library of Destruction and Hope: The First One Hundred Volumes of *Dos Poylishe Yidntum,* 1946–1954." Abstract prepared for Association for Jewish Studies, 34th Annual Conference, Los Angeles, California, December, 15, 2002.

16. See Naomi Seidman, "Elie Wiesel and the Scandal of Jewish Rage," *Jewish Social Studies*, 3, No. 1 (Fall 1996): 1–19.

17. Wiesel, *All Rivers Run to the Sea*, 163.

18. Wiesel, *All Rivers Run to the Sea*, 189.

19. See Ellen Fine, *Legacy of Night: The Literary Universe of Elie Wiesel* (Albany: State University of New York, 1982); Simon Sibelman, *Silence in the Works of Elie Wiesel* (New York: St. Martin's Press, 1995); and Colin Davis, *Elie Wiesel's Secretive Texts* (Gainesville: University Press of Florida, 1994).

20. See Michael Berenbaum, *A Vision of the Void: Theological Reflections on the Works of Elie Wiesel* (Middletown: Wesleyan University Press, 1979); and Robert McAfee Brown, *Elie Wiesel: Messenger to All Humanity* (Notre Dame: University of Notre Dame Press, 1983).

21. Elie Wiesel, *Souls on Fire: Portraits and Legends of Hasidic Masters* (New York: Random House, 1972), 255.

22. Elie Wiesel, *Messengers of God: Biblical Portraits and Legends* (New York: Random House, 1976), xiv.

23. David Booth, "The Role of the Storyteller — Sholem Aleichem and Elie Wiesel," *Judaism: A Quarterly Journal of Jewish Life and Thought,* 167, 42, 3 (Summer 1993): 304.

24. Ibid., 306.

Mosaics and Mirrors: Wiesel, American Autobiographies, and the Shaping of a Storied Subject

ZOE TRODD

"Let us tell tales. That is our primary obligation.... And now let me tell you a story."[1]

Storying the Self I:
"Traces and scars on the surface of history"[2]

"From the depths of the mirror, a corpse gazed back at me. The look in his eyes, as they stared into mine, has never left me."[3] So Elie Wiesel ends the French / English version of his autobiography, *Night*. He acknowledges that the attempt to make "question and answer ... become *one*,"[4] with which the narrator began *Night,* has ended with the self divided in *two*. The mirror image confirms Wiesel's sense of himself as object, of "looking ... into the eyes of another or with the eyes of another," as Bakhtin puts it.[5] It is comparable to the moment in *Night* when he sees himself "[i]n every stiffened corpse," or when the dead boy on the gallows represents a part of himself destroyed.[6] Similarly, his father's face seems "the

15

face of someone else" and then "another invalid" really *does* arrive to lie in his "father's place."[7]

The narrator of *Night* had put his real self into hibernation on entering the camp: he walks in his own funeral procession, and then offers his identity as that of an eighteen-year-old farmer rather than a fourteen-year-old student, so creating a self-imposed distance from his own story as it unfolded real-time. He had "become a completely different person," feeling that: "the child that I was, had been consumed in the flames," so that "[t]here remained only a shape that looked like me."[8] That shape, the corpse, now stares at him from the mirror, and forces a double-consciousness: he sees himself as another sees him, just as he had watched himself from a distance in the camp, knowing that "[t]he main thing was not to think about it.... Leave thoughts for later."[9]

But in storytelling these thoughts left "for later" return to reclaim the image in the mirror as character and subject. In an interview Wiesel remembered that when he looked in the mirror that day he thought that "since everything changes — even the face in the mirror changes — someone must speak about that change. Someone must speak about the former face and that someone is I. I shall not speak about all the other things but I should speak, at least, about *that* face and *that* mirror and *that* change."[10] Speaking of "that change," he set out to construct a new subject-self, even embodying the shift in this interview: the two "I"s are still mirrored across the period ("that someone is I. I shall not speak") but he does move from third-person ("that someone") to first-person ("I shall not speak"). He said once of his stylistic shifts between first and third-person, that the "change between 'I' and 'he'" make the "question of all questions ... not, 'Who are you?'" but "'Who am I? Who is the "I" in me?'" and that this "dialogue, this quest of the real 'I,' which can never be solved, I try to transmit in my novels." He continued: "when my father died, I died. That means that one 'I' in me died."[11] His storytelling has been the search for the lost "I."

The original ending of *Night,* published in Yiddish as *Un di Velt Hot Geshvign*, emphasizes the shift to a subject-self that Wiesel would then attempt. He writes: "I dragged myself over to the mirror that hung on the wall. I wanted to see myself. I had not looked in a mirror since leaving the ghetto. A skeleton gazed back at me, skin and bones. I saw a picture of myself after death. At this very moment the will to live awakened in me. Not knowing why, I raised my fist and broke the mirror, broke the image that dwelt there. I fainted. From that moment on my health improved."[12] No longer an observer of his object-self, he breaks that self into pieces. The camp inmate who seeks "his ghostlike reflection in the soup" is killed for it, in the French / English version,[13] and here the narrator banishes the same impulse to see himself as other, in this original ending to *Un di Velt Hot Geshvign*.

Upon smashing the mirror he begins to recover, and finds a "desire to live." He is, François Mauriac explains in his foreword to *Night,* "a Lazarus risen from the dead."[14] The mirror-smashing marks the end of the faith, as expressed in the original beginning of *Un di Velt Hot Geshvign*, that "a holy spark glowed in each one of us; that the image was *mirrored* in our eyes, and that it resided in our soul."[15] But it also reverses his sense earlier in *Night* that the camp experience had "deprived me, for all eternity, of the desire to live"[16]; he raises a fist, the same size as a heart, and replaces broken heart with shattered glass, destroying the self-as-other, and enabling a self "in my own image." Though the outside had invaded his inner realm, so expressed at the moment in the camp when his hair is clipped and a thought "buzzed all the time in my head"[17] (as though the sound of the *clippers* is "in" his head), here he reclaims an internal life.

He faints after breaking the mirror, suggesting a further loss of connection with the self and symbolizing his exile: in an interview he expressed the sense of being "displaced," of feeling "I am here and I am not here," which prevents any image of the self in the mirror at all — for the exile is in "continuous movement."[18] But Wiesel's career after *Night* has been a process of rebuilding the mirror, this time in his own image and with the traces and scars of a storied subject — the shards of broken glass forming what he calls "the mosaic" of his method (with essays that explain novels and "novels [that] explain the essays," for "[t]hey are all connected; each is part of one and the same mosaic").[19] Isis-like, he would spend the following decades reassembling the fragments of the broken mirror in his *own* combination of plots; seeking re-memberment, reconnection, and the path out of exile via his writings, interviews, and speeches.

The shattered self-image of the mirror is slowly rebuilt into a mosaic-story with traces and scars on its surface, for, as he notes in his essay "Ethics and Memory," "[t]o remember is to acknowledge the postulate that time does leave traces and scars on the surface of history."[20] Even in *Night,* in the "thick dirty smoke" left "behind" by the first train of Jews out of Sighet, or the "red mark" left on his father's cheek by the gypsy,[21] Wiesel sees clues that begin a process of question-and-answer. His mosaic of stories and traces since *Night* have marked a changing, storied subject-hood, further banishing the absolute and frozen mirror-object. Story-telling re-members the shattered self of the mirror-image into a storied self with "traces and scars on the surface" of its history.

Mikhail Bakhtin writes of an "empty time" or "hiatus" that "leaves no traces anywhere," but Wiesel finds instead what Jean Baudrillard calls the "residue of history."[22] Wiesel knows, as Walter Benjamin puts it, that "[l]iving means leaving traces"— and dying too.[23] And he resists a narrative of Holo-caust evaporation through texts that set the multiple voices of the self in dia-logue, and also leave traces *of* that dialogue — in a process comparable to that of Native American autobiographers who also wrote in the face of erasure and emphasized, for example, the tracks left by spirits after their visit and dialogue in *Black Elk Speaks,* or the "little rock" that Black Bear brings back from his spiritual encounter and dialogue in Mary Crow Dog's *Lakota Woman.*[24] Crow Dog finds signs of gain and loss, "wear and tear," along his-tory's loops and trails, and Wiesel similarly salvages ruins as traces.[25]

Indeed, many Native autobiographies make traces and tracks speak stories, and in return use words like "bird's track and fish-fin studies on the sand," as Charles Eastman explains in *From the Deep Woods to Civilization.*[26] He adds elsewhere that tracks are a "language" that tell a "history," foot-prints the "wood-dwellers autograph" that can be "read" if not "illegible," and Carlo Ginzburg even speculates that "the actual idea of narration ... may have originated in a hunting society, relating the experience of deciphering tracks."[27] In reconstructing and narrating a storied, subject-self, Wiesel also deciphers tracks to find narrative, and writes story out of trace. He seeks, he explains, to "rebuild with memories, with ruins, with efforts, and with moments of grace"; to assemble a mosaic of memory-fragments and ruins.[28]

Storying the Self II: "I feel his gaze on my face"[29]

"I think of the young Jewish boy from the Carpathian Mountains. He has accompanied the old man I have become throughout these years of quest and struggle." Wiesel ended his lecture at Northwestern Univer-sity with an image of the doubled self, one of the many occasions on which he has referred to himself in the third-person during talks and interviews.[30] For, since *Night,* he has used the third-person voice to express a storied, dialogic self composed of fragments, ruins, and echoes. Within this self, "the voices of [his] friends and the voice of the violin [of my friend Juliek] become one," so that he feels: "I no longer know who I am," and asks, "[w]ho am I? The hero of my tales? The voice of that hero? Who am I?"[31] One friend's voice in particular haunts his writing — "Moshe comes back all the time [in my books] as a warning, a reminder, an echo and often as an inspiration," he has said.[32]

In another speech he asked: "[t]he boy that began to talk to you tonight, where is he? Did he dream or live his dreams of fear and fire? ... For a very long while I resisted accepting this story as mine."[33] This boy, his other self, speaks to him from the depths of the mirror, with a "gaze on [Wiesel's] face" — in a 1983 lecture he summoned the boy again:

> Thirty-eight years ago to the day — April 11, 1945 — a young Jewish boy awakened and realized he was alive.... [He] has since then dedicated his life to writing stories and telling tales, to trying to find the language to describe events that defy language.... On that April 11, 1945, a young Jewish boy in Buchenwald tried to understand whose dream he was dreaming.... And all my books really are ways of speaking to that young boy. I feel his gaze on my face. I hear him asking me: "What have you done with your life?"[34]

Wiesel sometimes fears the confrontation with the past self that autobiography demands, finding that it sets past and present into an eternal, static loop that joins tale to tail-end of tale. He writes in *The Eternal Light:*

> I did return to Sighet once.... I went back to the home that used to be the home of my parents, my home.... I became afraid, afraid that the door might open and a little *yeshivah* boy with side curls resembling me would come out and ask me innocently, "Tell me, stranger, what are you doing here? What are you doing in my dreams and in my childhood?" I was so afraid of being judged by that child, I was so afraid of shattering the dream and killing the child once again that I did not dare go in. I retreated and began running, running away from the street, from the town from all the places that once were ours.... I ran so much that I reentered my own tale, and this is the tale of the tale itself.[35]

But more often he tells readers and audiences of his yearning to merge past and present selves, to go through the looking-glass and live *as* the child: "As for my stories, you must see beneath every word the child I was and that perhaps I would still like to be today," he comments.[36]

Wiesel's sense of *self as other* sets him in the ethnic–American autobiographical tradition as well. Mary Antin shifts to the third-person to acknowledge a moment of shame and sin in *The Promised Land*, only returning to what she calls "the honest first person" several pages later.[37] As an onlooker within her own life, she sometimes does "not know what was going on in my own heart," experiencing a radical discontinuity of self because she lives in the "borderland between the old life and the new" with the hyphenated double-consciousness of a Jewish-American.[38] Or, in the opening to *A Son of the Forest*, William Apess describes himself in the third-person ("Apess ... was born"), and then often uses the language of spectatorship to express his emotions ("my crimes were arrayed before me").[39] Eastman expresses a double identity in *From the Deep Woods* through first- and third-person pronoun shifts, most notably when he feels ashamed, like Antin ("He was called 'Baby'"), or when he wants to distance himself from shameful acts: he uses "we" and "us" when the United States betrays the Sioux, but "them" when describing the massacre of 1862.[40]

Similarly, in his collaborative autobiography with John Neihardt, Black Elk offers a dialogue between "little" self and "bigger" self, like Wiesel who says he is "speaking to that young boy."[41] For Black Elk, there is a self *narrating* from "high hill of my old age," "from a lonely hilltop," and the self *narrated,* who is "too young to understand."[42] And he too imagines himself as others see him. Each time he refers to himself as a "pitiful old man" he includes the phrases "you can see," or "you see me," and during his vision experiences a separation of selves, seeing "a sick boy that was myself" and a "someone" that is him.[43] Or, in *Lakota Woman,* Crow Dog feels a "spectator" on her life, refers to herself in the third-person and views herself at one point as "the strange woman lying dead in my bed."[44]

These four Native autobiographers, Apess, Eastman, Black Elk, and Crow Dog, use the mirrored self to express bicultural and bi-temporal identities. As in Wiesel's universe of texts, these autobiographies contain a dialogic nexus of exchange between individual and community, public and private, subject and object, past and present, and myth and history. The act of looking inside oneself as though "into the eyes of another or with the eyes of another," as Bakhtin puts it, *appropriates* the language of mirroring, used by writers like James Fenimore Cooper to taxonomize his fictional cultures.[45] Wiesel explores the idea of bicultural mirroring, explaining in interviews that what happens to the Jews will later happen to the world — they are a barometer and prophetic mirror. So, in *Night,* the Jewish camp inmates run down the road of history, followed by guards who eventually seem to flee as well.[46]

When whites sought an indigenous identity via selective appropriation and imitation of Native American culture, using what Apess terms "The Indian's Looking Glass for the White Man" in his 1834 essay of the same title, Native writers turned to "the mirror," like Crow Dog does at one point, to find "who and what" *they* were.[47] But when this mirror gave back what Ralph Ellison called "an image drained of all humanity," as it did for African Americans, Native Americans, and Wiesel at the end of *Night,* these autobiographers set up a shifting reflective surface of their own.[48] Ellison's narrator in *Invisible Man* hears the "crashing of huge sheets of glass" during the riot towards the end of this fictional autobiography and observes the smashed "mirrored façade of one store." Black boys watch "their distorted images as they danced before the jagged glass"; they dance before the smashed national mirror, in which a black man had discovered "an image drained of all humanity" when he approached "for a glimpse of himself," Ellison explained.[49] Invisible to those around him, IM has felt "surrounded by mirrors of hard, distorting glass," and later trapped within a "glass aquarium wall,"[50] but this moment at the end of the book is, as for Wiesel when he smashes the mirror, the reconfiguration of a destructive vision — that "mirrored façade."

The dialogic self doubles and fragments in the rippling layered surfaces of Wiesel's works, *Invisible Man*, and several Native American autobiographies; a mode of repetition-with-difference eventually shatters the closed circle of mirror-imaging in *Lakota Woman,* for example. Reality threatens to become the mirror-image of a fictionalized culture in the wake of Native-white encounter for Crow Dog: she encounters a replica of the Mayflower and ponders the forms of white culture on the pages of catalogues, from the added distance of "an outhouse."[51] Whites expect a Buffalo Bill Wild West Show; people try to look like Marlboro ads; a sheriff walks right out of a Grade B Western; and scenes look like Vietnam films or a "cheap World War Two Movie."[52] Protesting this fictional culture, AIM activists eventually set fire to an imitation pioneer log cabin and turn the American flag upside-down.[53] Modern Native culture that tries to mirror or repeat the past as a closed, mirroring loop seems as watered-down as these fictions: at one point young Indian men try to hunt and can only bring in an old bull.[54]

Throughout the siege at Wounded Knee, however, the past returns in full force — "like the old days."[55] The activists fight on the anniversary of the Custer battle, ghosts rise from a mass grave, and later Crow Dog hears "women crying, babies screaming, cannon shots" when she walks "along Cankpe Opi Wakpala where our women and children had been killed in 1890."[56] She wonders: "Is it the vision of a tragedy still to come, of history repeating itself?" To her husband this closed loop of history seems natural, for the Crow Dogs have "no shortage of legends"; the past is not "ancient history" for them but "what happened only yesterday."[57] Leonard's "acute sense of history" means he repeats the 1884 surrender at the courthouse and gradually makes the Sun Dance more severe until it repeats the ritual of 150 years ago.[58] But Mary knows "[no] big deeds of some ancestors."[59] Grappling with "problems of identity" she looks in "all the Lakota history books" for details of her past and tries to measure up to the standards of "the old buffalo days."[60] She learns that modern Natives might create their *own* legends through historical repetition-with-*difference,* in an open loop.

She sees Indians count coup on armored cars, lay trails of urine and pepper for dogs, and make AIM a new Ghost Dance with its own songs.[61] She learns that the land is good for "talking of great deeds done in the past" but that they "can't live forever off the deeds of Sitting Bull or Crazy Horse," and notes: "You have to make your own legends now."[62] So she creates and recounts her "own legends": the birth of her baby during a firefight, where her breasts are as hard as the muzzles of the feds' guns, her own birth backwards, her article which is the "worst thing ... in the school's long history," her shoplifting which is "like counting coup," and her tracking of Leonard when he is moved from jail to jail.[63] She even decides to have her baby at Wounded Knee "no matter what," so as to place her new legend and new life amid the closed loop of ghosts and slaughter.[64] In these ways she gathers up "the broken pieces of the sacred hoop and put them together again," to make a legend of fragments and objects, "odds and ends," like her house, and Wiesel's storied self.[65] The reassembled hoop comprises layers of past and present, old and new stories; in the manner of the Ghost Dance story, told by an Indian to a dreamer who tells a leader in the presence of Dick Fool Bull who tells Crow Dog who tapes him! Mary now relays the taped story to her collaborator Richard Erdoes, who re-tapes and transcribes it — completing a loop of seven stages.[66]

For Wiesel, too, there is an ongoing dialogue between the two selves of a bi-cultural identity, and between past and present selves, young boy and adult man. His doubled self expresses a repetition, but in smashing the mirror he begins a *repetition with difference* across his stories. This resists a philosophy of the present as a frozen mirror-image of the past, while affirming the continuing presence of the past as a way to build a storied subject, and as a way to acknowledge the "traces and scars on the surface of history." For him, as for Crow Dog, life loops on, albeit looking radically different to life before the shattering of the mirror and the Holocaust's rupturing of history. He wrote in the introduction to *Messengers of God* that: "Everything holds together in Jewish history ... all events are linked.... And so, faithful to the promise, the storyteller does nothing but tell the tale: he transmits what he received, he returns what was entrusted to him. His story does not begin with his own."[67] Applying this philosophy to his own storytelling, he explained in an interview that he tries to link past to present: "the present and the past are the same to me ... in our tradition and in Hebrew past and future can be interchanged — it's almost the same word."[68]

This implies a mirror-imaging of present and past, or past and future — but here the "almost" is important. *Night* reverses and parodies the story of Exodus, as he explained in another interview: "it's ironic because in Scripture the clouds were meant to protect the Jews. In the desert, after the Exodus, there were clouds and they protected the Hebrews. But now they did not protect them. How could they? They *were* the clouds."[69] He also called his autobiography "the binding of Isaac in reverse, where the father is sacrificed and not the son," and imagined "Auschwitz as its own Hannukah lamp with its six huge chimneys, throwing flames to the clouds. These six chimneys were to me six Hannukah candles."[70] In addition, we might see the "selection" of the sick as a twist on the Jewish selection, for Yom Kippur, the day of judgment before God, becomes the day of selection before the camp doctor; or the bread in the railway car as a new kind of manna, and Moshe knocking on doors in vain while "the year 1943 passed by" as enacting a new kind of Passover.[71]

Like Crow Dog, Wiesel knows that, as Mary Antin put it, "[w]e are not born all at once, but by bits," and that "[o]ur souls are scarred with the struggles of successive births, and the process is recorded also by the wrinkles in our brains, by the lines in our faces." Antin adds: "Look at me and you will see that I have been born many times."[72] The mirror is rebuilt through a reflective, shifting dialogue with myth and story that scars the soul and records its process; it is rebuilt through the gaze into the face born many times. For Antin, these successive births work against the idea of a linear life, marking instead the journey that is "millions of years on the way" along a "zigzag path of human possibility."[73] These patterns of loops and spins repeat across Native autobiography and across Wiesel's mosaic of stories told and retold. He explained in an interview: "The Bible is a story and story to me is the repository of humanity that one generation leaves for another." His mission is to "find the original story ... and retell it once more," for "when we tell stories, really, we do not tell stories, we *re*tell stories."[74] His retold-stories are repetitions with difference, images of the past but marked now with the traces and scars of time's passage: a mosaic in the mirror.

Storying the Self III: "The good story ... was to remain unfinished"[75]

"Still I go on.... Life goes on." Crow Dog affirms the continuing existence of Native life and stories.[76] She knows that her looping movement of storytelling through time and space challenges the confinement of the modern Indian, "fenced in" amid "railroad tracks and ... barbed-wire fences," far from the "outside world" and in a "vacuum" or "attic cell."[77] The "corner is where the Indian lives," she writes, but her looped "roaming" across land and through storied layers toward her own legend makes her "more Indian."[78] Like the turtle woman who is "constantly on the road," or the turtle at the end of Eastman's autobiography who is "at home" because he carries his home on his back, Crow Dog finds a shifting borderland space that she can call home, beyond the confinements of stereotypes and old stories.[79] Legends beat there like the heart of the turtle after it is dead.[80]

With its looping repetition-with-difference, Wiesel's storytelling method also belongs alongside the storytelling genius of Vietnam veteran and writer, Tim O'Brien. Like Wiesel, O'Brien addresses the questions of how to narrate events that defy language, how to speak to the young boy of his past and the self in the mirror, and how to move along the surface of his own history. He writes in his autobiographical collection of stories, *The Things They Carried:* "I'm skimming across the surface of my own history, moving fast, riding the melt beneath the blades, doing loops and spins, and when I take a high leap in the dark and come down thirty years later, I realize it is as Tim trying to save Timmy's life with a story."[81] Storytelling sometimes *objectifies* the self for O'Brien: "By telling stories, you objectify your own experience. You separate it from yourself," he writes.[82] But, believing ultimately that "stories can save us," O'Brien finds they are "a way of bringing body and soul back together"— the body and soul divided for Wiesel in *Night,* where he remembers: "I could feel myself as two entities — my body and me."[83]

His "loops and spins" and the mosaic of cracked but connected story in *The Things They Carried,* express trauma and the rupture in history occasioned by the Vietnam war: "the looping aspect of my writing is important," he explained in an interview. "To tell stories in a linear way would be deceitful. The trauma doesn't end, it comes back in memory, returns and returns, often with a different take on the original event; horror, outrage, disbelief. War and trauma don't end in a literal sense, they reverberate across time, and my repetitions are a way to get at this psychological truth. And they match the looping subject, the circular war."[84] As with O'Brien here, Wiesel's form matches his subject. His challenge is to narrate an event that seems to have no narrative coherence — that interrupted history like it did his father's story: "The good story he had been in the middle of telling us was to remain unfinished," he remembers in *Night,*[85] and toward the end of the narrative, his father's last words are again unintelligible, the story still unfinished.

For Wiesel, the Holocaust does not belong in any story sequence but is like the page in *Night,* "*torn* from some story book, from some historical novel about the captivity of Babylon or the Spanish Inquisition."[86] And his mosaic of stories and the divided self retain the sense of a history torn. Loren Baritz expands on this idea of pulling apart and then reconstructing history: "Because of America's rejection of the past, of the fierce commitment to the notion that this land will start anew, the American Jew is pulled apart. To be a Jew is to remember. An American must forget."[87] Pulled apart, Wiesel re-members himself through stories.

His work explores the Holocaust as a rupturing of time and history, but his restored fragments and storied loops that move from subject to reflection and back, and retell but do not create stories anew, heal the break. He explained in one interview that "during the Holocaust the covenant was broken," and in another that "the war represents the year zero and Auschwitz is as important as Sinai."[88] In *Night* he shows "the end, the finality of the event," explaining to yet another interviewer that "Everything came to an end — man, history, literature, religion, God. There was nothing left." But he added: "And yet we begin again with *Night....* I am still searching. I am still exploring. I am still protesting."[89]

In *Night* the apocalypse repeats, rather than effecting a single, final break: "Yet another last night. The last night at home, the last night in the ghetto, the last night in the train, and, now, the last night in Buna," he writes.[90] For, with O'Brien, Antin and Crow Dog, Wiesel challenges the linear construction of history that erases the past from the present: the long run in *Night* is also that of Jews through history, but he affirms that "[w]e're not going to run like this till the end of the world," along the "endless road" following "blind destiny."[91] Though *Night* seems initially a quest for knowledge, with the traditional mentor figure and "initiation" that moves toward "the end of the road,"[92] in fact Wiesel's story enacts not the movement of a *Bildungsroman*—towards a place in society—but rather a parodic movement *away* from society, faith, origins, and identity.

When the living recite the *Kaddish*, the prayer for the dead, for themselves, and then follow "a hearse at our own funeral,"[93] the expected chronology of life then death is disrupted. This thanatognomonic movement haunts much Holocaust writing and is literalized by Martin Amis in *Time's Arrow*, where Wiesel's repeatedly expressed dislike of the phrase "to kill time," and the idea that Hitler will kill the Jews "before the clock strikes twelve, before they can hear the last stroke"[94] is also echoed by Amis's description of the stopped clock at Auschwitz.[95] Reversals of time's arrow and disruptions of history and chronology appear across the narrative of *Night*. Moshe closes "his eyes, as though to escape time," and later the narrator loses "all sense of time," realizes that the "stomach alone was aware of the passage of time," and thinks that he "had been running for years."[96] Characters repeatedly experience a tragedy of timing, for example, "by the time we had managed to open the window, it was too late"; "our eyes were opened, but too late"; "I had lost my crown for nothing"; "liberated ... two days after the evacuation"; or lose control of time ("I had not time to think.").[97] They try in vain to "conquer time and space and submit both to their will."[98] The narrator feels himself changing too quickly ("Had I changed so much, then? So quickly?") and moves from 14 years old to 18 in a flash, while his father moves from 50 to 40, and throughout, time twists, so that "seconds ... seemed like an eternity," speeds up so that it "passed very quickly," slows down to pass "very slowly," and stops, during the "endless night."[99]

Wiesel uses these temporal disruptions and tragedies of timing to indicate the paradox of time stopping, when "Night enveloped ... human history" and the sun refused to rise, as he explained in an interview, "while the Jews *remained* bound on time's wheel of fire, caught in a cog of the Nazi wheel of history."[100] "The wheel of history turned...," he writes in *Night*, echoing Shakespeare's "wheel of fire" in *King Lear,* confirming the parallel to *Lear* with his eight uses of the word "Never" in one passage that echo Lear's eight negatives in "No, no, no life.... Never, never, never, never, never."[101] Within a form that traditionally traces the progress of the self, Wiesel's autobiographical story collapses time's passage. He narrates the end of history and the beginning of time *beyond* time — the life of the corpse in the mirror.

But he also reclaims the negative (those eight nevers) as silence. "If I could ... communicate a Silence through silence I would do so.... I try to communicate that Silence with words," he explained.[102] The fissures in time's passages become the white space between words and the cracks between the fragments of his mosaic. He believes that writers can "never express in words — coherent, intelligible words" the story of the Holocaust, for the "language of night was not human; it was primitive, almost animal," and "*negated* all other language and took its place."[103] Words became meaningless during and after the Holocaust — the word "furnace" was "the only word which did have any meaning" in the camp, remembers the narrator in *Night,*[104] and Wiesel has insisted that "[w]ords had been degraded. Words had been betrayed. There had been a kind of aggression against the word itself during the war," or that "[w]ords are no longer innocent; words are dangerous. We have learned that in our time."[105]

He added in a lecture that "words are no longer innocent," but that "silence is filled with new meaning." If, as he posits, "[l]anguage had been corrupted," then "it had to be invented anew and purified." He continued: "Had any one of us told the whole story he would have been proclaimed mad."[106] So his writing tells not "the whole story" but a story in pieces. Wiesel "writes in order to find out not only the words but the silence within the words, not only the stories but the life beyond the stories."[107] The mirror is shattered, but the silences and codes of a hidden story remain unbroken, for "[w]e speak in code, we survivors, and this code cannot be broken."[108] Fragments and the gaps and silences between the fragments, may make a true story, for "[t]he full story of the Holocaust" cannot be told — "[a]ll that we know is fragmentary."[109] His fragmented language, the ellipses, long dashes, interruptions, and inserted pauses, tells the story, as in *Night* when the narrator's father repeats Nazi lies but his silences speak the truth; or when the silent gestures of his mother and sister as they move toward the cattle cars, and the silent gaze later between father and son, communicate a wordless understanding.

Storying the Self IV: "to reconcile the two attitudes"[110]

"Now we've burned our bridge behind us," joked someone.[111] American Indian Movement activists at the 1973 siege of Wounded Knee had just burned a wooden bridge so that federal agents could not sneak behind a group of Native American women and children. This figural and literal burning of a bridge between two cultures recalls the moment in 1915 when Haitian writer Edmond Laforest tied a Larousse dictionary around his neck and leapt to his death from a bridge; Henry Louis Gates, Jr. calls Laforest's bridge-suicide "a symbolic, if ironic, statement of the curious relation of the marginalized writer," and "an emblem of [the] relation of overwhelming indenture."[112] As expressions of the impossibility of bridging an "impassable gulf" between cultures, or of negotiating a non-destructive cultural encounter, both moments also recall the end of Aldous Huxley's *Brave New World* when John the Savage, who is raised on a Native American reservation and encounters the works of William Shakespeare, ties a noose around his neck and jumps to his death from the archway of a light-house.[113]

Colonial theorists focus on these binary dynamics of resistance or absorption that burned cultural bridges and drowned reciprocal exchange in the white noise of imperialism. But they ignore dialogic exchanges that negotiated the contact zone and built a bridge across the gulf. As Wiesel explains: words may "enrich life or unleash death. But they must be links, not spears; offerings, not swords; tales of bridges to be built, not destroyed."[114] Or, in *Hope Against Hope*, he insists that words must be a "bridge ... a connection, a burning connection. And this connection should not separate me from you — rather, the opposite."[115] As witness and storyteller, he has offered *himself* as the bridge that burns but connects — the link between cultures, and between past and present — while seeking a connection between subject-self and third-person object-self of the mirror. He told an interviewer that his "position in the Jewish community is really the position of a witness from within and defender from without." This position, he continued, comes from his commitment to "the duties and privileges of a storyteller — of a writer. From the inside ... I am critical. If Jews are criticized or attacked from the outside, then I try to defend them. What I try to do (it's very hard) is to reconcile the two attitudes."[116]

In rebuilding the self in the mirror as a subject-self of multiple temporalities, a storied self that bears the traces and scars of history, he has constructed a *witness-self*, too. After the war, he says, he felt "the obsession to tell the tale, to bear witness that every person shared and nourished and had to put forward," and so the autobiographical imperative becomes the witness imperative. *Night* was therefore "an autobiographical story" but also "a kind of testimony of one witness speaking of his own life, his own death."[117] Wiesel's storytelling is inseparable from his philosophies of the self-as-subject and the self-as-witness. His self-definition as a witness takes up the forced vision of the self as object, in order to witness by choice, translate the mirror-vision of a doubled self into a "writer-witness," and restore the self as subject.[118] As a writer-witness he performs the two meanings of "witnessing"—*observing*, but also *bearing witness*, a dual role that combines what he describes as the two "key expressions in my mythology, in my universe ... the eye [and] silence": the witnessing eye is also the witness whose silences between words tell the story.[119]

As witness and storyteller, Wiesel implants a sense of audience within his narrative voice. In retelling stories, he begins a dialogue with the stories and with himself: "I try to tell stories and understand the stories I tell," he says of the two-part story-telling process.[120] He tells himself stories as he writes, seemingly speaking aloud to himself as audience: "When I write, it is as if I am telling a story. When I wrote *A Beggar in Jerusalem*, I wrote it in one great sweep. And the amazing thing — as I was writing, my lips were moving. The book is a tale because I told it as I wrote it. Afterwards I was hoarse for a week."[121] He is not writer but storyteller, and so his storied self is also a dialogic self of stories: "the word 'writer' does not really apply. I see myself much more as a storyteller," he told an interviewer.[122]

Another audience and mirror for his stories is God, but this only adds another fragment of "I" identity to the subject-self. A head-note to one of his novels reads "God made man because he loves stories," and Wiesel later remarked in an interview: "When I said [that] ... he who? He man or he God?" The "I" who loves stories is both man and God, for: "Ultimately we are two: I and God, I and I." Proposing a doubled self of addresser and addressee in one, he continues: "Who is the other 'I'? It's when I speak and I say 'I,' I address myself to the other 'I' but then I speak *for* him as well." The witness and storyteller knows not "I-It or I-You or I-Thou" but "now ... I-I."[123]

But in spite of this self-audience or "I-I," Wiesel reaches out for the "I-You or I-Thou." His "prayer which fits storytellers of all times, of all places" is as follows: "My only prayer, God, is that You give me good listeners." For, he continues: "the listener is part of the tale, what Buber called the I-and-Thou. When one tells a tale, one relives it. One does not talk to the listener. One talks with the listener."[124] Even his continuing dialogue with the storyteller Moshe, whose voice mingles with his own to form multi-vocal stories, involves the reader: "today when I write, I wonder whether it is not [Moshe] who is writing in my place, whether the voice I think is mine is really his. Perhaps it is his, the tales are his tales, and what he has seen I have seen, and now I try to make you see."[125] He is listener and teller at once, bridging the gap between Moshe and the reader, who must listen and tell in turn.

The reader is important to the process of rebuilding the shattered mirror into a mosaic of stories and voices. To rebuild the *other* in himself he must believe in the *other* of the reader, for "if there is hope it comes from the other ... we are the hope of the other."[126] As a witness to the self, Wiesel tells stories that make the reader a witness too. His work is full of examples of bad readers and audience, like the people in the opening of *Night,* who reject Moshe's story, or the boy who "was convinced later that were he to survive, he would tell the tale; he was convinced that if he would tell the tale history would be redeemed.... Part of the tale was told and man did not change."[127] Even the original ending of *Un di Velt Hot Geshvign* records the world's failure to respond: "Now ten years after Buchenwald, I often ask myself: Was is worth breaking the mirror? Was it worth it? And the world was silent."[128] The world's silence is like a mirror without a reflective surface, refusing to give back an answer to the question, and so Wiesel must build new mirror and audience.

Asked in 1999 whether it had been worthwhile to smash the mirror, Wiesel answered: "I asked myself this question even then, and today the answer is — yes."[129] Storytelling has rebuilt the "voice within me," and the storied self of multiple voices and persons offers the "answers *within* yourself," but storytelling has also constructed the voices *without,* the reader worthy of the story.[130] Bakhtin's idea that "[e]ach utterance is filled with echoes" makes language itself a chamber of trails and traces. He writes:

"Each utterance is filled with echoes and reverberations of other utterances.... At the base of the [almost a memoir genre] lies ... the dialogic nature of human thinking about truth. The dialogic means of seeking truth is counterposed to official monologism, which pretends to possess a ready-made truth."[131] Wiesel, who acknowledges, but tries to close the distance between past / present and text / audience through his echo-chambers of voices, times, and traces, involves the reader as a dialogic participant, "trail[ing] every word."[132]

He inscribes his texts with an awareness of audience, like Apess, who notes that certain facts are "given not with a view of appearing great in the estimation of others," or are related "to show the reader how we were treated," and poses a series of rhetorical questions to the reader[133]; or Black Elk, who implies questions from readers and emphasizes the "you" throughout *Black Elk Speaks*.[134] On five occasions Black Elk acknowledges an audience just after explaining that he must tell his vision in order to use it. "If I thought I was doing it myself ... no power could come through," he explains, for "a man who has a vision is not able to use the power of it until after he has performed the vision on earth for the people to see."[135] Black Elk shows and performs his vision, realizing it through his audience. The "power was in the meaning," he says, but then amends this: the "power of it was in the *understanding* of its meaning."[136] The reader must "live that story," and become like the singing birds at the end of the book. Black Elk teaches his vision as though a song, so that "some little root of the sacred tree still lives."[137] "Nourish it then, that it may leaf and bloom and fill with singing birds," he tells Neihardt and his audience.[138]

As a performance, Black Elk's narrative makes words into events or acts, the whole universe a symbol that may be contained in a hat, and saying something makes it true, and thoughts make reality, he says.[139] Just as Wiesel insists that "Words can be acts ... words are important as events, as forms of action, as calls for action. God had to say for the world to be created.... Tales change people."[140] The world is an event in process for Wiesel and these Native storytellers: "words make the trail," and create what Eastman calls in *Indian Boyhood* a "living book."[141] The dialogic process of performative narration, involving Black Elk, his translating son, Neihardt, Neihardt's transcribing daughter, tribal members who participate in the storytelling, and the readers filling Black Elk's utterances with their own echoes, challenges the rule of "everybody for himself and with little rules of his own," everyone with "his own little vision that he followed."[142]

Black Elk narrates his life-story as "fulfillment of a duty," to "save his Great Vision for men."[143] Eastman reveals himself to know and save himself: "I showed myself," he writes, and on this occasion is asked, "Are you a Sioux?" "Yes," he answers, and the exposure and self-definition saves his life.[144] Crow Dog uses autobiography as a ritual: a rebirth like the Sweat Lodge ritual, a circular rite like the Ghost Dance, and a journey like the Yuwipi ceremony. Her autobiography is a way to remember, revise, and pass on her inheritance: she becomes "wholly Indian" and cries "A Voice I will send."[145] These autobiographies, and Wiesel's combination of witnessing, storytelling, remembering, and self-narrating, collapse the assumption that the American autobiographical tradition, with its solitary heroes and individualized identities, is somehow impossible to translate into the relational matrix of Native culture, or the communal memory of Jewish culture. In fact, the Bakhtinian, dialogic self of these Native autobiographies, and of Wiesel's body of work, is that of the autobiographical participant-observer writ large. Encountering past and ideal selves, private and public selves, essential and constructed selves, states of being and processes of becoming, autobiographical models, and fragments of life amongst the whole, Euroamerican autobiographies have often expressed a national consciousness and the individual in relation to national type or community. They have been an important part of nation-making — asking, what is this American, this new man?[146] The American Adam has answered, with Black Elk: "Behold this day, for it is yours to make."[147] In Euroamerican autobiographies too, the self has encountered self in the mirror, smashed that mirror, and known that "the end of all exploring will be to arrive where we started, and know the place for the first time."[148] American autobiographers have reconstructed the self and revisited the past in order to move toward the future, in an open loop of dialogic encounter — gazing upon the self in the mirror, and feeling the gaze of a young child upon their faces.

Notes

1. Elie Wiesel, "Art and Culture After the Holocaust," opening address, International Symposium on the Holocaust, New York, June 3, 1974, in *Against Silence: The Voice and Vision of Elie Wiesel,* ed. Irving Abrahamson (New York: Holocaust

Library, 1985), Vol. 2, 88; Wiesel, *Legends of Our Time*, in Harry James Cargas, *Conversations with Elie Wiesel* (South Bend, Indiana: Justice Books, 1992), 99.

2. Elie Wiesel, *Ethics and Memory* (Berlin, New York: Walter de Gruyter, 1997), 15.

3. Elie Wiesel, *Night,* trans. Stella Rodway (New York: Hill & Wang, 1960), 109.

4. Ibid., 3.

5. Mikhail Bakhtin, *Problems of Dostoevsky's Poetics* (Ann Arbor: Ardis, 1973), 287.

6. Ibid., 85; 62.

7. Ibid., 102; 106.

8. Ibid., 34.

9. Ibid., 88.

10. Cargas, *Conversations*, 88.

11. Ibid., 109; 110.

12. Final chapter of *Un di Velt Hot Geshvign* [*And the World Remained Silent*] (Buenos Aires: *Farband fun Poylishe Yidn in Argentine*, 1956), excerpted in *Against Silence,* Vol. 3, 59.

13. Ibid. 57.

14. Wiesel, *Night*, xi.

15. Opening of *Un di Velt Hot Geshvign*, excerpted in *Against Silence*, Vol. 3, 57. My emphasis.

16. Wiesel, *Night*, 32.

17. Ibid., 33.

18. Interview in *Parabola* 10 (1985): 2.

19. Cargas, 147; Ekkehard Schuster and Reinhold Boschert-Kimmig, *Hope Against Hope: Johann Baptist Metz and Elie Wiesel Speak Out on the Holocaust* (New York: Paulist Press, 1999), 74

20. Wiesel, *Ethics and Memory,* 15.

21. Wiesel, *Night*, 3; 37.

22. Bakhtin, *The Dialogic Imagination* (Austin: University of Texas Press, 1981), 91; Jean Baudrillard, *In the Shadow of the Silent Majorities* (New York: Semiotext(e), 1983), 37.

23. Walter Benjamin, *Charles Baudelaire* (London: New Left, 1973), 169.

24. John Neihardt and Black Elk, *Black Elk Speaks: Being the Life Story of a Holy Man of the Oglala Sioux* (Lincoln: University of Nebraska Press, 1979, 1932), 179; Mary Crow Dog and Richard Erdoes, *Lakota Woman.* (New York: Grove Weidenfeld, 1990), 152.

25. Crow Dog and Erdoes, *Lakota Woman*, 262. Crow Dog puns on "tear," referring to the Trail of Tears.

26. Charles Eastman, *From the Deep Woods to Civilization* (Lincoln: University of Nebraska Press, 1977, 1916), 74.

27. Eastman, "The Language of Footprints," 1917, in *Indian Scout Craft and Lore* (New York: Dover, 1974), IV; Carlo Ginzberg, *Clues, Myths and the Historical Method* (Baltimore: John Hopkins, 1989), 96, 103.

28. Elie Wiesel, "How and Why I Write," interview with Heidi Anne Walker, *Journal of Education,* Spring, 1980, excerpted in *Against Silence,* Vol. 2, 118.

29. Elie Wiesel, "Answer to a Young Boy," lecture to National Press Club, Washington D.C., April 11, 1983, excerpted in *Against Silence,* Vol. 1, 196; 198.

30. Elie Wiesel, "The Holocaust as Literary Inspiration," *Dimensions of the Holocaust: Lectures at Northwestern University* (Evanston, Ill.: The University, 1977), 17.

31. Elie Wiesel, "The Call to Life," excerpted in *Against Silence,* Vol. 3, 62.

32. Cargas, *Conversations,* 3.

33. Elie Wiesel, "The Perils of Indifference," April 12, 1999, White House Symposium, in *Why Freedom Matters: The Spirit of the Declaration of Independence in Prose, Poetry, and Song from 1776 to the Present,* ed. Daniel R. Katz (New York: Workman Publishing, 2003), 90.

34. See n. 28.

35. Wiesel, excerpted in *Against Silence,* Vol. 3, 65.

36. Cited in ibid., 289.

37. Mary Antin, The *Promised Land* (New York: Penguin Books, 1997, 1912), 99; 101.

38. Ibid., 216; 198.

39. William Apess, *A Son of the Forest,* in *On Our Own Ground: The Complete Writings of William Apess, a Pequot* (Amherst: University of Massachusetts Press, 1992), 1; 19.

40. Ibid., 23.

41. Neihardt and Black Elk, *Black Elk Speaks,* 8.

42. Ibid., 8; 276; 2; 49.

43. Ibid., 276; 279; 210; 47; 45.

44. Crow Dog and Erdoes, *Lakota Woman,* 200; 185.

45. See the mirroring of characters in *The Last of the Mohicans* and the novel's two-part structure.

46. Wiesel, *Night,* 81.

47. Crow Dog and Erdoes, *Lakota Woman,* 9.

48. Ralph Ellison, *The Collected Essays of Ralph Ellison* (New York: Modern Library, 2003), 82.

49. Ralph Ellison, *Invisible Man* (New York: Vintage Books, 1952), 537; 513.

50. Ibid., 3; 239.

51. Crow Dog and Erdoes, *Lakota Woman,* 189; 21.

52. Ibid., 90; 116; 120; 195; 218; 136.

53. Ibid., 121; 150.

54. Ibid., 134.

55. Ibid., 167.

56. Ibid., 195; 84; 145.

57. Ibid., 9; 177.

58. Ibid., 238; 258.

59. Ibid., 8.

60. Ibid., 9; 17; 176.

61. Ibid., 135; 139; 73; 77.

62. Ibid., 11

63. Ibid., 3–4; 8; 35; 61; 224.

64. Ibid., 126.

65. Ibid., 155; 172.

66. Ibid., 151.

67. Elie Wiesel, *Messengers of God: Biblical Portraits and Legends,* trans. Marion Wiesel (New York: Random House, 1976), xi.

68. Cargas, *Conversations,* 108

69. Ibid., 56

70. Ibid., 162; 55.

71. Wiesel, *Night,* 95; 6.

72. Antin, The *Promised Land,* 72.

73. Ibid., 48.

74. Cargas, *Conversations,* 130.

75. Wiesel, *Night,* 10.

76. Crow Dog and Erdoes, *Lakota Woman,* 56; 262.

77. Ibid., 6; 148–9; 18; 26; 32.

78. Ibid., 51; 72.

79. Ibid., 25.

80. Ibid., 24.

81. Tim O'Brien, "The Lives of the Dead" in *The Things They Carried* (Boston: Houghton Mifflin, 1990), 273.

82. O'Brien, "Notes," in *The Things They Carried,* 179.

83. Ibid., 265, 267; Wiesel, *Night,* 81.

84. O'Brien, interview with the author, July 12, 2005.

85. Wiesel, *Night,* 10.

86. Ibid., 14. My emphasis.

87. Loren Baritz, "A Jew's American Dilemma," *Commentary,* 33, 6 (June 1962): 525. For the importance of memory and history in Jewish writing, see also Alvin H. Rosenfeld, *Midstream: A Monthly Jewish Review,* 21, 4 (April 1975): 54 "we are not allowed to indulge ourselves ultimately in fabrication. Whenever we ... overextend ourselves in imaginative play, history calls us back to our senses: thunderously. For that is the fate of the Jews, to vouch for the truths of history."

88. Cargas, *Conversations,* 56; Cited by Joyce Hackett, "The Territory of Trauma," in *Boston Review,* December 2001.

89. Interview with Morton A. Reichek, *Present Tense,* Spring, 1976, excerpted in *Against Silence,* Vol. 3, 243.

90. Wiesel, *Night,* 79.

91. Ibid., 82; 83.

92. Ibid., 89.

93. Ibid., 31.

94. Ibid., 76.

95. See for example, Cargas, *Conversations,* 155.

96. Ibid., 5; 34; 50; 68.

97. Ibid., 12; 21; 54; 78; 27.

98. Ibid., 63.

99. Ibid., 37; 29; 13; 10; 24.

100. Ibid., 54. Wiesel adds: "Night is a symbol of that period."

101. Ibid., 107; 32; William Shakespeare, *King Lear,* V. iii. 367–370.

102. Cargas, *Conversations,* 5.

103. "Why I Write," in *From the Kingdom of Memory: Reminiscences* (New York: Summit Books, 1990) 14–15. My emphasis.

104. Wiesel, *Night,* 36.

105. *The Eternal Light* (1970), excerpted in *Against Silence,* Vol. 3, 61; Cargas, 85.

106. Wiesel, "The Holocaust as Literary Inspiration," 6; 8.

107. In March 1980, cited in *Against Silence,* Vol. 3, 285.

108. Wiesel, "The Holocaust as Literary Inspiration," 7.

109. Elie Wiesel, "Jewish Values in the Post-Holocaust Future: A Symposium," *Judaism*, 16 (Summer 1967): 283.

110. Cargas, *Conversations*, *33*.

111. Crow Dog and Erdoes, *Lakota Woman*, 132.

112. Henry Louis Gates, Jr., "Writing 'Race' and the Difference it Makes," *Critical Inquiry*, 12 (Autumn 1985): 13. See also Ralph Ellison on the "Negroes in the North" who encountered white America and "fell into a great chasm," *The Collected Essays of Ralph Ellison*, 323.

113. In "The Future of the Red Man" Forum 23 (1897): 698–708. Simon Pokagan writes against the idea of an "impassable gulf." For more on bridging the cultural divide via literature, see W.E.B. Du Bois in *The Souls of Black Folk* (Chicago A.C. McClurg, 1903): "I sit with Shakespeare and he winces not. Across the color line I move arm in arm with Balzac and Dumas ... [etc]."

114. Speech on receiving the King Solomon Award, American-Israel Cultural Foundation, New York, November 20, 1977, excerpted in *Against Silence*, Vol. 2, 107.

115. Wiesel, *Hope Against Hope*, 67.

116. Cargas, *Conversations*, 33.

117. Cargas, *Conversations*, 87, 86.

118. As he described himself in an interview, ibid., 88.

119. In the *U.S. Catholic Jubilee*, September 1971, 30.

120. "Answer to a Young Boy," lecture to National Press Club, Washington D.C., April 11, 1983, excerpted in *Against Silence*, Vol. 1, 197.

121. Cited in *Against Silence*, Vol. 3, 291.

122. Cargas, *Conversations*, 84.

123. Ibid., 111; 109.

124. Lecture, February 18, 1970, Washington University, excerpted in *Against Silence*, Vol.2, 55–57.

125. Excerpted in *Against Silence*, Vol. 3, 62.

126. Cargas, *Conversations*, 170.

127. Wiesel, "The Holocaust as Literary Inspiration," 5.

128. Final chapter of *Un di Velt Hot Geshvign*, excerpted in *Against Silence*, Vol. 3, 60.

129. Wiesel, *Hope Against Hope*, 63.

130. Wiesel, *Night*, 62; 3. My emphasis.

131. Mikhail Bakhtin, *The Problem of Speech Genres* (Austin: University of Texas Press, 1986), 91; *Problems of Dostoevsky's Poetics*, 110.

132. Bakhtin, *The Dialogical Imagination*, 187.

133. Apess, *A Son of the Forest*, 4; 5.

134. Neihardt and Black Elk, *Black Elk Speaks*, 203; 208–209.

135. Ibid., 209; 208.

136. Ibid., 210; 216. My emphasis.

137. Ibid., 1; 280.

138. Ibid., 280.

139. Ibid., 240; 5; 94; 104; 86.

140. Interview, December 3, 1970, excerpted in *Against Silence*, Vol. 2, 60–61.

141. Diane Glancy, *Claiming Breath* (Lincoln: University of Nebraska Press, 1992), 4: "The Word is important in Native America tradition. You speak the path on which you walk. Your words make the trail. You have to be careful with words.

They can shape the future"; Eastman, *Indian Boyhood* (Lincoln: University of Nebraska Press, 1992), 115.

142. Neihardt and Black Elk, *Black Elk Speaks*, 219; 37.

143. Ibid., xi.

144. Ibid., 12.

145. Crow Dog and Erdoes, *Lakota Woman*, 260.

146. See J. Hector St. John De Crevecoeur, *Letters from An American Farmer* (1782), letter 3.

147. Neihardt and Black Elk, *Black Elk Speaks*, 42; R.W.B. Lewis, *The American Adam* (Chicago: University of Chicago Press, 1955), 81.

148. T. S. Eliot, *The Four Quartets* (1942). See also Eudora Welty, *One Writer's Beginnings* (Cambridge: Harvard University Press, 1984), 102. "It is our inward journey that leads us through time — forward or back, seldom in a straight line, most often spiraling.... As we discover, we remember; remembering we discover; and most intensely do we experience this when our separate journeys converge. Our living experience at those meeting points is one of the charged dramatic fields."

Creative Ambiguity in Wiesel's Storytelling

ROSEMARY HOROWITZ

Elie Wiesel's postwar life in Paris coincided with a particularly vibrant period in modern French literature and philosophy. Of that time, Wiesel says:

> I was intrigued and stimulated by the intellectual and artistic ferment of Paris. Still working on my education, I was an insatiable patron of the library. Never have I read so much. I devoured the works of Malraux, Mauriac, Paul Valery, George Bernanos, Ignazio Silone, and Roger Martin du Gard. I read everything by Camus ... and Sartre....[1]

Given this reading list, the Wiesel scholar Jack Kolbert, concludes that Wiesel was clearly influenced by the French Existentialists. Kolbert goes on to write that the philosophy of Albert Camus seems to have had the greatest impact on Wiesel.[2] The attraction to Camus is perhaps due to Wiesel's attempts to understand his wartime experiences, even if those experiences ultimately defy understanding and have no overarching meaning. Since the memory of the war was constantly with him, Wiesel's interests in narrative time seem similar to those of the French New Novelists, the group of writers who explored the relationship between past and present in their fiction.[3] And even now, years after leaving Paris, questions about how to live with uncertainty, disconnectedness, and disorder are still integral to Wiesel's writing. About this, Colin Davis writes that for Wiesel:

> The ambiguity inherent in writing and thought — their shared failure to occupy the open space of truth — is a point of departure, not an end.

> Storytelling, for Wiesel, takes place in the wake of a crisis of meaning and belief, but is not paralyzed by that crisis. It must act, affect, and alter. Storytelling may not deliver unambiguous messages, but it must still be a form of action in and on the world. The story does not communicate clear meanings; instead it confronts the reader with opacity and enigma, the ambiguity of experience and of the narrative of experience.[4]

Despite the uncertainty of life, one point that is supremely clear to Wiesel is that the lack of certainty should not deter one's action. Action imparts a measure of meaning to life, and to Wiesel, one form of action is storytelling. In addition, he hopes that his stories promote his readers to action. Overall, the question of how to act in the face of ambiguity underlies much of Wiesel's storytelling. And moreover, in his fiction, the ambiguity in the storytelling structure parallels the theme of ambiguity in the stories. Aspects of his writing style — the framing devices, the embedding of stories, the unreliability of narrators, and the sequencing of events — provide a means of exploring the subject of ambiguity.

Like the postmodernists, Wiesel is concerned with ambiguity; thus my discussion of the structural and thematic elements in his novels is informed to an extent by postmodern theory. One critic, Ken Ireland, notes that postmodernists purposely manipulate reader expectations: "Contemporary, especially Postmodern authors challenge the notion of certainty in various ways, thereby instilling uncertainty in readers, and encouraging them to impose their own order on texts."[5] One way in which postmodern authors challenge certainty is by acknowledging the instability of narrative frames. William Nelles's study of narrative levels, for instance, discusses ways in which the embedding of stories affects narrators and readers.[6] With respect to narrative strategies that introduce ambiguity, Nelles remarks:

> While embedding is frequently a latent source of unity and closure, it also has the potential to produce fragmentation and open-endedness ... narrative embedding often has the paradoxical effect not only of producing the illusion of a more profound realism or aesthetic unity ... but also of undercutting that illusion at the same time.[7]

Thus, the interplay between the internal and external frame may be exploited as a fictive strategy to increase ambiguity.

Another way that postmodern writers undermine certainty is by introducing temporal discontinuity. Noting that the linear unambiguous storyline is only one narrative strategy, Brian Richardson proposes a typology of non-realistic temporalities found in fiction. One type of story is the circular story, which "instead of ending returns to its own beginning, and thus continues indefinitely."[8] This indefiniteness means that the story has no permanent conclusion. An analysis of Wiesel's work reveals that he skillfully selects those narrative strategies that instill uncertainty in his narrators, as well as in his readers, in order to express his message of ambiguity.

Framing for Ambiguity

The narrative frame defines the borders of a text, and the choice of one narrative framework instead of another provides different degrees of resolution to a story. In general, a completed closed frame offers the most certainty; an open frame offers the least. In Wiesel's world view, resolution is an unobtainable goal. He expresses the belief that definite answers are impossible to achieve by the ways in which he frames his stories. Often, Wiesel uses an incomplete outer frame to underscore an indefinite ending. And, even when he closes the outer frame and brings the story back to its original setting, closure is not still gained because the outer frame is left incomplete. His stories with open outer frames amplify the uncertainty even further.

Dawn is an example of novel with an incomplete closed frame. The novel opens with Elisha, the main character, standing at a window, one autumn night in Palestine. He hears a crying child outside and thinks about the execution of John Dawson, an English officer, which will take place the next morning. While standing at the window, he also thinks about a beggar that he met years before. From the beggar Elisha learned that the night reflects one's thoughts, loves, and dreams. With that in mind, Elisha recalls the faces that he sees at night and thinks: "I looked out the window, where a shadowy face was taking shape out of the deep of the night. A sharp pain caught my throat. I could not take my eyes off the face. It was my own."[9] The action in the book takes place during one night, and the book ends the next day at dawn after Elisha shoots Dawson. The ending passage of the book is similar to its opening one. Elisha is again standing by the window and thinking:

> The night lifted, leaving behind it a grayish light the color of stagnant water. Soon there was only a tattered fragment of darkness, hanging in midair, the other side of the window. Fear caught my throat. The tattered fragment of darkness had a face. Looking at it, I understood the reason for my fear. The face was my own.[10]

Killing Dawson, while perhaps useful to the political and military cause, makes Elisha an executioner. By killing his enemy, Elisha turns himself into the type of person he detests. In effect, he symbolically kills his innocent self when he kills Dawson. Thus, carrying out the orders does not bring Elisha relief. On the contrary, it brings him tremendous anguish. He becomes afraid of himself. He has exchanged places with the enemy and gains no peace. His inner turmoil and the outer violence continue without end.

A Beggar in Jerusalem is an example of a circular frame, which provides no lasting resolution. The novel explores the attempted annihilation of the Jews in Europe during the Holocaust and the fights for Israel. David, the main character, opens by addressing the reader:

> Look: I am watching you. I am speaking to you, yet I am sure of nothing. Not even of the moment which unites us, you and me. I cling to you to become one with you, only to rise to the surface again, alone, expelled from time, not from the tale.... Anyway, do come closer. The beggar insists. Please.... At night I dwell among madmen, visionaries, vagabonds of all types. My friends, my companions. I'll tell you about them. You will listen and decide for yourself.[11]

Right from the start David describes his state of mind. He is unsure about what he is doing and saying, and thus questions himself throughout the novel. His use of the word "anyway" after the ellipsis suggests that despite all doubts, we should at least listen. The story ends with the same people in the same place. David says:

> While accepting ambiguity and the quest arising from it, the beggar at times would like to lose his memory; he can not. On the contrary: it keeps growing and swelling, storing away events and faces until the past of others becomes one with his own.... For him everything is question, including the miracle that keeps him on the surface. That is why I am still here on this haunted square, in this city where nothing is lost and nothing dispersed. An indispensable, necessary transition.... For tales, like people, all have the same beginning.[12]

David remains in the square hoping for answers. But, there are none, and the story ends in the old city of Jerusalem at night, where it starts and with whom. The ending does not supply an answer to the book's key question: "How can one work for the living without by that very act betraying those who are absent?"[13] No matter what else happens, the question remains, and it is perpetual. The question is the only thing that is fixed.

Open outer frames reinforce ambiguity even further, and these are readily found in Wiesel's novels. Even his love stories, the genre that typically offers closure, do not provide resolution. *The Accident* provides an example. The book opens with an unnamed narrator and his girlfriend Kathleen in New York City on their way to a movie. As they cross the street to the theater, a taxi strikes and injures the narrator. He is taken to a hospital, which is the setting for the remainder of the novel. During his hospital stay, the narrator thinks about the events that led up to his accident. He thinks about many things: his first meeting with Kathleen, the concentration camps, his family, his childhood, his suffering, his death, and God. Near the end of the novel, he realizes that he will never be free from his past. In contrast, Kathleen believes that their love could eventually overcome his past. Kathleen starts the following exchange:

> "And you'll let me make you happy?"
> "I'll let you make me happy."
> "And you promise to forget the past?"
> "I promise to forget the past."
> "And you'll think only about our love?"
> "Yes."[14]

Even as the narrator agrees to Kathleen's requests, he knows that he is lying. Instead of thinking about the future with Kathleen, he is thinking about the train that took his family to the death camps. And so even if love could possibly supplant his horrible memories, he notes that his accident happened the next day. The final chapter makes it clear that the dead have power over the living and that the narrator may have to choose one over the other. With that ending, the novel eliminates love as an antidote to uncertainty.

The Fifth Son is another novel in which the open frame reflects the message of ambiguity. Ariel, the main character in the novel, is traveling to Germany to learn about his father's past. Among other things, he learns that his parents had another son who was killed in the ghetto. Near the end of the novel, Ariel finds his brother's killer and promises to recite the account of those who suffered during the Holocaust. He makes this pledge:

> I shall speak. I shall tell the tale.... I shall describe the solitude of the survivors, the anguish of their children. I shall relate the death of my little brother. I shall set forth, I shall recall the wounds, the moanings, the tears, I shall speak of the voices of dusk, the mute violence of night. I shall recite the Kaddish of dawn.[15]

His promise to keep the knowledge of the murderer alive is reassuring, but the book does not sustain that reassurance. Ariel wants to understand the murderer's motive and knows it will take time. The meeting with the murderer is so powerful that it forces Ariel to release his own anger, as well as the anger of generations of Jews. To a degree, his entire life was in preparation for that one single encounter. Ariel is rewarded with a measure of calmness. He seems to have achieved his life's goal. However, the novel does not end on that note. Ariel's calm does not last. The final chapter takes place ten years later. Ariel thinks:

> Still, it's no good deceiving myself. I look upon my life not as a failure but as a defeat. Son of survivors, I feel ill at ease in a complacent world that, in order to rest easier, has repudiated me even my birth. For me all is constraint: language and silence, love and the absence of love. What I wish to say, I shall never say. What I wish to understand, I shall never understand.[16]

That Ariel cannot fulfill his earlier pledge implies the impossibility of speaking about horrific events. Indeed, the open frame underscores the point that no amount of time is sufficient for what Ariel needs to relate. He will never be released from his obligations to the living and to the dead. Those are persistent.

Unlike many of the novels, *The Judges* seemingly holds out the possibility of a resolution. During the novel, which spans one night, five airline passengers stranded in a snow storm are questioned by their host. He asks them about their lives and instills fear in them with his relentless interrogation. He wants them to evaluate the worth of their lives and says that he will condemn the least worthy to die. By the end of the book, the judge is killed, the storm passes, and the passengers resume their flight. This signals an apparent return to normalcy. However, this return to normalcy is short-lived. The novel ends with a series of questions that Razziel, one of the passengers, poses to himself. The questions that he asks himself are similar to those the Judge asked the stranded passengers earlier. So even though the judge is dead, his questions still remain. At the end, closure remains elusive because the questions are unanswered.

Despite Wiesel's refusal to provide answers, in his world, there is one honorable manner of gaining some personal, if not communal closure — tell the story to someone else. That happens in many of his novels, where one narrator takes over the message or the question from another at the end of the work. Books such as *The Town Beyond the Wall* and *The Oath* show that although the situations and people change, the messages and the questions remain. *The Oath* begins and ends with an encounter between an old man who has promised never to speak about the terror that he saw in his hometown of Kolvillag and a young man who is trying to undercover the secret of the town. The old man explains that he is sworn to secrecy and cannot recount the terrible history of the Jews who lived in the town. However, during the course of the novel, the old man tells the young man what happened, and in doing so eases his own burden. By the end of the work, two men return to their homes. The younger understands that he has been changed by the information and that he has become responsible for the older man's secret. Now, the younger carries the knowledge of the destruction of Kolvillag. In order to free himself of the responsibility, the young man will have to tell the story to some else. He is the bearer of the tale until he transmits it. Above all, what matters is the transmission of the story.

The Town Beyond the Wall makes a similar point. At the beginning of novel, Michael is in prison, dreaming about his hometown. Throughout the novel, he thinks about his town and the events that lead to his arrest. At the end of the novel, Michael is still in jail, suspecting he is going insane. However, in his cell, there is a young man who does not speak, and in order to keep his own sanity, Michael tries to communicate with his fellow inmate. In order to break though the man's muteness, Michael makes wild gestures to the inmate, yells at the man, and tells him stories. Although the novel ends with Michael still in prison, he has succeeded in communicating with the other man. With that accomplished, the inmate will pass on Michael's message about indifference, the worst human behavior. The ongoing action of telling means that the story has no end.

In much of his fiction, Wiesel's reliance on ambiguous external frames suggests that closure is not a realistic goal. Striving for certainty is futile because ambivalence is an inherent part of all encounters. Ultimately, the ambiguity in the framework of the novels leaves open the possibility that there are no answers. Rather, there are only ongoing questions about meaning.

Embedding for Ambiguity

To include an inner story within an outer framework, authors may nest a story within a story or provide occasions for telling stories. Depending on an author's purpose, Nelles notes that the technique of embedding increases the open-endedness of a story. This is seen in Wiesel's novels, where embedding magnifies the ambiguity

The structure of *The Testament* provides an example of the way in which Wiesel's nested stories reinforce his message of ambiguity. The book opens with a first person preface signed by E.W. The preface describes a meeting between E.W. and Grisha Paltielovich Kossover in Israel in 1972. This preface is followed by a letter to Grisha from his father, Paltiel. Then, a third-person narrator describes Grisha reading "The Testament," the document that Paltiel wrote in prison. Interspersed with the third person, there are excerpts from the prison document. Another narrator, Zupanev, a stenographer working in Paltiel's prison, also speaks to Grisha. Within the novel, Zupanev's story appears in italicized print. The alternating narrators fragment the novel, and the layering of preface and letter on top of the core story blurs the boundary between fact and fiction. The initials E.W. suggest Elie Wiesel, giving the impression that Wiesel and Grisha had an actual meeting in Israel during which they discussed the real poet, Paltiel. Including a letter from Paltiel to Grisha further suggests a work of history. In this way, Wiesel draws our attention to the possibility that the work is historical. The fictional nature of the narrative is thrown into doubt, reinforcing the confusion about the meaning of the story.

Occasions for storytelling provide further opportunities to amplify ambiguity. That happens when storytellers fail to clearly articulate their points. Instead of advancing the plot or giving insights into the characters, Wiesel's storytellers often end up confusing their listeners, and sometimes, even themselves. This confusion stems in part from the source of material for a story. Often, the storytellers draw from biblical, historical, and personal sources, without making distinctions between the reliability of those sources. In some cases, storytellers may not have first-hand experience of the events they are recounting. They are not necessarily the witnesses to the events they describe. And even if they are witnesses, they may give their account in associative, not in linear order. That makes the stories hard to follow and obscures the message.

A Beggar in Jerusalem contains numerous examples of the difficulties of judging a story. For instance, Itzik's stories, as David says, are

> Unlike those told by his companions, they grow out of the immediate present. The others, having chosen to be contemporaries of their ancestors, are unwilling to limit themselves to dates and locations. For them, chronological truth or nominal truth is only accidentally related to truth. What do they care if the events they relate happened to other witnesses, in an epoch long since gone? We don't care either. If Itzik sticks to his own memories, it's because he was never good at history.[17]

By defining different types of storytelling truths, David glosses over differences between lived experiences and historical events. He notes that his companions are not necessarily bound to a specific time or place. Their reliance on material from other times and places makes it hard for listeners to follow their account. That is not their concern, however, because they are not responsible for figuring out the meaning of their tales. That is task for listeners.

In addition to blending their sources, storytellers test their listeners even further by refusing to give answers about the truth of a story. As a result, along with confusion, there is anger. Sometimes storytellers grow angry when they are pressed to defend a story. Listeners grow angry as well. The storytelling round between Itzik, Shlomo, Yakov, Moshe, Velvel, Zalmen, and David that follows the introduction of Itzik provides an example of the way the anger stems from a storyteller's elusiveness. In one scene, the men are sitting by the Western Wall trading stories about fear. A pilot, who is listening to them, questions Itzik's war story:

> A young officer, an Air Force lieutenant, opens his eyes wide: "You ... you really fought in the war?"
>
> "Come on now, sonny!" Itzik reprimands him. "A little respect, if you don't mind! I sniffed powder long before you, and a hell of a lot more than you ever will!'
>
> Taken aback, the officer mumbles a few words of apology, then clears his throat: "I didn't mean to offend you, but...."[18]

Itzik reacts harshly to the pilot's probing question, and even goes so far as to scold the pilot. Not only does the storyteller fail to answer the pilot's question at that point, but later in an exchange with Velvel, another man in the group, the pilot becomes more frustrated in his attempts to get definite answers. After Velvel tells his story about a bombing in Jerusalem, the narrator David notes:

> The pilot, our only visitor from the outside world, displays his good manners; he greets Velvel's little story with a short outburst of laughter. Yet, not knowing what to make of it all, he looks annoyed, irritated. He wants to get up and leave, but Itzik, leaning on his arm, holds him back. "Come on, sonny! You're not going to insult the other speakers, are you?"[19]

The answers given by the beggars do not satisfy the pilot. When the storytellers fail to provide the pilot with satisfaction, his initial response is to leave the group. However, Itzik criticizes that behavior. By reacting with annoyance and irritation, the pilot reveals the limits of his tolerance. As the storytellers continue to mix biblical, dream, historical, and personal sources, the pilot continues his attempts to leave. What matters to the pilot are the answers; what matters to Itzik and the others are the stories. Even if a story tests the boundaries of tolerance, listening is still required.

The Accident takes the position that storytellers and listeners are bound by the act of listening. In the novel, the narrator asks Sarah to talk about herself. As she starts her story, he remembers that

> I did nothing, I listened. Attentively. I was sitting on the edge of the bed, next to her half-undressed body, listening to her story. My clenched fingers were like a vise around my throat. Now, every time I think of her, I curse myself, as I curse those who did not think of her at the time of her undoing.... I think of her and I curse myself, as I curse history which has made us what we are: a source of malediction. History which deserves death, destruction. Whoever listens to Sarah and doesn't change, whoever enters Sarah's world and doesn't invent new gods and new religions, deserves death and destruction.[20]

This encounter brings Sarah no relief, and telling her story brings her no comfort. In fact, the narrator leaves the room even before she is finished with her account. Later on, he looks for her unsuccessfully. What happens to her is never known, but what happens to him is revealed as the novel progresses. He is changed by her story and wants to find meaning in it. He wants to find an explanation for the cruelty of life, as well as a reason for the death of his family members, including his mother Sarah. Just like his friend Gyula, the narrator hopes to find definite answers to life's mysteries. But at the end of the novel, he is left with the ashes of the burnt portrait. Perhaps only death gives life its significance.

Not content with one level of ambiguity, Wiesel uses the internal frame and the embedded story to add a second level. Functioning like the external frames, his internal frames and embedded stories also thwart attempts of his characters and his readers to reconcile the indefinite messages in the stories. Given the importance of storytelling and listening in the novels, perhaps meaning is found in the acts of storytelling and listening. Perhaps, the exchange between people, not necessarily the message, imparts a degree of meaning.

Narrating for Ambiguity

Narrators serve many roles, but generally they anchor a story. By contrast, Wiesel's narrators compound the uncertainty in the novels. Some of his narrators doubt their own sanity. They claim to be delirious, feverish, or possessed. With that claim, they dismiss their own ramblings as nonsense. Other narrators doubt their own waking experience. They say that an event was a dream. The dream state, with its fleeting and chaotic images, becomes their means of undermining their own tale. And still others question their own memory. The degree to which they claim that their memory is faulty provides another means of dismissing their own accounts.

The sanity of the narrator is a factor in *Twilight*. The work opens with Raphael, the main character, volunteering in the Mountain Clinic, a psychiatric hospital in which the patients believe that they are characters from the Bible. Raphael wants to understand the causes and manifestations of madness. During his stay in the clinic, Raphael remembers his own childhood. He does not reach any understandings, and at the end of the assignment, he is asking the same questions that drew him to the asylum originally. These questions remain despite everything. Raphael questions his state of mind three times in the opening passages. He senses that he is going mad and does not know how to judge his own thoughts, feelings, and actions. He says: "I am going mad, Pedro. I feel it. I know it."[21] He says, more definitively: "I am going mad, Pedro. Now I am sure."[22] And finally, he asserts: "I am convinced Pedro, that I am going mad. I may even be mad already."[23] Thus, if a madman has a truth to tell, it is overshadowed by the madness.

Later in the novel, when Hayim returns to the ghetto after his failed attempt to escape to Palestine and tells his father, Aharon, about the failure, focusing on what he saw along the way, and in particular, about the deportation with the Hungarian Jews to a forest near Kolomey, where a mass execution of the Jews occurred. Aharon advises his son to tell a number of prominent Jews in the ghetto about the executions. As Hayim speaks:

> A stunned silence followed his account. Dr. Breitman, the physician, shook his head over and over. Rabbi Perl studied his fingers. The former president of the community, the timber merchant Jakobson, looked perturbed. Without a word, he got up and left. The others followed him out of the room. Aharon and his son looked at one another. "You did your duty," Aharon said. "If they refuse to listen, that's their mistake. As for us, we shall do what we can."[24]

To Aharon, the educated, community leaders would surely understand the significance of Hayim's account and listen despite their feelings. However, without a single question, they left the room. In doing so, the community rejected Hayim, and by leaving the room, they thwarted Hayim's plans to relay the information. His story was beyond the bounds of acceptability.

Later the novel presents the story of the massacre at Kolomey again, but as a memory. Raphael remembers the evening when he heard his brother's story:

> Raphael's brother Hayim was describing the massacre at Kolomey. The men listened in disbelief. And he watched them as they listened. Like the others, he wondered if his poor brother had lost his mind.... Raphael listened but was too young to understand. He understood the words, but not the enormity of their meaning. It was as though the words detached themselves from one another and flew in different directions. A clear blue day, the crackling of machine guns, men shooting, men dying, women watching as their children were murdered. It all seemed unreal.[25]

Raphael explains Hayim's words in terms of madness. Madness became the method of reconciling the beautiful day with the horrible deaths. In that way, Raphael protects himself from the unwanted information.

The state of the narrator's memory is a key element in *The Forgotten*. The novel revolves around Elhanan Rosenbaum, who is losing his memory, and his son, Malkiel. Before Elhanan totally loses his memory, he decides to tell Malkiel about the past. The books opens with a section entitled "Elhanan's Prayer," in which Elhanan asks God to spare his memory, and it continues with "Malkiel's Words," a passage in which Malkiel identifies himself and his desire to remember his father. After these two opening passages, the story begins with Malkiel at his grandfather's grave site in his ancestral hometown. Malkiel is asking his grandfather for help in dealing with Elhanan. During the novel, to a degree, Malkiel learns about his father's life. Knowing that his father is losing his own memory and that one cannot really understand another's life fully, Malkiel says:

> Of course I'll bear witness for you. But my deposition will pale before yours. What shall I do father? Your life and memory are indivisible. They cannot survive you, not really. I know that whoever listens to a witness becomes one in turn; you told me that more than once. But we are not witnessing the same events. All I can say is, I have heard the witness.[26]

Malkiel knows that he cannot faithfully retell his father's story because their experiences are vastly different. Thus, when Malkiel talks about his father, he does so with limits. That adds another layer of interpretation to the account. In addition, Elhahan's degenerative disease affects his memory, and this makes it even more difficult to assess his accounts. He is quite aware of this and shares his doubts to Malkiel:

> "I'm afraid," my father said, his eyes half shut. "Everything in my head is muddled. Names, dates, words. I see a face in front of me and I recognize, but I don't know if it belongs to the present or the past. Who are you, Tamar? Which period of my life do you belong to? Are you perhaps Talia? Am I reliving my past even as it deserts me?"[27]

Elhanan's condition affects his clarity, and the result is that this creates uncertainty in what he tells his son. At the end of the novel, Malkiel is at his grandfather's grave site saying goodbye. He tells his grandfather about Elhanan's worsening condition and promises to remember his father. However, Malkiel is prevented from fulfilling that promise. The book ends with Elhanan's farewell to his son:

> I did not tell you the essential. Yes, Malkiel, I am still lucid enough to admit it: there is something important, vital, that I especially wanted to

pass on to you, perhaps a kind of testament. And each time, I said to myself, That can wait. I said to myself, That is so essential that I won't forget it, even if I forget the rest. And now I've forgotten that, too.[28]

So even though Malkiel promises to bear witness to his father's life and the scene at the grave site suggests closure, his father has not disclosed his final message. In the end, Malkiel does not know the most important aspect of his father's life. In this way, then, the father's last words undercut the value of Malkiel's pledge. Malkiel is unable to keep his promise to remember his father's life.

Doubts about the narrator's health are an issue in *The Gates of the Forest*. When Gregor starts to talk to Maria about murder, revenge, and God, she considers this blasphemous and says:

Be quiet child, be quiet for the love of heaven! Why must you talk like this? Whom do you want to insult and why? I hardly know you; you seem a different boy, a different man, with a strange voice and a strange soul. It's as if someone, a demon I don't know, has taken hold of you — it's that demon trying to give me pain and make me angry. It's not your fault, little one.... You need rest, food, sleep. You need someone to care for you.... You have a fever. You talk like a sick man....[29]

Gregor is trying to tell Maria about what he saw during the war but his words upset her. She offers him material comforts for his emotional turmoil because she is unable to understand his mental state. That knowledge is outside her comprehension. Gregor knows that her ministrations will not chase away what he sees, namely, the heads of assassinated children. Later in the novel, Gregor doubts himself and his own understanding of events. He tells the group of partisans what happened to their leader Leib.

At Zeide's command, he began for the third time to tell his story. From the beginning? From the beginning. Gregor wanted to protest but he restrained himself. He was becoming feverish, but continued.... We'll start again.... In the beginning God created the heaven and the earth, and that evening Leib was supposed to meet me in the restaurant. Do you understand? I don't. Never mind. Let's go on. As Gregor spoke he became someone else. Listening to his own voice, he found it false. This isn't the true story; you're holding that back.[30]

Gregor's doubts his own story because the unreality of the situation makes him question himself. Gregor's fevered state as represented by his physical condition calls into question that trustworthiness of his account.

Throughout the novels, listeners are constantly assessing the stories. A listener may decide that the narrator is a madman. If so, the tale is rejected because the speaker is deemed untrustworthy. By definition, if a person is mad, then he or she is not reliable. Along with labeling the narrator as a madman, listeners may also say that a narrator is sick or dreaming. Those provide two other excuses to reject unwanted information. Wiesel further complicates the role of the narrator by injecting the possibility that his madmen are seers who have special insights. In that case, they are not necessarily out of touch with reality. Thus, madness does not absolutely undermine their credibility. With that assertion, listeners have to contend with another level of ambivalence. Coupled with the tentativeness of the narrator and the doubts of the listeners are the assessments of the readers. Readers have the same option as the listeners to accept or reject a tale. These ongoing possibilities invite uncertainty.

Sequencing for Ambiguity

Like in the work of the French New Novelists, Kolbert finds a pattern of "chronological experimentation" in Wiesel's novels. Usually, the sequencing of natural phenomena offers overarching continuity to a story, but not in Wiesel's novels. As Gregor says in *The Gates of the Forest,* the "sequence of events has a mystery all its own."[31] In Wiesel's novels, this mystery takes the form of temporal ambiguity.

In contrast to those authors who use the cycle of seasons as a unifying structure, Wiesel uses it to undermine coherence. An example is *The Gates of the Forest,* which is divided into four chapters: Spring, Summer, Autumn, and Winter. In the first chapter, Spring, Gregor is hiding in the woods during a time of war. A stranger, Gavriel, appears in the woods, and for several weeks, the two men hide out together, sharing stories about their lives. After telling Gregor his secret, Gavriel lets himself be captured by a group of soldiers, so that Gregor may escape from the woods. While the soldiers are distracted by Gavriel, Gregor runs for safety to the home of his former servant, Maria, a Christian. Spring is the hopeful season, the time of possibilities. Gavriel's presence offers Gregor the possibility of a new beginning. Released from the woods as a result of Gavriel's tactics, Gregor runs toward his home. However, given that Gregor has been abandoned by his father in the woods, a low point in any child's life, the first chapter seems more like Winter, not Spring. Wiesel's opens with hope, which is soon worn away in the novel.

The second chapter takes place in Maria's village. As a Jew, Gregor is in danger, so Maria persuades him to pretend to be her nephew. Until his secret is discovered and he must flee, Gregor lives among the villagers. In this chapter, Maria offers Gregor peace and protection. The "ripening" that traditionally occurs during the summer also occurs within people, and Gregor sees that people mature during a war. In chapter three, Gregor returns to the woods where he encounters a group of Jewish partisans. Their leader, Leib, is an old friend. When Gregor realizes that the partisans do not know about the planned massacre of Jews, he tells Gavriel's account of the final solution to Leib. After a failed attempt to rescue Gavriel results in Leib's arrest and the partisans grow close, Gregor falls in love with Clara, Leib's lover. In this chaper, Leib's arrest and Yehuda's death are the beginning of the end of the group of partisans. Their fate parallels the season. Chapter four reunites Gregor and Gavriel. They talk about Clara, and Gregor describes the difficulties of living with Clara and wishes that he were back in the woods, where life was simpler. However, Gregor does not return to the woods. Instead, he chooses to continue with his life. The novel ends with Gregor saying the Kaddish and by doing so affirming life, with all its suffering. The love between Gregor and Clara is over, and they are each suffering in their situation. At the end, Gregor decides to commit himself to find peace. The peace he wants is elusive, but he promises to try. However, with its title of Winter, the chapter suggests that Gregor may not achieve his goal.

In fiction, the cycle of the seasons is similar to the cycle of the day insofar as each often symbolizes hope. However, in *The Night Trilogy*, which includes *Night*, *Dawn*, and *The Accident*, and is alternatively called *Night, Dawn, Day*, the daily cycle does not fulfill its promise of hope. About the connections between the works, Wiesel notes: "Written between 1955 and 1960, these three narratives were created separately. Though the first is a testimony, the other two serve only as commentaries. However, they are all written in the first person. In 'Night,' it is the 'I' who speaks; in the other two, it is the 'I' who listens and questions."[32] Disregarding Wiesel's insistence that *Dawn* and *The Accident* are in response to *Night*, book publishers regularly try to force unity on the works. The publishing history of the three works shows the problem with that approach.

In 1956, Wiesel published his Yiddish-language memoir, *Un di Velt Hot Geshvign* [*And the World Remained Silent*]. Two years later, he published *La Nuit* [*The Night*]. Its English translation was issued in 1960. The next year, *L'Aube* [*The Dawn*] was translated and published as *Dawn*. The work *Le Jour* [*The Day*] was also published that year. The following year, *Le Jour* was issued under the title *The Accident*.

In 1969, the three works were published as the trilogy, *La Nuit, L'Aube, Le Jour* [*Night, Dawn, Day*]. In 1972, a version of the trilogy, entitled *Night, Dawn, The Accident: Three Tales* was published. That was followed in 1985 and 1987 by editions of the works under the title: *Night, Dawn, Day*. Later editions of the three works were published as *The Night Trilogy: Night, Dawn, The Accident*. Attention to the publishing history of three works and their shifting titles reveals a fundamental discrepancy between the titles and the contents of the books. Choosing the daily cycle as an image for the trilogy suggests uplift and hope. However, the contents of the stories do not fulfill that promise. Rather, the shifting titles point to an uneasiness with the focus on uplift. Expectations for resolution are frustrated by this constant shift. Davis also notes that in the trilogy "there is no unambiguous movement from darkness to light, despair to hope. Wiesel's 'trilogy' appears to set itself a teleological program with which it fails to comply."[33] In the preface of the English edition, published in 1985, Wiesel comments on the choice of title. He writes: "Entitled *Le jour* (Day) in its original French version, it follows Dawn and Night. It is an ironic title, to be sure, indicating not the end of the darkness, but its hold over those seeking to find a bit of warmth, a bit of light."[34]

To further amplify uncertainty, Wiesel uses memory as a plot device to create temporal instability. Unlike authors who presuppose linearity, for Wiesel, the past and present are inseparable; memory imposes its own order on events. In *Dawn*, for instance, the story of how Elisha, a victim, turns into a killer, the past intrudes on Elisha's present behavior and thoughts. While recounting the military training that he underwent in Palestine, Elisha remembers other formative events and people, including his childhood teacher, his family, and the concentration camps. He remembers everyone who has helped shape his life. Bringing images of these people to Elisha dramatizes the ways in which those who helped form our character are always with us. In a chilling scene, Elisha speaks with a number of important people in his life, such as the beggar, his father, his teacher, his mother, and himself as a child. They tell him that they have gathered to attend the execution, because as part of Elisha's life, they are implicated in the murder of the Englishman. As Elisha feels his mother's touch, Gideon, the leader of the unit, interrupts Elisha's reverie. However, even while Gideon speaks about the pending execution, Elisha continues to think about the past. Memories are not time-bound, so they interrupt Elisha's present. More importantly, the past becomes the witness to the present. This undermines the possibility of a straightforward life for Elisha. Rather, it suggests that he will never be freed from his burdens. This discounts the comforting notion that somehow the past may be put behind.

To sum up, Wiesel's novels upset the cycle of the seasons, the cycle of the day, and the linear flow of time. In doing so, they create a discrepancy between the natural world and its usual order. This dislodges the expectations of characters in the stories, as well as readers of the stories.

Conclusion

Ultimately, then, what is absolutely clear from Wiesel's refusal to provide answers is that he wants to use the disparity between our expectations as readers and his theme of uncertainty to jolt us from complacency into action. Transmission, not resolution, is his point. However, like Raphael, in *Twilight*, we may refuse the message and claim that the narrator is sick, mad, or dreaming. Like the prominent Jews in the Rovidok ghetto, we make turn away from the storyteller. Nevertheless, Wiesel passes the message to us. What we do with it is our responsibility.

Notes

1. Elie Wiesel, *All the Rivers Run to the Sea,* trans. Marion Wiesel (New York: Alfred A. Knopf, 1996), 189.
2. Jack Kolbert, *The Worlds of Elie Wiesel* (Selinsgrove: Susquehanna University Press, 2001), 186.
3. Ibid., 186.
4. Colin Davis, *Elie Wiesel's Secretive Texts* (Gainesville: University Press of Florida, 1994), 51.
5. Ken Ireland, *The Sequential Dynamics of Fiction: Energies at the Margins of Fiction* (Madison, N.J.: Fairleigh Dickinson University Press, 2001), 153.

6. William Nelles, "Stories within Stories: Narrative Levels and Embedded Narrative," in *Narrative Dynamics: Essays on Time, Plot, Closure, and Frame*, ed. Brian Richardson (Columbus: Ohio State University Press, 2002), 339–352.

7. William Nelles, *Frameworks: Narrative Levels and Embedded Narrative* (New York: Peter Lang, 1997), 149.

8. Brian Richardson, "Beyond Story and Discourse: Narrative Time in Postmodern and Nonmimetic Fiction," in *Narrative Dynamics: Essays on Time, Plot, Closure, and Frame*, ed. Brian Richardson (Columbus: Ohio State University Press, 2002), 48.

9. Elie Wiesel, *Dawn*, trans. Frances Frenaye (New York: Hill & Wang, 1961), 126.

10. Ibid., 204.

11. Elie Wiesel, *The Beggar of Jerusalem*, trans. Lily Edelman and Elie Wiesel (New York: Random House, 1970), 5–6.

12. Ibid., 210–211.

13. Ibid., 210.

14. Elie Wiesel, *The Accident*, trans. Anne Borchardt (New York: Hill & Wang, 1962), 306.

15. Elie Wiesel, *The Fifth Son*, trans. Marion Wiesel (New York: Summit Books, 1985), 214.

16. Ibid., 219.

17. Wiesel, *Beggar in Jerusalem*, 45–46.

18. Ibid., 47.

19. Ibid., 48.

20. Wiesel, *The Accident*, 289.

21. Wiesel, *Twilight*, trans. Marion Wiesel (New York: Summit Books, 1988), 11.

22. Ibid., 14.

23. Ibid., 27.

24. Ibid., 112–113.

25. Ibid., 210–211.

26. Elie Wiesel, *The Forgotten*, trans. Stephen Becker (New York: Summit Books, 1992), 148.

27. Ibid., 188.

28. Ibid., 236.

29. Elie Wiesel, *The Gates of the Forest*, trans. Frances Frenaye (New York: Holt, Rinehart and Winston, 1966), 58–59.

30. Ibid., 162–163.

31. Wiesel, *Gates of the Forest*, 87.

32. See Elie Wiesel, *Night, Dawn, The Accident* (New York: Hill & Wang, 1972).

33. Davis, *Secretive Texts*, 63.

34. Elie Wiesel, *The Accident*, trans. Anne Borchardt (New York: Hill & Wang, 1985), xi.

Elie Wiesel:
Telling Stories
of Children and Loss

KATHERINE LAGRANDEUR

> The little girl sat on her lap and listened to stories. Zdena felt her forty-year-old breasts and belly go warm against the weight of the child. The grief we carry, anybody's grief, Zdena thought, is exactly the weight of a sleeping child. — Anne Michaels, *Fugitive Pieces*

In *A Jew Today*, Elie Wiesel offers the following story about one of his students. The student says to Wiesel:

> "Your protagonist's story is mine. My father is sad and silent; his wife and their children perished *there*. My mother is sad and silent; her husband and their children perished *there*. After the Liberation my mother and father met and were married. I am their son — but every time they look at me, I know it is not me they're seeing."[1]

We find this story in Part V of *A Jew Today,* which is entitled "Legends of Today." We may assume this story happened because Wiesel tells it again in the second volume of his personal memoirs.[2] In *A Jew Today*, this specific legend is located among ten others, all of which have Jewish suffering as a central theme. The first and last legends in the chapter are from Jewish tradition. The first is from the time of the Hasidic rebbe Dov Ber, the Great Maggid of Mezeritch, who lived from 1704–1772; the last legend dates back to the Expulsion from Spain in 1492. The other nine legends, situated between the two traditional narratives in the chapter, are more recent stories in Jewish history; they describe conditions of Jewish suffering during and after the *Shoah*. These recent legends share another theme in common as well: they all describe the impact of the *Shoah* on Jewish families, and particularly on Jewish children.

I have discussed elsewhere the seemingly contradictory juxtaposition of these traditional and recent legends in order to understand what they might tell us about the covenant between God and Jews after Auschwitz. I suggest that we should refrain from considering the traditional narratives as a framework for understanding the more contemporary stories, despite the fact that these older stories are situated at the beginning and the end of the chapter, as though they were serving as both an introduction and a conclusion to the more recent narratives. I argue that it is rather the recent stories that should guide our reading. They should be considered *central* texts, as their physical location in the chapter might suggest, because the meaning of the two traditional legends needs to be reconsidered in a post–Holocaust context. In particular, we need to reconsider any conclusions that the traditional stories may allow us to draw about the complicated alliance between Jews and the God of Israel in light of what the modern legends tell us about the suffering of Jews, and especially about the suffering of Jewish children, during and after the *Shoah*.[3]

In this chapter, I would like to put aside the traditional legends in the chapter and give my full attention to the other nine "legends" in order to offer a closer reading of what they tell us about Jewish children and loss. I would like to suggest that the genius of these legends resides not only in the glimpses they offer readers into the impact of the *Shoah* on Jewish children during and after the war, but also in the way they point to how we should read stories from *Shoah* victims and survivors. In other words, these legends each *tell stories* and *tell us how to receive stories* from victims and survivors of the *Shoah*.

The Weight of the Shoah: Voices of Victims and Survivors

Let us return here to the legend above about the Jewish student whose parents lost spouses and children during the Second World War. This is one of three stories in the chapter "Legends of Today" that give voice to the experiences of children of Holocaust survivors. There are also three legends that share stories about survivors who are coping with the fact that they lost children during the war. The other three legends confront readers with stories from victims and survivors who were children or teenagers during the war, in other words from individuals whose primary social role at that time of their lives was still located within the family, as someone's child. Although these nine legends tell different stories about Jewish children and loss, they all evoke the same kind of feeling, a grief that bears down and cannot easily be articulated, what I would like to call *the weight of the Shoah.*

In the story told by the Jewish student to his teacher, which is the second "legend of today" in the chapter, this weight is experienced most heavily in moments where the son's parents do not see him when they are looking at him. In her book *Family Frames*, Marianne Hirsch proposes that "looking," along with photography, is one of the nonverbal relational processes by which a family constitutes itself as an "affiliative group." She draws on Roland Barthes' discussion of the photo of his mother as a child in the winter-garden to further suggest that individuals not only constitute affiliative ties, but also their own subjectivity, through the act of looking at members of their family: "Barthes's look is affiliative and identificatory. His desire is to recognize not only his mother but himself, not only to recognize but to be recognized by her."[4] Hirsch's discussion may offer us some insight into the weight that bears down on the parents and the son in the "legend of today" introduced above. What weighs down on the parents, I would suggest, is the impossibility of looking at the children they have lost and along with it, the impossibility of constituting themselves as subjects. In other words, along with their children and spouses, the parents have lost their selves. When looking at their living son, they are forever occupied in the necessary yet ultimately impossible process of trying to reconstitute families and selves that no longer exist, but whose existence they must seek in order to become whole again. The son, in turn, experiences his own sense of alienation regarding his family and his self because he cannot engage with his parents in the "affiliative and identificatory" process of looking that would allow him to recognize and be recognized by family members. We are left instead with the weight of a *family that cannot ever be* and a *son who cannot ever become.*

Elie Wiesel offers readers another narrative about the impossibility of looking, and its effect on familial affiliations, in the chapter's sixth legend. In this tale, the familial affiliations are not *doomed never to become* as they are in the second legend; they are rather *deliberately severed* by a child who can no longer bear to look her father in the eyes after he has chosen her as the one to sacrifice if the Nazis came to arrest his children. The legend is about the brutal hunt for children in the Lodz ghetto and a mother and father who are trying to make a decision about which of their two children to hide: Alter, their son, or Blimel, their daughter. Wiesel describes this situation as follows:

> Shraga and his wife succeeded in discovering an almost secure hiding place for one of their children. But which child should they save? ... Then the danger passed. Shraga and his family were safe. All remained alive. But from that day on, Blimel, without knowing why, without having been told, avoided her father's eyes.... "And then, one night, they took her away," says Shraga. "I saw her leave. She turned away. So as not to look at me."[5]

The father chose to save Alter because the son could carry on the family name. As events unfolded, the daughter did not have to be sacrificed by the parents. Having been chosen as the child who her father would not save when the Nazis rounded up Jewish children, Blimel chooses *not to look her father in the eyes*, while she is still living with him and at the moment when she is taken away from him. By *not looking* at her father, she breaks away from the ties that bind her to him and becomes at the same time alienated from her own personal identity. Here again, the affiliative and identifactory nature of looking has been torn asunder by the unspeakable horrors that the *Shoah* imposed on victims and survivors.

Lawrence Langer insists that we must refrain from judging the decisions that were made by Holocaust victims and survivors when they were confronted with what he calls a "choiceless choice," a moment when an otherwise decent human being needed to make decisions that were doomed to be unethical, when an individual was forced to choose between what was bad and what was even worse.[6] In his view, we must change our expectations of the family when we read Holocaust testimonials because victims and survivors were often in situations beyond imagination where it was impossible for them to respect the same family values that they would have honoured outside of the war.[7] Langer adds that we must avoid using traditional consoling language, such as "spiritual resistance" or "martyrdom," to try to understand the behaviour of these individuals. He asserts that we need instead a new language, what he calls a *language of the inconsolable*, to help us express the agony and difficulty of these moments of "choiceless choice."[8]

This is how I would suggest we read Shraga's decision to hide Alter rather than Blimel if the Nazis came to round up his children: as a decision that needed to be made despite how terrible it was because *not deciding* would lead to an even more terrible plight. Indeed, Shraga himself acknowledges the horrifying yet choiceless nature of his decision when he says, "May heaven forgive us ... but I must choose." But perhaps Blimel, too, was confronted with a "choiceless choice." Perhaps the only way the child could save the dignity of the relationship she once had with her father, and the dignity of the daughter she once was thanks to her family, was by turning away from the parent her father had become through no choice of his own. By alienating herself from the parent the Nazis had created through their force and will, she is perhaps unconsciously reclaiming instead her relationship with the father she once had, the father who could make choices that were not choiceless, the father who could allow himself to embrace each of his children without fearing for their lives.

A daughter's relationship with her father is complicated because of a "choiceless choice" in the seventh "legend of today." In that story, a daughter of a survivor confronts her classmates and teacher with her desperate struggle to find an argument in defense of her father, who had been a *kapo* in the camps. The young woman asks questions in the hope that she will *not* have to condemn her father's actions during the war: "But can we blame them? Were they all volunteers, profit-seekers? Is there nothing to be said in their defense? ... Can we really blame them for having compromised more than the others, for having succumbed before the others?"[9] Here too, we feel the weight that is carried by a child confronted by a decision made by her father during the Holocaust. In this case, the father made choices that undoubtedly put other Jews at risk, and probably even cost some of them their lives, so that he may prolong and ultimately save his own life. Unlike Blimel, however, this daughter cannot distance herself from her relationship with her father in order to reclaim an affiliation with him that predates the war. This daughter's father *has already been* and *will always have been* a *kapo*; in other words, the daughter is doomed to carry with her forever the weight of her father's "choiceless choice" and all that it implies.

We find another story where the weight of the *Shoah* is passed on from a survivor to a child born after the war in the ninth "legend of today." In this narrative, a survivor's daughter torments her mother by asking her why she had decided to have children after the war when she knew what the world does to children, and why she had to be the one to whom her mother had given birth. The daughter asks her mother:

> "You were my age and you knew life, didn't you? You knew what evil man is capable of, didn't you? ... Why did you give birth to me? You who are so intelligent, you knew what the world does to its children — why, then, did you insist on giving birth? And why did it have to be me, tell me?"[10]

Despite the series of questions from the daughter, the mother does not answer. Like the student who wrestles with her father's choice to be a *kapo* during the war, this daughter struggles to justify her survivor mother's actions. In her case, however, her struggle has to do with life rather than with death. While the student tries to find ways to justify her father's decision to risk others' lives to save his own, this daughter struggles to understand her mother's decision *to give life* after the war and particularly, with her mother's choice *to give life to her*. The trauma of the *Shoah*, then, bears down not only on those who experienced it first hand, but also on those who were born afterwards. Indeed, the daughter has so completely absorbed her mother's pain that she finds it difficult to live, as though mother and daughter have become one in a symbiosis of grief. And this weight, the weight of a daughter who finds life unbearable, becomes another source of grief for the survivor mother and renders her, as Wiesel writes, "[s]pent and silent."

I would like to expand Langer's idea of a *language of the inconsolable* here to include all the grief that is unsayable yet undeniable around the *Shoah*, what I call an overall *poetics of loss* that pervades Holocaust texts.[11] This is how I think we should read the mother's fatigue and silence in the story above, as a grief that cannot be expressed or assuaged, but which is all-consuming and incontestable, as a grief in need of a language of the inconsolable.

We find a similar grief in the second "legend of today," which introduces readers to Shimshon, a survivor whose wife and three children were killed by the Nazis. Like the survivor mother whose daughter wishes she had not been born, Shimshon is confronted with a daughter who is so overcome with the weight of the *Shoah* that she prefers not to live. In this situation, however, the daughter experienced firsthand the horror of the war and moreover, she was only six years old at the time. About the daughter, Wiesel writes,

> She saw the killers, she saw them kill — how did she translate these visions in her child's mind? One morning she asked her mother to hug her. Then she came to place a kiss on her father's forehead. And she said, "I think that I shall die today." And after a sigh, a long sigh: "I think I am glad."[12]

The father in this legend carries a grief that is triple in its depth: the trauma of having personally experienced the horrors of the *Shoah*; the sorrow of having lost his wife and children to the war; and finally, the anguish of knowing that his six-year-old child, despite her young age, had already discovered the meaning of life and had found it to be so wanting that she was glad to die. In the third "legend of today," Benjamin, another survivor, is likewise burdened with the knowledge that life had lost all meaning for the young Jewish children under his care during the war. As their teacher, he could not make them understand the meaning of things outside of their existence as children confined to the ghetto and targeted for murder. He remembers the lessons in the ghetto with his students:

> "I have spoken to them of apple trees. What is an apple tree? And what is nature? Spring? Fields of flowers in bloom? And what does happiness mean? Serenity? And what is a piece of cake? Confronted with their questions, I feel wretched, foolish. And I know that they will die without ever knowing." And Benjamin wearily lowered his gaze. "When words have lost all meaning for children, it is a sure sign of disaster."[13]

Benjamin cannot fully embrace life after the war and turns down every offer to teach because teaching is too painful a reminder of the weight of the children he once knew who could not find meaning in words. All the children knew was death. Similarly to Shimshon, who is always in a state of "unspeakable and contagious melancholy," Benjamin remains forever "helpless and confused" as well as "[u]nable to cope with life, unable to work." Each survivor seem to be experiencing what Freud might call *melancholia*, an experience brought on by a death, or in this case by a sorrow, so devastating to the *ego* that it becomes incapable of freeing itself from a state of mourning. According to Freud, *melancholia* may lead the afflicted to experience insomnia, feelings of inferiority, a lack of appetite, and sometimes and most significantly, a loss of willingness to live.[14] This *melancholia* seems to bear down as well on children of the *Shoah* and children of survivors; indeed, Shimshon's six-year-old child goes willingly to her death and in the eighth legend, the daughter of the survivor mother wishes she had not been born. One of the ways the weight of the *Shoah* seems to manifest itself, then, is through a ubiquitous *melancholia* that affects not only adults but also children who experienced the war firsthand, not only survivors but also the children of survivors who were born after the war.

Along with *melancholia*, silence would appear to be another expression of the weight that bears down on *Shoah* victims and survivors. Indeed, like the mother whose daughter wishes she would have never been born, survivors are often reduced to silence as a barrier against the pain of the *Shoah*. In the eighth legend, we encounter another kind of silence as well: a silence that is imposed on a five-year-old boy who must avoid making noise in order to protect his family's hiding place from the Nazis. That boy, Joel, learns to protect himself and especially how to be quiet, as all his family leaves him. Wiesel writes:

> Joel's father was the first to go, having ventured out to look for water one night.... And in the shelter Joel succeeded in crying without crying. His mother placed her hand over his mouth when a few days later Yekutiel was arrested. That same evening she, too, was taken. Joel the Redhead knew that he was going to burst with pain, but his Uncle Zanvel's hand was on his mouth. Zanvel, too, disappeared. And Joel was left alone in the darkness. His hand covering his mouth, he began to sob without a sound, scream without a sound, survive without a sound.[15]

Joel's silence in his hiding place, "his cave under the cave," becomes increasingly difficult to bear. The five-year-old boy must first teach himself to control the spontaneity of childhood and refrain from making noise since "to shout was dangerous." Next, he must force himself to express his sorrow without crying when his father dies. Finally, Joel must learn not to gasp in shock at the moment when his other loved ones are killed as well. Joel's need to be silent forces him to separate mind and body so that he can suppress all physical expression of his grief. Indeed, he must even contain primeval expressions of sorrow such as sobbing and screaming; in this way, he lives just below the surface of existence, in a constant state of ungrievable grief. Indeed, "his cave under the cave" could perhaps be considered a metaphor for his need to retreat physically and emotionally from a world that has taken away everything he has known in his five years of life, including his childhood, his family, and even his cry.

In the tenth legend, we encounter another survivor who confronts the fact that he has lost everything he has known because of the *Shoah*. In that tale, a son returns home after the war, only to discover that Ivan, the stableman, has moved into his home and refuses to return the house or its contents to him. After explaining to the stableman that he does not plan to claim any of his belongings, Yehuda-Leib is invited into his former house for a drink of brandy. As they drink together, Ivan offers Yehuda-Leib a present for having not asked for anything from the house:

> Ivan gets up, climbs to the attic and returns with a long object wrapped in a wool blanket. Yehuda-Leib feels dizzy. In the stableman's arms he recognizes the holy scrolls that belonged to his father, who had received them from his.... His head is spinning. My father's fortune, he thinks. This is what remains of my father's fortune.[16]

After receiving his father's Torah, the son runs into the woods and heads for the next town, repeating to himself that this one possession is all that remains, not only of the family's fortune, but of his father. In this legend, we confront the reality that most Jewish homes and belongings had been taken over by non–Jews during the war and were seldom given back to survivors upon their return. And so another weight is added to the many others that survivors carry with them, the grief of the impossibility of returning home and reclaiming a sense of family through the belongings their loved ones had left behind. In fact, Michael Marrus explains that, in many cases, it was dangerous for Jews to attempt to reclaim their belongings and even to return home in the first place, because of the outbreaks of violence they experienced at the end of the war at the hands of non–Jews.[17] In this sense, survivors are left without traces of their past, without a *place* where they can recreate in their minds their interactions with loved ones and without *things* around which they can reconstruct family memories. I would like to suggest that Yehuda-Leib's obsession with his father's Torah is a manifestation of his longing for a physical proof of his beginnings, what Derrida might call a *mal d'archive*,[18] which is not only an aching but also a passion for home, for origin, for absolute beginnings. Salman Rushdie points out that all human beings construct the meanings of their lives from fragments, but that this is particularly so for those who are exiled from their homelands and left with few reminders of their past lives. Because of this fragmentation, even the most insignificant object may resonate with symbolism for the refugee who is trying to reconstruct a sense of past and self.[19] In the case of Yehuda-Leib, the only object he has left and around which he may try to reconstruct his past is his father's Torah. In this case, however, the family object is not trivial; as the Torah, it stands as a reminder not only of Yehuda-Leib's personal origins as a member of a family, but also of his collective origins as a Jew. In this sense, it stands as a reminder that Yehuda-Leib's grief extends beyond the death of his family and the loss of his home; it includes the sorrow of the entire community of European Jews, all of whom were destined for murder under Nazi rule. His legacy, then, is the weight of the Torah, or the responsibility to choose life, despite how overcome with grief he may be, because his father and other Jews could not and because their memory must live on through his own life.

In the fifth "legend of today," we find another story of a son who is left fatherless after the war; in this narrative, the son witnesses his father's death in the concentration camps. The tale is about an officer who taunts the father with an offer of food to deny Judaism. When the prisoner refuses, the officer shoots him. As the prisoner falls, the onlookers hear his prayer:

> "*Adoshem hu haelokim, adoshem hu haelokim*—God is God, God alone is God." "You swine, you dirty Jew," screams the officer. "Can't you see I am more powerful than your God! Your life is in my hands, not in His! You need me more than Him! Choose me and you'll go to the hospital and you'll recover, and you'll eat, and you'll be happy!" "Never," says the Jew, gasping. The officer examines him at length. He suddenly seems fearful. Then he shoots a second bullet into the man's other shoulder. And a third. And a fourth. And the Jew goes on whispering, "God is God, God is..." The last bullet strikes him in the mouth.[20]

The son in this story is left with even less than a Torah to help him recall memories of his father. His only legacy, in fact, is the *prayer* his father recited at the time of his murder. And yet, the son explains that it is difficult for him to understand why his father decided to say this prayer because it was actually unlike him to do so: "I was there," his son tells me. "I was there, and the scene seems unbelievable to me. You see, my father ... my father was a hero.... But he was not a believer."[21] There are many compelling ways to interpret the atheist Jew's recital of the prayer of martyrs. We could consider it to be new-found faith in the face of certain death; we might read it as a way to defy the Nazi and take away his power, if only for a passing moment; we could suggest that the prayer stands as an accusation against God who chooses to remain silent while His creation suffers. However, I would like to suggest that the force of this legend resides elsewhere, not in our *understanding* of the atheist Jew's new-found faith, but rather in the *mystery* of his gesture, in our inability to bestow upon it any definitive reading. As mystery, the gesture opens itself up to endless interpretations; it turns the non-believing/believing Jew's last moments into a *story*. In this way, the son plays a significant role in this legend: he becomes at once the receiver of his father's story and the storyteller who keeps the story alive. His legacy, finally, is to bear witness to his father's suffering and death.

Sharing the Weight: Listening to Stories

The legend of the non-believing/believing Jew may be read as a metaphor for what I would like to suggest to be three underlying principles that resonate throughout Elie Wiesel's writing: The drama of the *Shoah* belongs first and foremost to victims and survivors; in other words, *it is their story to tell*; it is impossible to explain the *Shoah* in definitive terms; the fact that it happened remains incomprehensible; and we have a responsibility to listen to their stories and to bear witness to their deaths and suffering. In sum, the storytelling genius of Elie Wiesel resides in his decision to discuss the *Shoah* through the mystery of victims and survivors' stories rather than through reasoned accounts and explicatory narratives. In this way, Wiesel avoids reductive conclusions about the *Shoah* that could dishonor victims and survivors, especially those victims and survivors who were children during the war. In this respect, Wiesel aligns himself with Rabbi Irving Greenberg who offers the following statement to guide discourse on the Holocaust: "No statement, theological or otherwise, should be made that would not be credible in the presence of the burning children."[22]

The legends in *A Jew Today* emblematize Wiesel's principles and should be read as stories about victims and survivors and as a call to listen to their stories. Indeed, we must remember that there is another person in the story of the non-believing/believing Jew, and that is the narrator to whom the son tells his story and who passes it on to us, the readers: "'I was there,' his son tells me."[23]

In fact, almost all of the legends point consciously to a narrator who receives the stories from the survivors. Though he is never intrusive, he lets his presence be known to us, and he does so in a number of ways. In three legends, including that of the non-believing/believing Jew, the narrator explicitly reminds us that he is the receiver of the story that he is sharing with us: "I like to listen to him." and "She flares up, stares at us."[24] At other moments, the narrator steps into the text to describe how he knows the storyteller, what his relationship is to him: "my friend Shimshon"; "one of my best students"; and "I am his pupil."[25] In the story of the student whose parents never saw him when they looked at him and in the story of Benjamin, the teacher who could no longer bring himself to teach after war, the narrator also explains to us how he responds to the story he is being told. In the latter story, the narrator tells us that he likes to listen to Benjamin who calls upon the narrator to use his imagination when he is listening to him: "I like to listen to him. He always begins with the same word: 'Imagine....'"[26] This insistence on the word "imagine" reminds us to listen to the incomprehensibility and the mystery of what the survivor is telling us; we are to "imagine." This suggests that we are not to analyze, we are not to explain, and we are not to conclude. Indeed, the narrator's role as storyteller is displaced in favour of another role in the "legends of today," which is the *receiver* of stories. His primary role in these stories is to listen to stories that are being told by others; indeed, perhaps this is why Wiesel chose to call these stories "legends," to press upon us the importance of our roles as receivers of these narratives, to insist that we read them. Etymologically speaking, "legends" are, first and foremost, "things to be read."[27] In this way, these texts may be read as a metaphor for storytelling in general; they remind us of the relationship between storyteller and receiver, of the importance of the exchange between them. We learn that the grief of the *Shoah* does not belong to survivors and victims alone, but also to us, who have a responsibility to listen to their stories and to share the weight of their experiences.

Bearing the Weight: Listening with Silence

We also have a responsibility, however, to listen to their stories in a particular way. In the legend of the student whose parents do not recognize him when they look at him, the narrator provides some guidance as to how we should carry out our responsibility to listen. After the son of survivors cried out in agony that it is not he his parents see when they look at him, the narrator responds to his student's story with silence and does not contradict what he has said: "I don't dare tell him he is wrong — he is probably right. I don't say anything. There is nothing I can say."[28] What is implied here, I believe, is that in order to remain respectful of victims and survivors, we must let them tell us what they experienced and we must refrain from speaking out of turn and offering "consoling language," to return to Langer, that "would not be credible in the presence of the burning children," to return to Greenberg. In other words, we must resign ourselves to the fact that there is nothing we can say or do that would be appropriate, *except listen to them.* Michael Roth compares Claude Lanzmann's film *Shoah* to the period of *shivah,* the seven-day period of mourning when Jews sit with the bereaved in order to listen to them talk about their deceased loved ones. He suggests that the film creates a space where survivors can speak about the loss of their loved ones, and I would add the grief of the *Shoah* in general, in order to try to work through their pain and continue on with their lives. Roth insists that during *shivah,* we must listen to the afflicted in a particular way. It is not our place to start a conversation; on the contrary, our responsibility is to wait in silence and let the afflicted speak first:

> We sit with them (there is nothing we can do) while they describe the horrors of *not dying* with their brethren; we sit with them (there is nothing we can do) while they describe watching their loved ones go to their deaths; we sit with them (there is nothing we can do) while their torturers explain in gruesome detail the mechanics of murder, the technical problem of killing so many so quickly without leaving too many traces. But there are traces, and they speak to us; they are made to speak to us, and we must force ourselves to stay, to remain seated with them.[29]

I would suggest that this is how Wiesel would want us to read the "Legends of Today," and indeed, all stories about victims and survivors, with the same silence and reverence we would reserve for a *shivah.* Perhaps this is where a *language of the inconsolable* can be expressed in the end, in narrative's moments of silence and communion, where storyteller and receiver join to bear together the grief of the *Shoah* and the weight of a burning child.

Notes

1. Elie Wiesel, *A Jew Today*, trans. Marion Wiesel (New York: Vintage Books, 1978), 155–156.

2. Elie Wiesel, —*Et la Mer N'est Pas Remplie: Mémoires, 2* (Paris: Seuil, 1996), 290.

3. For an in-depth discussion, see my article "Élie Wiesel : Raconter la Foi et l'Existence Juives Après Auschwitz," *Diversité Culturelle et Désir d'Autobiographie dans l'Espace Francophone*, ed., Driss Aïssaoui, 70 (Spring 2005): 31–40.

4. Marianne Hirsch, *Family Frames: Photography, Narrative and Postmemory* (Cambridge: Harvard University Press, 1997), 9.

5. Wiesel, *A Jew Today*, 158–159.

6. Lawrence Langer, *Preempting the Holocaust* (New Haven: Yale University Press, 1998), 136.

7. Lawrence Langer, "Family Dilemmas in Holocaust Literature," *Michigan Quarterly Review*, 26, 2 (Spring 1987): 387–389.

8. Ibid., 396–397.

9. Wiesel, *A Jew Today*, 159.

10. Ibid., 161.

11. I first introduce the idea of a poetics of loss in Wiesel's writing in my PhD dissertation. See Katherine Annette Lagrandeur, *Poétique de la Perte dans l'Oeuvre Autobiographique d'Elie Wiesel* (Ottawa: National Library of Canada, 2003).

12. Wiesel, *A Jew Today*, 155.

13. Ibid., 156–157.

14. Sigmund Freud, "Mourning and Melancholia," in *On the History of the Psycho-analytic Movement (1914)*, Volume 14, trans. Joan Riviere and ed. James Stracey (London: Hogarth Press, 1957), 243–246.

15. Wiesel, *A Jew Today*, 160.

16. Ibid., 162–163.

17. Michael Marrus, *The Unwanted: European Refugees in the Twentieth Century* (New York: Oxford University Press, 1985), 335–336.

18. Jacques Derrida, *Mal d'Archive: Une Impression Freudienne* (Paris: Galilée, 1995), 142.

19. Salman Rushdie, "Imaginary Homelands," in *Imaginary Homelands: Essays and Criticism, 1981–1991* (London: Granta Books/Penguin Books, 1991), 11–12.

20. Wiesel, *A Jew Today*, 157–158.

21. Ibid., 158.

22. Michael Berenbaum and John K. Roth, *Holocaust: Religious and Philosophical Implications* (New York: Paragon House, 1989), quoted in Berenbaum and Roth 303.

23. Wiesel, *A Jew Today*, 158.

24. Ibid., 157; 159.

25. Ibid., 154; 155; 157.

26. Ibid., 157.

27. See "legend" in the *Shorter Oxford English Dictionary, Volume 1, A–M*, Fifth Edition (Oxford: Oxford University Press, 2002), 1569.

28. Wiesel, *A Jew Today*, 156.

29. Michael S. Roth, "Shoah as Shivah," in *People of the Book: Thirty Scholars Reflect on their Jewish Identity*, ed. Jeffrey Rubin-Dorsky and Shelly Fisher Fishkin (Madison: University of Wisconsin Press, 1996), 410.

The Storyteller and
His Quarrel with God

ALAN L. BERGER

The epigraph to Elie Wiesel's *The Gates of the Forest* reads: "God made man because he loves stories"; however the Nobel Peace laureate attests "My preoccupations in literature are as much theological as they are literary, and may be more of the former than the latter."[1] Consequently, the stories that Wiesel tells weave a rich theological tapestry as they interrogate God — and humanity in the wake of Auschwitz — while continually seeking to tell "legends of our time."[2] The God intoxicated youth from Sighet who entered the fiery gates of Auschwitz emerged from the conflagration to become the *maggid* [one who relates] of the Holocaust. Wiesel's stories are his *Din Torah* or trial of God. Like Job, the author does not doubt God's existence; rather, he is obsessed with God's silence and with divine injustice. "I entered literature," testifies Wiesel, "through silence."

At the outset it is crucial to note that Wiesel's tales are prayers. He approvingly cites the great hasidic storyteller, Rebbe Nahman of Bratzlav, who observed, "*De mes contes, faites prièrs.*"[3] Wiesel shares Reb Nahman's aspirations, writing that hopefully "no one will be able to distinguish between the ones [stories] and the others [prayers], not even myself, and, myself less than anyone else."[4] Storytelling in the form of scripture, midrash, aggadah, and hasidic tales — the milieu in which Wiesel was raised and which he wholeheartedly embraces — is a normative means of conveying Jewish theology. Richard Rubenstein writes that Wiesel is "undoubtedly the most important Jewish storyteller of the twentieth century." Moreover, this role "does not diminish [Wiesel's] stature as a religious thinker."[5]

Wiesel the storyteller is drawn to traditional sources. It is not surprising that he finds in rabbinic commentaries an inexhaustible reservoir of tales relating the elusive and complex nature of the divine-human encounter. The term midrash means "investigation." It comes from the root *drsh*, "to seek." What Wiesel seeks is a way to account for theodicy and to find an acceptable image of deity. Midrashic texts are themselves open-ended, admitting a variety of interpretations on the part of those who desire to keep the connection between classical teachings and the realities of the present. Professor Byron Sherwin comments on Wiesel as a maker of midrash:

> Though Wiesel's work is characterized by a constant tension between the devout Yeshiva student he once was and the skeptical Holocaust survivor he has become, it is this very tension that qualifies his work as a modern Midrash. Like earlier Midrashim, Wiesel's work manifests an attempt to relate new experiences to former faith.... The Auschwitz story is juxtaposed to the Hasidic story. The biblical story confronts the Holocaust story. Wiesel's spiritual pilgrimage brings these stories together.[6]

Wiesel's stories are, however, simultaneously a protest against — and an affirmation of — God. As Anson Laytner observes, "For Wiesel, argument with God serves as the basic operative and redemptive element in his ongoing search for a meaningful and functional post–Holocaust interpretation of Judaism."[7] Consequently, the author's stories and tales are both a rejection of despair and a challenge to God and humanity. Wiesel's faith, as expressed in his tales, is paradoxical. The author attests that: "If I said I believe in God as I used to believe when I was a child, I would be lying. If I say I don't, I would be lying, too."[8] In the trenchant words of Harry James Cargas, Wiesel's faith "requires defiance, eschews submitting to or defending God, does not allow for a definition of God...."[9]

In what follows I discuss selected works of Wiesel and what their respective presentations of God reveal about the author's relationship to the deity. I do so while emphasizing the role of story in post–Auschwitz religion. I first turn to his canonical memoir *Night* as the foundation of his *din Torah*. His memoir signals the end of Wiesel's unquestioning fealty to traditional ways of imaging God and to normative explanations of evil and suffering. *Night*, writes Wiesel, was his testing of unbelief, although

God was present.[10] What began was a lifelong story of the author's search for a credible image of God and a way of linking the past to the post–Holocaust era. Next, I discuss the question of Auschwitz and the function of religion. I then turn my attention to three of Wiesel's other works; *Ani Ma'amin, The Trial of God*, and his two volume autobiography, *All Rivers Run to the Sea* and *The Sea Is Never Full*.[11] The first two are the author's most sustained trials of God. The autobiography reveals his most recent reflections on the post–Auschwitz divine image and the role of faith. While each of these books represents a different genre — cantata, play, and memoir — all may be understood as radical *midrashim* or troubling legends, telling the complex and paradoxical story of God's relationship to the *Shoah*. I conclude with a meditation on the implications of Wiesel as a post–Holocaust storyteller.

Night

Wiesel's now classic memoir *Night*, composed after a ten year period of self-imposed silence, is paradigmatic for the writer's subsequent tales. Three images shape this work. Wiesel begins as a deeply religious youth certain that the deity operates in history. God is then portrayed as a young boy hanging on a gallows in Auschwitz-Birkenau. *Night* ends with the author gazing into a mirror and seeing the image of a corpse. Hovering over the text is the all encompassing image of night itself during which the lives of his Father [Shlomo], Mother [Sarah], and little sister [Tzipporah] were consumed by the flames of the *Shoah*. Yet, incredibly, the author does not lose faith during the Holocaust. Wiesel's stories present changing images of deity which reflect his post–Holocaust understanding of the role of God and the existence of death camps.

Wiesel's quest for deepening his relationship with God begins prior to the Holocaust. Reflecting on the question of his mentor Moshe the beadle who asks the youth why he prays, Wiesel incredulously muses, "Why did I pray? A strange question. Why did I live? Why did I breathe?" The Beadle, however, teaches his disciple a crucial two-fold lesson about the role of questions in religious life. "Man," he observes, "raises himself toward God by the questions he asks Him." Moreover, Moshe shares with his young pupil the true nature of divine-human dialogue, "man questions God and God answers. But we don't understand His answers." The wise beadle continues his instruction revealing to his rapt pupil the source of ultimate truth, "You will find the true answers, Eliezer, only within yourself!"[12]

The mysterious beadle embodies the theological stance that leads to Wiesel's subsequent quest. This is so for three major reasons. He is emblematic of the fate of the unheard and disbelieved witness. Additionally, the beadle's emphasis on questions rather than answers underscores Wiesel's own distrust of answers. Answers divide people and, radicalized as in National Socialism's "Final Solution," are frequently fatal. Third, returning to Sighet after escaping a mass execution, Moshe, reports Wiesel, had changed. "There was no longer any joy in his eyes. He no longer talked to me of God or of the cabbala, but only of what he had seen."[13] In Wiesel's stories *personal experience* challenges normative teachings about the purpose of suffering and the ways of God with man.

Wiesel describes *Night* as a memoir written "to testify, to stop the dead from dying, to justify my own survival."[14] Theologically, he juxtaposes traditional Jewish teachings about theodicy and about history as the arena for the unfolding of God's plan with the murder of the chosen people. The tale Wiesel tells inverts biblical themes such as the Exodus and the *akeda* [binding of Isaac]. Death, the anti–Exodus, not redemption awaits the Jewish people in *l'univers concentrationnaire*. Sons abandon fathers. Wiesel searches for a Jewish anchor amidst the ethical, moral, psychic, and theological chaos of the Holocaust. André Neher succinctly states the crux of Wiesel's theological dilemma, writing that "the tragic grandeur of Wiesel's work lies in [the] desperate effort to make the Bible, in the face of Auschwitz, say what it cannot say, because it said what it did when Auschwitz had not yet come into existence."[15] In sociological terms, he seeks a *nomos* (well ordered universe) amidst the chaos of anomie.

Those who cannot abide the conflict between traditional Jewish teaching about theodicy and the anomie of Auschwitz are unable to continue. Wiesel, in *Night*, reports two cases of prisoners who, ultimately, lose faith. Akiba Drumer, a hasid, believes the traditional assertion that God tests those whom he loves. Moreover, the relentlessness of divine punishment signifies the abundance of God's love for the Jewish people. But Akiba eventually loses his faith. Consequently, he "lost his reason for struggling and had begun to die."[16] Further, a learned Polish rabbi concludes that even though humans cannot know the deity's intentions, because of Auschwitz it is no longer possible to believe in a merciful God.

Wiesel in Auschwitz experiences a series of dark epiphanies. He discovers that the world is far from being a revelation of divine intentions. Reflecting on his entrance into the kingdom of night, he observes:

> Never shall I forget that night, the first night in camp, which has turned
> My life into one long night, seven times cursed and seven times sealed.
> Never shall I forget that smoke. Never shall I forget the little faces of the
> Children whose bodies I saw turned into wreaths of smoke beneath a
> Silent blue sky.
> Never shall I forget those flames which consumed my faith forever.
> Never shall I forget that nocturnal silence which deprived me, for all
> Eternity, of the desire to live. Never shall I forget these things, even if I
> Am condemned to live as long as God Himself.
> Never.[17]

The incantatory tone and ritual intensity of Wiesel's observation reveal the *nomos*-shattering nature of Auschwitz-Birkenau.

Wiesel's story of the destruction of his pre–Auschwitz belief reaches its apogee when describing the hanging of three prisoners in the camp. The prisoners are forced to march past the condemned. Two of the victims are adults and die quickly. The third is a child whom Wiesel describes as a "sad-eyed angel." It takes the youth a long time to expire. Responding to a prisoner's question, "Where is God? Where is He?" Wiesel writes of hearing a voice within him say, "Where is He? Here He is — He is hanging here on this gallows...."[18] This is perhaps the memoir's most frequently cited passage. And it is most misunderstood.

Professor David Patterson notes how deeply the status of the child is ingrained in the Jewish soul.[19] The Jerusalem Temple and, in fact, the entire world, exists owing to the merit of the children. Wiesel himself attests to what is at stake with the murder of Jewish children when he writes:

> The death of a man is only the death of a man, but the death of a child
> Is the death of innocence, the death of God in the heart of man. And
> He who does not drink deeply of this truth, who does not shout it from
> The rooftops, is a man devoid of heart, of God.[20]

Consequently, the death of the child in *Night* emblemizes the death of Wiesel's childhood [child like?] belief in God, and National Socialism's savage and systematic trampling on the dignity and sanctity of life itself.

But Wiesel, as noted earlier, embraces paradox. He is not claiming that "God is Dead." While his youthful image of God is murdered in Auschwitz, God is eternal. Wiesel rebels against God during *Rosh HaShanah* in Auschwitz-Birkenau, writing, "I was the accuser, God the accused. I was ... terribly alone in a world without God and without man." Although describing himself ontologically as "ashes," the author writes, "yet I felt myself stronger than the Almighty, to whom my life had been tied for so long."[21] What image of God is plausible in a Holocaust planet? All of his subsequent tales deal with the tension between the believer that he was and the survivor that he is.

As a teller of tales, Wiesel can continually raise the issue of God's role in history and present various images of the divine without either exhausting the question or arriving at a definitive response. For Wiesel the *Shoah* is the "question of questions. It is both man's way of questioning God and God's way of questioning man. And there is no answer coming from either side. There cannot be."[22] His stories transmit this question from generation to generation [*ledor vedor*]. The post–Auschwitz question, which for Wiesel remains open, is how to accept God's presence when the deity neither intervenes to stop the suffering of His people nor triumphs over evil. Wiesel told an interviewer that ever since *Night* he has been trying to find "an occupation for God. Just as I was always obsessed with the question of what God was doing then, I want to know what God is doing now."[23]

Auschwitz and the Function of Religion

The sociologist Peter Berger describes adherents of religion as residing under a "sacred canopy" whose protection enables them to understand their lives and to make sense of the world. In this view, religion and its rituals — including the telling of tales — provides a plausibility structure which yields the purpose of life, a plausible theodicy, and the meaning of death. "In religious terms," observes Berger, "the sacred order of the cosmos is reaffirmed [repeatedly] in the face of chaos."[24] In Judaism, the Torah and the Aggadah are the blueprint for living life under the guidance of a divinely inspired *nomos*. Dwelling outside of the teachings of these sources or ignoring them is symbolically to live in chaos or anomie. Auschwitz is *the* anomic situation in which the victims find themselves.

Theodicy is the major challenge in "radical and ethical monotheism." A plausible theodicy is one which permits "the individual to integrate the anomic experiences of his biography into the socially established *nomos* and its subjective correlate in his own consciousness."[25] The biblical Job adopts a theodicy which involves absolute submission to God as totally other. In the case of Job, Berger, inauspiciously, terms this submission "religious masochism," citing the following verses: "Though he slay me, yet will I trust in Him," and "I despise myself in dust and ashes." It is precisely this traditional notion of total surrender to God that Wiesel rejects. Characteristic of modernity is the challenge of personal experience to traditional assertions. The Nobel laureate advocates protest — but a protest from within — which, for him, is the only authentic form of post–Auschwitz belief. "I say," he writes, "that anyone who was a believer and did not protest was not a true believer. To give validity to his belief he had first to shout his disbelief in his disbelief."[26]

Wiesel's religious orientation was so strong that survival itself depended on adherence to traditional forms of piety. Recently he told a television reporter that he had no idea how to behave in a secular world. "The only secular world I knew was Auschwitz. But I knew everything about the religious world. I know what to do in the morning, in the afternoon, and in the evening."[27] Wiesel could not live outside the sacred canopy of Judaism. Telling tales of his protest theology and presenting different images of the deity, Wiesel the writer is doing nothing less than "beginning history again."

Night gives rise to the primary theological paradox suffusing all of Wiesel's subsequent tales. If the pre–Holocaust paradigms for understanding theodicy and the role of God are no longer credible, and one cannot abandon faith, how is it possible to live as a Jew? "In the beginning," he writes, "there was the Holocaust. We must therefore start all over again. We have to write a new Talmud just as we did after the destruction of the Second Temple."[28] For example, in *The Accident* he specifically calls for the invention of new gods and new religions. Reflecting on the theological implications of the sexual degradation of Sarah by Nazi officers in Auschwitz-Birkenau, Wiesel writes, "Whoever enters Sarah's world and doesn't invent new gods and new religions deserves death and destruction."[29] More precisely, in my view, he is articulating the necessity of imaging God in a different manner after Auschwitz.

Ani Ma'amin

Ani Ma'amin: A Song Lost and Found Again and *The Trial of God [As It Was Held on February 25, 1649, in Shamgorod]* are two of Wiesel's most overtly theological works. They move from the *despair* of *Night* to a more nuanced and aggressive *protest* against divine indifference, while advocating *human action* to secure justice. Each work presents the reader with a distinct post–Auschwitz image of the deity at variance with biblical images. Both the cantata and the play question traditional teachings about the relationship between divine and human covenantal partners. Both texts articulate a type of protest from within. Each work tells a tale which reaffirms the open ended nature of questioning God. Moreover, those hearing these tales are themselves bound to ponder what type of divine image is plausible following the murder of two-thirds of European Jewry.

Wiesel's cantata takes its title from one of Maimonides' thirteen principles of Jewish Faith which attests: "I believe [*Ani ma'amin*] with perfect faith in the coming of the Messiah, and even if he tarries, I shall wait for him on any day that he will come, I believe." This work, which is dedicated to his son, and set to music by Darius Milhaud, was performed in Carnegie Hall just weeks after the 1973 Yom Kippur War. The title is especially fraught in light of Wiesel's observation that he "learned that Jews on their way to Treblinka and Birkenau had sung that song, as if to defy death."[30]

The cantata is a contemporary re-working of *Midrash Lamentations Rabbah*, which portrays the reaction of the Patriarchs, Moses, and Rachel to the destruction of the first Jerusalem Temple. Each is moved by Israel's suffering and her steadfast faith. All protest to God on behalf of the Israelites. Wiesel's version omits two extreme possibilities found in the original; the covenant has been broken or the destruction is a preface to the coming of the Messiah.

Ani Ma'amin is in the form of an extended dialogue between the patriarchs and God. Abraham, Isaac, and Jacob call God's attention to or call God to account for the suffering of the Jewish people during the *Shoah*. As witnesses, the patriarchs plead with God to intervene. A chorus, comprised of the Jewish people throughout history, laments, asking the age-old questions of theodicy, what is the source of evil, does suffering have a meaning, and when will the agony cease. Nevertheless, and in spite of the entreaties of the patriarchs and the lamentations of the chorus, God remains silent.

The Patriarchs, however, refuse to silence their protest. A heavenly voice is heard defending God. Echoing the now discredited assertions of God as both wholly other and a *mysterium tremendum*, an omnipotent and unaccountable deity, the voice declares:

> God knows,
> That is enough.
> God wills,
> That is enough.
> God takes
> And God gives back,
> That is enough.
> God breaks
> And God consoles,
> That is enough.[31]

Unlike Job, the patriarchs refuse consolation. Wiesel emphasizes the tension between divine promise and the shattering impact of the Holocaust. The patriarchs, on the one hand, maintain their belief that God will ingather the exiles and give the Jews "A place among the nations." On the other hand, "Israel's children, Israel's heirs, will remain unconsoled." There can *never be consolation* for the Holocaust. Each of the patriarchs, in turn, respond in a manner that enfeebles God in the face of evil. Abraham queries, "Be consoled for Belsen and Ponar?" Isaac asks, "Be rewarded for Birkenau?" And Jacob muses, "Be forgetful of Majdanek, Sachsenhausen and..."[32]

God's defender changes tactics. Instead of defending the deity, the heavenly voice attacks man for destroying what God has created. "Does God not have the right," asks the heavenly interlocutor, "to question you, in turn, to ask of man, what have you done with my creation." The patriarchs are crushed. Not by the question, but by what it implies. Abraham, Isaac, and Jacob understand that God knows that His people are suffering unspeakable cruelties "and remains silent." Wiesel writes, "And the silence of God is God."[33] The patriarchs then express their defiance by returning to earth in order to tell the Jewish people that there is no divine justice, their faith in traditional theodicy is unwarranted. God does not act in history. The patriarchs do not justify God at the expense of man. Rather, they stand with the Jewish people and defy God's indifference.

Wiesel, however, is too subtle a thinker and storyteller to leave the matter there. The tale continues. Unknown to Abraham, Isaac, and Jacob, God is deeply moved by the faithfulness of the Jewish people who continue to bear witness; a child while standing before the murderer's machine gun, a Jew who continues to believe despite being in the depths of the Holocaust, and a death camp inmate who upholds his messianic yearning. Wiesel paints a portrait of people who, despite every reason to abandon faith, embrace it nevertheless. In response to the peoples' Holocaust plight, "God," writes Wiesel, "permits a tear to cloud his eyes."[34]

The patriarchs are unaware that "God accompanies them weeping, smiling, whispering: *Nitzhuni banai*, my children have defeated me, they deserve my gratitude."[35] Writing in *Five Biblical Portraits*, Wiesel makes an observation that indicts God for failing to see and understand the gravity of His people's situation. The author prefers changing the punctuation of the Hebrew to read *Natzchuni banai*, "please, children defeat me!" Although God loves to be defeated by His children, writes Wiesel, this refers only to debates.

Wiesel's image of the deity in *Ani Ma'amin* sparked great controversy. Many Jewish thinkers find this image unsatisfactory. The position of Michael Berenbaum typifies this reaction. He contends that God, in the cantata, is "pathetic and frighteningly amoral." Moreover, the deity's tears come too late and are not in any case perceived by the patriarchs.[36] On the Christian side the reaction tends to be different. Robert McAfee Brown notes that by the end of the cantata God "has become a listening God" who is deeply moved by the plight of His children. Furthermore, the fact that God follows the patriarchs to earth "to participate in their suffering" means that the deity does not abandon His people.[37] The controversy will continue as long as humanity engages the issue of God's role in history.

Wiesel's tale images God as an impoverished deity, able neither to put an end to the Holocaust nor to provide a credible response to the millennial question of theodicy. Instead, God is imagined in anthropapathetic terms. He Himself is in search of redemption or, at least, forgiveness. Following the teachings of the sixteenth century Kabbalah of Isaac Luria, the cantata strongly suggests that God's salvation depends on human initiative. It is the people's faith that keeps God alive. A midrash reads that God tells the people of Israel, "You are my witnesses, says the Lord"— that is, if you are My witnesses, I am God, and if you are not My witnesses, I am, as it were, not God" (Midrash Psalms, on Psalm 123:1). Wiesel's cantata compels asking, if the song that was lost — in Auschwitz —

is again to be found, how will the people sing it after the Holocaust? Yet the author himself observes that at the end of the cantata the chorus expresses something of his own belief, "which is a belief against and in spite of everything."[38]

The Trial of God
[As It Was Held on February 25, 1649, in Shamgorod]

Wiesel's three-act play *The Trial of God* is based on an episode that occurred in Auschwitz-Birkenau. Three learned prisoners, "great masters in Talmud, in Halakhah, in Jewish jurisprudence" convened a rabbinic court putting God on trial. Witnesses were called for the prosecution. And for the defense. After several nights, the head of the tribunal announced the verdict: guilty. Following a silence lasting "a minute or an infinity," the head of the "court" said, "And now let us pray *Maariv*."[39] This story is important for several reasons. First, that it occurred in the midst of a radically anomic setting attests to the sustaining power of faith. Moreover, the fact that God is found guilty means that He is believed accountable. Third, the story reveals the paradoxical nature of faith. Although the deity is guilty of injustice and silence, we continue to believe, in spite of God.

Wiesel refrained from writing about this incident for many years. The awesome nature of the trial meant that it could not be reduced to mere literature. Thus, the author confides that he placed the event further back in time. The play is set against the background of the Chmielnicki pogrom of 1648–49. Three wandering minstrels [*Purim spielers*] arrive at an inn in the city of Shamgorod on the eve of Purim, a holiday which is replete with disguises and secrets, and which commemorates the defeat of a genocidal plan against the Jewish people. Unbeknownst to the three wanderers, a devastating pogrom has killed all the city's Jews dead except for Berish the innkeeper, whose wife and sons have been murdered, and his daughter Hanna who has suffered a breakdown as a result of being raped and tortured by the murderous crowd. In the space of three acts, a decision is made to hold a trial of God, a defender of the deity needs to be found, and the trial itself reveals an awful truth about the classical Jewish concept "we are punished because of our sins" [*u'minei hata'einu*].

As in the Holocaust, God is conspicuous in Shamgorod by His

absence. The play resonates with overtones of the Job story. Berish, a righteous and generous man, agrees to the minstrels' request to celebrate Purim, only on condition that they participate in a trial of God. Berish is the prosecutor. The three minstrels are judges. After great difficulty, Sam, a mysterious stranger, volunteers to defend the deity. During the course of the trial it becomes apparent that once again pogromists are preparing to attack. A priest, whom Berish knows, comes to the inn to warn of an impending pogrom. Although he urges the Jews to hide, his offer of shelter is tinged with ambiguity, underscoring Christian antisemitism. Berish declines his offer. The trial must continue.

Berish rejects Sam's contention that since God spared Berish during the pogrom, why be against the deity. The innkeeper articulates Wiesel's theology of protest, proclaiming:

He annihilated Shamgorod and you want me to be for Him? I can't. If He Insists upon going on with His methods, let Him — but I won't say Amen. Let Him crush me, I won't say Kaddish. Let Him kill us all, I shall shout and Shout that it's His fault. I'll use my last energy to make my protest known. Whether I live or die, I submit to Him no longer.[40]

Robert McAfee Brown observes that "Berish is a strange affirmer" of God. Berish, continues McAfee Brown, is a "Job who refuses consolation and continues to accuse and defy." Berish articulates Wiesel's position; Jews may "oppose God as long as it is done in defense of His creation."[41]

Berish protests not only the personal injustice done to his family and to the Jews of Shamgorod, but the historical manifestations of God's injustice to the Jewish people. Responding to Sam's admonition that in the face of suffering, our Jewish ancestors were quiet, Berish contends:

For them, too, I'll demand justice. For the widows of Jerusalem and the Orphans of Betar. For the claves of Rome and Capadoccia. And for the Destitute of Oman and the victims of Koretz. I'll shout for them, against Him I'll shout. To you, judges, I'll shout, "Tell Him what He should not Have done; tell Him to stop the bloodshed now. Discharge your duties Without fear.[42]

Like the patriarchs in *Ani Ma'amin*, Berish takes the side of the Jewish people against divine injustice. His anger stems from the fact that he persists in believing. As the murderers approach the inn, Berish again proclaims his fidelity as a Jew and his anger at God's lack of justice.

I lived as a Jew, and it is as a Jew that I shall die — and it is as a Jews
That, with my last breath, I shall protest to God! And because the end is
Near, I'll tell Him that He's more guilty than ever.[43]

Berish, like Eliezer in *Night*, is the accuser and God the accused. The three
minstrels are taken by Sam's defense of the deity. One of them, Mendel,
goes so far as to term Sam a *tzaddik*, a saint and a righteous and holy man.
He begs Sam to save the Jews from the murderous crowd gathering near
the inn. The play ends with the revelation that Sam is actually Samael or
Satan. God is being defended by the Devil.

The Wiesel's play makes several important points about the divine image.
Unlike the thwarted genocide reported in the Scroll of Esther, which is
read on Purim, the Holocaust was not averted. Moreover, this Scroll does
not mention the name of God. Rather, Queen Esther and her uncle
Mordecai outwit Haman — the evil prime minister who issued the decree
of extermination. While it is true that certain rabbinic commentators see
God's presence in the tale — deriving the Hebrew *Hester* [hidden or hiding God] from Esther, Purim celebrates the triumph of the Jewish people with or without God. During the *Shoah,* however, no such victory
could be proclaimed either by God or His people. Moreover, the play
rejects suffering as a virtue. It is neither just nor justified. Quite the contrary is the case: suffering demands that humans argue with and defy
God. The fact that Sam/Satan advocates acceptance of suffering as
punishment for sin makes him "not God's emissary but man's adver-
sary."[44]

The trial of God will continue as long as humanity itself exists.
Mendel, the presiding judge, observes, "Who will continue the thread of
our tale? The last page will not be written. But the one before? It is up to
us to prepare testimony for future generations.... The verdict will be
announced by someone else, at a later stage. For the trial will continue —
without us."[45] Unlike the deity portrayed in *Ani Ma'amin*, God in *The
Trial of God* sheds no tears for His people and appears unmoved by their
plight. This deity bears greater resemblance to the divine image which the
young Eliezer portrays in *Night*. Wiesel's play bequeaths a legacy of eternal protest against divine injustice.

All Rivers Run to the Sea *and* And the Sea Is Never Full

Wiesel's two volume autobiography, *All Rivers Run to the Sea* and *And the Sea Is Never Full,* revisits the author's work and takes stock of his life. Bearing witness to his witness in *Night*, Wiesel attests that the memoir "was an autobiographical story, a kind of testimony of one witness speaking of his own life, his own death."[46] The death to which he refers is that part of himself which, as a child, prohibited him from interrogating the divine. Reviewing the testimony of *Night*, Wiesel asks three questions in *All Rivers Run to the Sea*; "Was I explicit enough? Did I miss what was essential? Did I serve memory well?" His response "...if I had it to do all over again, I would change nothing in my deposition."[47] Wiesel, whom Neher terms a "Diviner of Silence," grapples ceaselessly with the problem of divine silence during the Holocaust. This has the effect, attests Neher, of "reversing all religiously established values."[48]

Wiesel's search for a credible post–Holocaust divine image was influenced by several sources, including his study of subjects such as philosophy, literature, and Eastern religions. Perhaps the greatest impact on the young survivor was the influence of Shushani [Mordechai Rosenbaum], a bizarre, brilliant, and unusual teacher. Wiesel credits him with teaching two important lessons which helped formulate a plausible story of God and the possibility of belief after the *Shoah*. Lesson one: man is defined by what troubles him. Wiesel writes that he "needed to be forced to start all over again."[49] What divine image could replace that of the God of Wiesel's childhood who hung on a gallows? Wiesel reports elsewhere that Shushani berated him for searching in error. The youth's indictment of God was based on an inaccurate perception of the deity. "God," proclaimed the master, "means movement and not explanation."[50]

Lesson two emerges from Shushani's teaching method which upset both the believer and the heretic. This mode of thinking is clearly reflected in Wiesel's tales. The author's self-description of his writing, which he terms the literature of testimony, reveals his affinity with his late master:

I disturb the believer because I dare to put questions to God, the source
Of all faith. I disturb the miscreant because, despite my doubts and questions,
I refuse to break with the religious and mystical universe that has shaped
My own. Most of all, I disturb those who are comfortably settled within
A system — be it political, psychological or theological.[51]

Much later, Wiesel studies with the great Talmudist Saul Lieberman who observes that while one can and must love God, it is also necessary to challenge and be angry with Him. Lieberman also asserts that "one must also pity" the deity.[52] God, continues Lieberman, is the most tragic figure in the Bible. His creatures frequently betray and disappoint Him. Nevertheless, Wiesel observes that "God could have — should have — interrupted His own suffering by calling a halt to the martyrdom of innocents."[53]

As a mystic, Wiesel takes seriously the doctrine of evil advanced by the sixteenth-century Kabbalah. The teachings of Isaac Luria, transmitted by his disciple Hayyim Vital, imply that there is a flaw in creation itself which accounts for the existence of evil. Furthermore, in this telling, God is powerless to completely eradicate evil. On the mythic plane, Luria speaks of the "Breaking of the Vessels" [*Shvirat haKellim*] created to contain divine sparks at the origin of creation. Owing to the breaking of the vessels designed to contain these sparks, they were scattered over the earth and covered with matter. Consequently, Luria viewed the exile of the Jews as a mission, their task was to raise the divine light [*aliyoth haNitsosoth*] back to its heavenly source. When all the divine sparks are restored, the Jewish people will be ingathered to the land of Israel and God Himself will be redeemed. Raising the sparks will, eventually, result in a repair or restoration of the world [*tikkun olam*]. The redemption process may, however, continue for centuries. Wiesel contends that the Holocaust is a twentieth century manifestation of the "Breaking of the Vessels."[54]

Reflecting on *Ani Ma'amin*, Wiesel reveals the complexity of the post–Holocaust divine image. "The whole question of faith in God," he writes, "surely in spite of man and perhaps in spite of God, permeates the cantata."[55] Wiesel writes of being "haunted" by a phrase in the *Zohar*, the "Bible" of Jewish mysticism. There it is written that God follows the people of Israel into exile. The author wonders whether God will follow the Jewish people into Europe's death camps. Wiesel also comments on the question raised in *The Trial of God*. Berish accuses God of "hostility, cruelty, and indifference." Sam, God's defender, denies the pain of suffering and the injustice visited upon the Jewish inhabitants of Shamgorod. He is, attests Wiesel, "a fanatic, the enemy of God and man."[56]

Conclusion

Storytelling for Wiesel is both affirmation and protest. Furthermore, in elevating memory to the status of ontology — "If we cease to remember, we cease to be"— the author compels both divine and human covenantal partner to remember the *Shoah*. "It's in God's nightmare," writes the author, "that human beings are hurling living Jewish children into the flames."[57] Wiesel's post–Auschwitz prayer to God reverses the classical *Shema Yisrael* [Hear O Israel] prayer; it is now God who is required to listen. Wiesel writes, "I no longer ask You for the life of that child [Wiesel before the Holocaust], nor even for his faith. I only beg You to listen to him and act in such a way that You and I can listen to him together."[58]

As noted earlier, Wiesel is still seeking to find an occupation for God. Consequently, his tales present a myriad of divine images.[59] Today he speaks of a "wounded faith." But Wiesel never renounced his faith in God. Rather, he has "risen against His injustice, protested His silence and sometimes His absence, but my anger rises up within faith and not outside it."[60] Rebellion is itself, a form of belief. Nostalgia is the other side of Wiesel's anger. He observes the tension between his pre– and post–Holocaust faith writing, "*Ah, si seulement je pouvais aujourd'hui ouvrir mon âme à la prière, si je pouvais aspirer à la pureté comme je le faisis en ce temps-là....*"[61] Wiesel does not, however, stop at this point. He embraces what one scholar terms "defiant activism," which stresses humanity's role in seeking a more just world.[62]

Wiesel's tales employ traditional models, both in their midrashic and mystical versions. Like these models, his stories require continual interrogation. Their meaning is never completely revealed or exhausted. Each generation contributes its own particular understanding; not by answering, but rather by asking, its own questions. "The role of the text," comments Colin Davis, "is to solicit new interpretations for new situations."[63]

Consequently, Wiesel's stories are a way for him to continue his dialogue with God. But this, too, has its own linguistic dilemma. It is impossible to refrain from speaking, yet words themselves betray the experience.

Wiesel's tales of God after Auschwitz are nothing less than a continuing search for a credible way of residing under Judaism's radically altered post–Holocaust canopy. But the storyteller also involves his audience. Katriel, the protagonist in *A Beggar in Jerusalem*, observes: "Do you know that it is given to us to enrich a legend simply by Listening to it? It belongs as much to the listener as to the teller."[64] Listening to stories relating the author's quarrel with God simultaneously raises questions in the minds of the listeners. Wiesel's stories reach us more profoundly and touch us at levels that learned essays fail to reach. His interrogation of the divine refuses to restrict itself to an all or nothing position. It is Wiesel's gift as a storyteller that his tales focus on a "positive ambiguity" thereby enabling the listeners — no less than the teller — to raise and re-raise questions which are, like the deity, eternal.

Notes

1. Irving Abrahamson, ed., *Against Silence: The Voice and Vision of Elie Wiesel* (New York: Holocaust Library, 1985), Vol. 2, 139.

2. One of Wiesel's books is titled *Legends of Our Time,* trans. Stephen Donadio (New York: Schocken Books, 1982). Originally published in French as *Le Chant des Morts,* this collection of the author's reflections attests that all of Jewish history needs to be re-viewed through a Holocaust prism.

3. Elie Wiesel, *Paroles d'étranger: Textes, Contes et Dialogues* (Paris: Editions du Seuil, 1982), 166.

4. Ibid., 180.

5. Richard L. Rubenstein, "Elie Wiesel and Primo Levi," in *Perspectives on the Holocaust: Essays in Honor of Raul Hilberg,* ed. James S. Pacy and Alan P. Wertheimer (Boulder: Westview Press, 1994), 146.

6. Byron L. Sherwin, "Wiesel's Midrash: The Writings of Elie Wiesel and Their Relationship to Jewish Tradition," in *Confronting the Holocaust: The Impact of Elie Wiesel,* ed. Alvin Rosenfeld and Irving Greenberg (Bloomington: Indiana University Press, 1978), 119–120.

7. Anson Laytner, *Arguing With God: A Jewish Tradition* (Northvale, N.J.: Jason Aronson Inc., 1990), 214.

8. Harry James Cargas, "Positive Ambiguity: The Religious Thought of Elie Wiesel," *Spiritual Life,* Summer (1990): 79.

9. Ibid., 83.

10. Abrahamson, *Against Silence,* Vol. 3, 230.

11. Elie Wiesel, *Night,* trans. Stella Rodway (New York: Bantam Books, 1986); *Ani Ma'amin: A Song Lost and Found Again,* trans. Marion Wiesel (New York: Bibliophile Library, 1973); *The Trial of God (As It Was Held on February 25, 1649, in Shamgorod)* trans. Marion Wiesel (New York: Schocken Books, 1986); *All Rivers Run to the Sea: Memoirs,* trans. Marion Wiesel (New York: Alfred A. Knopf, 1995); *And the Sea Is Never Full: Memoirs, 1969–,* trans. Marion Wiesel (New York: Alfred A. Knopf, 1999).

12. Wiesel, *Night,* 2–3.

13. Wiesel, *Night,* 4.

14. Wiesel, *All Rivers Run to the Sea,* 239.

15. André Neher, *The Exile of the Word: From the Silence of the Bible to the Silence of Auschwitz* (Philadelphia: Jewish Publication Society of America, 1981), 216.

16. Wiesel, *Night,* 73.

17. Ibid., 32.

18. Ibid., 62.

19. David Patterson, *Along the Edge of Annihilation: The Collapse and Recovery of Life in the Holocaust Diary* (Seattle: University of Washington Press, 1999). See

especially the chapter "The Suffocation of the Child," 192–210. Wiesel observes that the destruction of his childhood began in the cattle car hurtling toward Auschwitz: "Life in the cattle cars was the death of my Adolescence. How quickly I aged." Wiesel, *All Rivers Run to the Sea,* 75–76.

20. Wiesel, *A Beggar in Jerusalem,* 99.

21. Wiesel, *Night,* 67.

22. Abrahamson, *Against Silence,* Vol. 1, 144.

23. Harry James Cargas, "Positive Ambiguity," 81.

24. Peter Berger, *The Sacred Canopy: Elements of a Sociological Theory of Religion* (New York: Anchor Books, 1969), 53.

25. Ibid., 58.

26. Abrahamson, *Against Silence,* Vol. 3, 229.

27. Elie Wiesel, "First Person Singular," Interview on Channel 2, Miami, Florida. October 24, 2002.

28. Abrahamson, *Against Silence,* Vol. 1, 206.

29. Elie Wiesel, *Night, Dawn, The Accident* (New York: Hill & Wang, 1972), 289.

30. Wiesel, *And The Sea Is Never Full,* 67.

31. Wiesel, *Ani Ma'amin,* 99.

32. Ibid., 103.

33. Ibid., 123.

34. Ibid., 131.

35. Ibid., 147.

36. Michael Berenbaum, *Elie Wiesel: God, The Holocaust, and the Children of Israel* (West Orange, N.J.: Behrman House, 1994), 117.

37. Robert McAfee Brown, *Elie Wiesel: Messenger to All Humanity,* rev. ed. (Notre Dame: University of Notre Dame Press, 1989), 159.

38. Abrahamson, *Against Silence,* Vol. 3, 94.

39. Ibid., 112.

40. Elie Wiesel, *The Trial of God,* 133.

41. McAfee Brown, *Elie Wiesel: Messenger to All Humanity,* 154.

42. Wiesel, *The Trial of God,* 134.

43. Ibid., 156.

44. Laytner, *Arguing With God,* 220.

45. Wiesel, *The Trial of God,* 156–158.

46. Harry James Cargas, *Conversations with Elie Wiesel* (South Bend, Ind.: Justice Books, 1992), 86.

47. Elie Wiesel, *All Rivers Run to the Sea,* 79.

48. Neher, *Exile,* 211.

49. Wiesel, *All Rivers Run to the Sea,* 336–337.

50. Wiesel, *Legends of Our Time,* 93. Shushani's notion of the deity is indebted to the Jewish mystical tradition. Byron Sherwin observes that "In Kabbalah nothing is static, everything is becoming. In non-mystical thinking God is a Being: in Kabbalah, He is Becoming." Byron Sherwin, "Elie Wiesel and Jewish Theology," *Judaism,* XVII (Winter 1969): 44.

51. Wiesel, *All Rivers Run to the Sea,* 124.

52. Ibid., 85.

53. Ibid., 105.

54. Ibid., 105. Wiesel is, however, equally concerned with human indifference

to the plight of the Jewish people during the *Shoah*. In *All Rivers Run to the Sea,* on the same page, he writes, "I will never understand their moral decline, their fall. There was a time when everything roused anger, even revolt, in me against humanity."

55. Wiesel, *And the Sea Is Never Full,* 68.

56. Laynter, *Arguing with God,* 220.

57. Wiesel, *And the Sea Is Never Full,* 361.

58. Wiesel, *All Rivers Run to the Sea,* 78.

59. Wiesel, *Legends of Our Time,* 190.

60. While this is not the place to list the various images of deity in Wiesel's work, a legend at the end of one of his novels is revealing. God granted man's wish to exchange places for "only a second." Man refused to resume his human condition. "So, writes Wiesel, "neither God nor man was ever again what he seemed to be." The liberation of one was bound to the liberation of the other. Consequently, "they renewed the ancient dialogue...." *The Town Beyond The Wall,* trans. Stephen Becker (New York: Schocken Books, 1982), 179. It is significant to note that in Wiesel's hasidic writings emphasize the role of the human covenantal partner. The way to God, writes, the author, leads through man.

61. Elie Wiesel, *Tous les Fleuves Vont à la Mer: Mémoires 1* (Paris: Éditions du Seuil, 1994), 37.

62. Laytner, *Arguing with God,* 214 ff.

63. Colin Davis, *Elie Wiesel's Secretive Texts* (Gainesville: University Press of Florida, 1994), 41.

64. Wiesel, *A Beggar in Jerusalem,* 107.

Wrestling with Oblivion: Wiesel's Autobiographical Storytelling as Midrash

Deborah Lee Ames

Elie Wiesel frequently identifies himself as one who must bear witness. He explains in an essay: "Why do I write? To wrest those victims [of the Holocaust] from oblivion. To help the dead vanquish death."[1] With those words, Wiesel's viewpoint looks Janus-like to the past, as he describes what happened to the Jews during the *Shoah*, and towards the future, as he strives to prevent the dead from being forgotten within our once and future memory. The only way to make sure that the survivors' accounts are not vanquished is to hear the stories they tell. *Shoah* survivors keenly know that the world did not want to hear their stories, neither during nor immediately after the Event, to say nothing of Holocaust deniers; even now, many people would prefer not to hear the disturbing details of the Third Reich's oppression of the Jews. Of the relatively few survivors who have published their autobiographies, Wiesel is the best known and the most prolific author. One reason Wiesel has reached a wide audience has been his masterful manner of telling a story. *Night*, other autobiographical accounts, his fiction, and even his essays are endued with the spirit of the storyteller, and not just any type of storyteller: Wiesel's reflective spirit and his theological attitude place him firmly within the midrashic tradition of storytelling.

The Midrash is a form of rabbinic literature wherein commentators throughout the centuries engage in exegetical, philological, and hermeneutical interpretations of the Hebrew Scriptures. Anything is open to interpretation; consequently, rabbis might focus their attention on a short passage, a line, a phrase, or an individual word. It is no exaggeration to say that every element that makes up Scripture is worthy of midrashic scrutiny. The term midrash is derived from the Hebrew word for search, a connotation that is most appropriate for the Midrash.[2] The Midrash records the rabbis' search for meaning within Scripture, and the compilation of rabbinic insights preserves the agreements, disagreements, elaborations, and speculations over any Biblical passage or phrase, forming, in a curiously modern way, an ancient form of hypertext. The Midrash preserves the dialogic interaction that spans countries and centuries.

Because the Midrash is a compilation of rabbinical exegesis, a reader may go to the bookshelf and pull out, for example, Genesis Rabbah, the midrashic commentary on Genesis, or the Midrash on Exodus. However, midrash is not limited to that singular denotation. In *Midrash for Beginners*, Edwin C. Goldberg explains that while the Midrash is "a specific body of classical rabbinical commentary on the Bible, edited from approximately the year 200 of the Common Era (C.E.) to the ninth century"[3] it is more than that because "any comment which is directly or indirectly related to the Bible is midrashic."[4] Jacob Neusner offers a threefold definition in his guide, *What Is Midrash?* When people talk about what the Midrash says about a particular portion of the Hebrew Bible, they could mean "a concrete unit of scriptural exegesis," or "a compilation of the results of that process," or "a process of interpretation."[5] Finally, Emil Fackenheim argues that midrash "reflects upon the root experience of Judaism"; furthermore, time is transcended because midrash looks upon the Biblical passage as both a past and a present event.[6] Thus midrash is at once a collected work of rabbinical thinking and a way of reflecting upon contemporary Jewish life.

What does this have to do with Elie Wiesel, particularly Wiesel the storyteller? Wiesel is a midrashic storyteller; the spirit of search, inquiry, and speculation that is at the heart of the Midrash is also at the heart of Wiesel's stories. Wiesel's writings link him to the midrashic tradition on several levels: he contextualizes the Holocaust as an event of Biblical proportions; he uses words as thoughtfully, sparely, and reflectively as did the midrashic commentators; and by his use of Scriptural allusions within the stories he tells, he creates a midrashic text wherein he explores the timeless nature of humanity and God.

The creation of the concentration camps, slave labor camps, and extermination camps that forced into reality the Nazi obsession with hatred and death is one of the best-known aspects of the Holocaust. Yet even we who read about the Event cannot grasp the full impact of such a world, such a life. The human-engineered nightmare was so other-worldly that *Shoah* writers struggled to find words descriptive enough to convey its uniqueness. Sixty years after the liberation of the death camps, debate still continues about what to call the Nazi-run era of torture and death: the most common designations are the Holocaust, the *Shoah*, the Event, and the *Hurbn*. Each term is appropriate in its own way; each, inappropriate. The lack of agreement upon a term suggests the magnitude of the disaster. In the same vein, when survivors describe their entry into the bizarre world of the camps, they use such terms as "planet Auschwitz," "the Holocaust Kingdom," "*l'univers concentrationnaire*," "the inferno," "beyond Dante's Inferno," and, most simply, "hell." Being plunged into this hell caused some writers to think of the Holocaust in Biblical terms, and, at first, readers may recoil at the linking of the Nazi Night and Fog with what many consider to be sacred Scripture. And yet — a phrase Wiesel favors — what other text reflects on the often-stormy, always mysterious relationship between a Deity and the chosen people? Wiesel asserts that a Biblical gravitas exists around the Event. "I think we live in Biblical times," he has simply said. "This is the conclusion I have reached."[7] He implies that linear time may be transcended with such observations as "in the beginning was the Holocaust"[8] and "[a]fter Auschwitz everything long past brings us back to Auschwitz."[9]

Wiesel is not alone in his assessment. Primo Levi establishes a correlation between the stories of the camps and the tales of the Bible in his first autobiographical work, *Survival in Auschwitz*:

> He told me his story, and today I have forgotten it, but it was certainly a sorrowful, cruel, and moving story; because so are all our stories, hundreds of thousands of stories, all different and all full of a tragic, disturbing necessity. We tell them to each other in the evening, and they take place in Norway, Italy, Algeria, the Ukraine, and are as simple and incomprehensible like stories in the Bible. But are they not themselves stories of a new Bible?[10]

Wiesel has never elevated his own stories to the canonical level of the Bible, but he is emphatic that the themes of the Hebrew Scriptures were embodied during the *Shoah*. He situates himself within a Biblical context, although he will at times discretely distance himself from that stance. Specifically, Wiesel identifies with Isaac, the second of the patriarchs, whom he considers the exemplum of the survivor. Whether Wiesel is telling his own story of his Holocaust experience or telling the story of Abraham obeying God's strange commandment to sacrifice his beloved son, the kinship Wiesel feels with Isaac is palpable. His identification with the second patriarch is woven throughout his writings: he treats it at length in his relatively early study of the *Messengers of God: Biblical Portraits and Legends*, and in his most recent memoir, *And the Sea Is Never Full*, the image of Abraham, Isaac, and the ram is brought up early in the first chapter.[11] Turning to *Messengers of God*, the subtitle for the chapter about Isaac clearly states Wiesel's interpretation: "The Sacrifice of Isaac: A Survivor's Story."

A brief review of the Abraham and Isaac story found in Genesis 22 may be in order. God instructs Abraham to sacrifice his "favored" son Isaac, the miraculous child of his old age with his infertile wife Sarah. Father and son, accompanied by servants, set out on their silent quest; they are eventually directed to Mount Moriah, where the sacrifice will take place. Isaac carries on his own back the wood for the sacrifice — the holocaust, a burnt offering — and is placed upon the altar of wood for his father to slay him. Abraham picks up a knife to kill his son. An angel calls out to Abraham, staying the patriarch's hand, thereby stopping the sacrifice. God provides a different acceptable sacrificial victim: a ram whose horns have trapped it in a bush. Abraham and Isaac depart the mountain, apparently separately; Scripture does not record any further interaction between the two men. Moreover, the writer of Genesis 22 hints that Isaac's mother Sarah died while he was gone. Some midrashic commentators presume that she died of a broken heart, knowing that her husband intended to kill their son.

The importance of Genesis 22 for Jewish and for Christian thinkers can scarcely be overstated, and, in a different context, we would wish to spend time analyzing both the Scriptural account and the theological commentary it has generated. It must be briefly noted that although Christians refer to the story as "the sacrifice of Isaac" because the Lord asked Abraham to sacrifice his son, most Jews eschew that designation (contrary to Wiesel's use of it as his chapter title), preferring instead the Hebrew term *akeda*, or *akedat* Yitzchak, "the binding of Isaac" because the son was bound before being placed upon the altar. The *akeda* plays a pivotal role in Wiesel's thinking and in his storytelling. "Here," Wiesel declares, "is a story that contains Jewish destiny in its totality.... Every major theme, every passion and obsession that makes Judaism the adventure that it is, can be traced back to it."[12] In telling contemporary audiences about Genesis 22, Wiesel cannot help but tell his own story, albeit inverted.

"In my own way," Wiesel admits, "I speak of Isaac constantly, in all my writings. In fact, I speak of almost nothing else."[13] Because Isaac is "the first survivor," his life has something "to teach us, the future survivors of Jewish history."[14] Those future survivors experienced, as did the Isaac of Genesis, the journey to the place of their planned extermination, the overarching anticipation of death, and the lonely walk away from the death site. Those future survivors found, as did Isaac, that to return home, to the same place, to the same manner, and to the same people, was impossible. Their homes have been destroyed or overtaken by others; family members are dead or scattered across a continent. Wiesel finds in the *akeda* a paradigm for his own Holocaust ordeal:

> That is why the theme and term of the *Akeda* have been used, throughout the centuries, to describe the destruction and disappearance of countless Jewish communities everywhere.... Of all the Biblical tales, the one about Isaac is perhaps the most timeless and relevant to our generation. We have known Jews who, like Abraham, witnessed the death of their children; who, like Isaac, lived the *Akeda* in their flesh; and some who went mad when they saw their father disappear on the altar, with the altar, in a blazing fire whose flames reached into the highest of heavens.[15]

Thus the *akeda*, according to Wiesel, occurred not only at Mount Moriah but also at Auschwitz. In *Night*, Wiesel records a moment when he, the young Eliezer, fears he will be separated from his beloved father. The two survive the selection together, and Eliezer was, "for the moment," as Wiesel puts its, "happy."[16] His father, however, did not experience the same emotion. "His voice was terribly sad. I realized that he did not want to see what they were going to do to me. He did not want to see the burning of his only son."[17] In *Messengers of God*, Wiesel identifies the emotion that Abraham must have felt was "anguish."[18] The tangible sadness that hovers over Eliezer's father in *Night* textualizes the patriarchal anguish. Other parallels exist between Abraham and Wiesel's father. In Genesis 22, the father wielded a knife, a knife by which Isaac was to be sacrificed. Wiesel employs the knife imagery, thereby drawing a subtle comparison between his father and Abraham. Wiesel's father, while in the concentration camp, is not sure how much more he can endure, and so he tries to prepare his son for his death. "'Look, take this knife,' he said to me. 'I don't need it any longer. It might be useful to you.' ... The inheritance."[19] The knife, virtually the only possession his father had in Auschwitz, links Wiesel's father with Abraham, whose iconography in the *akeda* often portray the patriarch with a knife hovering over the bound Isaac. By handing over his knife, Wiesel's father has also handed over the iconographic image of Abraham, passing the *akeda*'s burden to the son.

Again and again Wiesel returns to the *akeda*. In his cantata, *Ani Ma'amin*, he paints with words the following picture: "An old man / And his son / They speak / In a low voice. / The father believes in miracles: / Anything can happen, / Even at the last moment, / If only God wills it."[20] The son sings: "'Does it hurt, Father, say, / Does it hurt to die?'"[21] Here, Wiesel midrashically situates Abraham and Isaac at Mount Moriah and in the death camps.

André Nehur, in his provocative study of the Bible, observes: "If the *Akedah* [an acceptable variation of the transliteration of the word *akeda*] had been real (and we know now, through Auschwitz, that real *akedot* [plural form of *akeda*] do occur), then everything would have happened to Abraham and Isaac as is related in *Night*."[22] Abraham quietly led his son to a place where he trusted that God would provide; the twentieth-century parallel finds, during the dregs of the war's final days, the Nazis evacuate Auschwitz, taking the hapless prisoners on a death march. Eliezer, that is, the young Elie Wiesel, leads and exhorts his father, who is never named (what son would call his father by any name other than that of the father's role?), even as he, Eliezer, longs for the end of the agonizing death march: "My father's presence was the only thing that stopped me [from dying].... He was running at my side, out of breath, at the end of his strength, at his wit's end. I had no right to let myself die. What would he do without me?"[23] Wiesel intuitively understands that in movement, there is life; were they to stop, they would die. "The march continued," Wiesel states, not about his own march through the snow, but about the patriarch's journey toward Mount Moriah. "The two of them alone in the world, encircled by God's unfathomable design. But they were *together*."[24] He observes:

And so the father and the son walked away together ... the one to bind and the other to be bound ... the one to slaughter and the other to be slaughtered — sharing the same allegiance to the same God, responding to the same call. The sacrifice was to be their joint offering; father and son had never before been so close. The Midrashic text emphasizes this, as if to show another tragic aspect of the *Akeda*, namely, the equation between Abraham and Isaac.... Once more the key word is *yakhdav*, together: victims together.[25]

Wiesel, along with other *Shoah* autobiographers, often pay tribute to the fact that being together with either family members or friends who became members of their concentration camp family helped them cope with the trauma. Being together, even if they were "victims together," allowed them to endure, if not survive, hardships.

However, in the paradoxical universe that defines the Holocaust, the converse was also true; sometimes, being with a family member could add to the emotional distress. Abraham sings the following words to God in Wiesel's cantata *Ani Ma'amin*: "The Torah forbids / The slaughter of an animal / And its young / On the same day. / Yet — fathers and sons / Are massacred / In each other's presence / Every day. Is then a Jew / Less precious / Than a beast?"[26] The anguish felt by men, women, and children who endured their own physical and psychological pain was enhanced by watching the agony and death of beloved family members, a fact fully recognized and exploited by the Nazis.

For many religious Jews, the *Shoah* presented an agonizing conflict with faith. It must be said that some Jews did not experience such a crisis; Wiesel and other autobiographers recount tales of religious Jews meeting their deaths with unwavering belief in the benevolence of a good God, a trustworthy King of the Universe. We read in many *Shoah* memoirs stories of Jews proclaiming their faith even as they stand before the open pit that will become a mass grave; we read of Jews who mumbled the *Sh'ma* [Hear, O Israel] as they stand in line to the gas chambers. But part of the paradox that is contained within the *Shoah* is, as Wiesel puts it, the Holocaust does not make sense with God nor does it make sense without God.[27] A persistent motif in Wiesel's reflections is his struggle with God. In *Night* and elsewhere in his writings, he describes himself as a youth filled with religious zeal, but the sights that he saw while trapped within the Kingdom of the Night turned his love into anger. A memorable moment in *Night* occurs when young Eliezer observes the devout Jews around him who gather on the eve of Rosh Hashanah. He who had once been filled with a love for God notices his own emotional distance. "How could I say to [God]: 'Blessed art thou, Eternal, Master of the Universe, Who chose us from among the races to be tortured day and night, to see our fathers, our mothers, our brothers, end in the crematory? Praised by Thy Holy Name, Thou Who has chosen us to be butchered on Thine altar?'"[28] Isaac had not been "butchered on [God's] alter" because a ram was provided; why, asks Wiesel over and over throughout his writings, was no other sacrifice provided for the millions of Isaacs who lived during the *Shoah*? He admits that he is haunted by a midrash wherein the Archangel Michael showed God one suffering child in Egypt and God, deeply moved, brought the Hebrew people out of Egypt."[29] "And often I say to myself: *Ribono shel olam*, Master of the Universe, one child was enough to move you — and one million children were not?"[30] The historical fact and the theological trauma of such a universe propel Wiesel's writings and his search for justice.

Like Isaac, Elie Wiesel did survive the near-sacrifice. Unlike Abraham, Wiesel's father did not. Alfred H. Rosenfeld comments upon the inversion of the father and son roles in *Night*: "Wiesel, a storyteller very much within the line of the classic Midrashic writers ... [concludes] his memoir with an Isaac surviving the bloody altar but all the father figures dead."[31] Observing the parallels between the Biblical *akeda* and Wiesel's *Night*, Neher points out that Wiesel's experience is "an *Akeda* in reverse: not a father leading his son to the sacrifice, but a son conducting, dragging, carrying to the sacrifice an old, exhausted father."[32] Wiesel is Isaac; he has lived the *akeda* in his own flesh; he leaves the site of sacrifice without his father; death forbids that they will ever speak to one another again.

The enormity of the suffering and death — and Wiesel consistently acknowledges that it was not only Jews who were victims (and yet all Jews under Hitler's reign were victims) — compels silence. What use are words in the face of such an event? Here again Wiesel must struggle with a paradox:

> Let us tell tales. Let us tell tales — all the rest can wait.... The difficulty lies in the transmission. Not all tales can be, should be, communicated in language. Some, according to Rebbe Menachem Medei of Kotzk, can be transmitted only in silence, and others, more profound, not even in silence. What, then, is one to do?[33]

Wiesel grapples with the need for silence that is respectful, hushed, versus the silence demonstrated by the world that could not be bothered to speak out against injustice while the Nazis reigned.

And so Wiesel the storyteller seeks to tell a story using words laden with silence. He understands his role is to be a storyteller, yet he admits that his storytelling is about "the impossibility of communicating a story."[34] A storyteller who uses words, be they written or spoken, to tell the story thus faces an enormous challenge when trying to communicate that which defies comprehension. Wiesel, in his interview with Harry James Cargas, states that the story he has to share "will never be told because maybe only God can tell it — to himself, not even to [humanity]."[35] Furthermore, the story of the *Shoah* contains within it "mystery, almost a religious mystery, with theological implications."[36] For a writer such as Wiesel, who gives testimony concerning an historical event laden with theological conundrums, perhaps no other manner of telling the story is more appropriate than in the scholarly, creative, and condensed style of the Midrash.

Wiesel assesses the *akeda* as a "literary composition" that is "austere and powerful."[37] His own writings, but most particularly *Night*, may well be called "austere" and "powerful." The brevity of words and the force of the images are among the reasons why *Night* has become the premiere first-person account of the Event. The book's title — *La Nuit* as originally published in French, *Night* in English — of course allows for multiple interpretations, but Wiesel hints that a Biblical allusion is present. He states that the original French publisher wanted "a biblical phrase, perhaps something from the book of Jeremiah,"[38] but that eventually the image of night was settled upon. A reader might draw associations less with the book of Jeremiah but rather more with the first creation story in Genesis, as chaos swirled and night was separated from the day.

Moreover, Wiesel uses the following descriptive terms when he expresses how Scripture and the Midrash communicate insights via storytelling: "...the Midrash tries to compensate for Biblical terseness and offers a portrait both elliptical and striking."[39] Such descriptors — terse, elliptical, and striking — accurately describe Wiesel's own writing style. Although he says that the original version of the book he wrote in Yiddish, *And the World Remained Silent*, was over eight hundred pages, the final published version of that text was *Night*. With over seven hundred pages deleted, *Night* is the very definition of terse and elliptical. Staggering images are painted with only a few words; the barest brush of his use of words conveys overwhelming loss and tension.

His writing may be defined as elliptical not only in its approach to the subject (perhaps Emily Dickinson's advice, "Tell all the Truth, but tell it slant" may apply to Wiesel's testimony) but in his use of the ellipsis to suggest that silence alone may speak what needs to be said. The lacuna that silence offers when Wiesel barely touches on an image or the ellipsis that he frequently employs textualizes the tension as he navigates between the words that must be used and the enormity of the Event that demands silence. His characteristic use of the ellipsis hints at all that may not be said; his fondness for the phrase "and yet" implies that life's circumstances constantly and unpredictably change, just as our interpretations of those changes may also shift and refocus.

"As one plunges into Midrashic literature," Wiesel observes when discussing Genesis 22, "one feels its poignancy. It leaves one troubled."[40] Indeed, Wiesel's own storytelling of the *Shoah* is midrashic: terse, poignant, troubling. The six million Jews who died will die a second death, Wiesel often articulates, if their deaths are not remembered. Humanity does not wish to look at genocide; despite cries of "Never Again" to promote Holocaust awareness, genocide still exists in the world. In the literary world that Wiesel creates, he is dedicated to looking injustice, abuse, and tyranny in the face. "For me literature must have an ethical dimension," he asserts. "The aim of the literature I call testimony is to disturb."[41] Wiesel's literary genius may well rest in the fact that in telling a story, he can both engage and disturb the reader.

Wiesel does not disturb for the sake of using that power. He bears witness for a reason, for six million reasons. The dead, he states, "have their rightful place in all of his works."[42] In the timeless realm of Jewish thought, the *Shoah* dead "appear on Mount Moriah, where Abraham is about to sacrifice his son, a Holocaust offering to their common God ... the dead are part of every story, of every scene. They die with Isaac, lament with Jeremiah...."[43] The midrashic linking of past and present is at the heart of Wiesel's stories. "After Auschwitz everything long past brings us back to Auschwitz," he says. "When I speak of Abraham, Isaac, and Jacob ... it is the better to understand them in the light of Auschwitz."[44] But as Wiesel often notes, trying to understand Auschwitz, or even its reflected light, is a daunting task.

Arguably, no story bears greater significance than an account of the

Holocaust. Wiesel's autobiographical stories are important because so few survived the Holocaust; the compelling nature of his storytelling and the depth of his reflective nature cause him to be the primary voice of the *Shoah* survivor. His authorial presence emerges from his style of writing — his midrashic, terse, and haunting stories involving God and humanity — and in the *testimonio* — his need to bear witness. Within the disturbing, heartbreaking stories that necessarily constitute the *Shoah* accounts, Wiesel instructs us. By his storytelling, by his words as well as the lacuna that encapsulates silence, he transmits the story of the Holocaust, even when he speaks of other subjects. "So all those who are our students," he observes, "our children, our children's children, and who listen to our tale, become custodians of that tale."[45] Telling the story is one thing, but now that we, the listeners or the readers, have heard the story, the onus is upon us. Wiesel transfers responsibility and authority to us, who have become the custodians of the tale. Although he often states that literature and the Holocaust exclude one another, his writings tell memorable stories that invite readers to reflect upon theological questions and historical truths that we can spend a life time reflecting upon, yet without any real hope of an epiphany. As the Midrash records the search for meaning, so too does Wiesel's storytelling encourage us to join the search.

Notes

1. Elie Wiesel, *From the Kingdom of Memory: Reminiscences* (New York: Schocken Books, 1990), 21.

2. Jacob Neusner, *What Is Midrash?* (Philadelphia: Fortress Press, 1987), ix.

3. Edwin C. Goldberg, *Midrash For Beginners* (Northvale, N.J.: Jason Aronson Inc., 1996), xii.

4. Ibid., xi–xii.

5. Neusner, *What Is Midrash?*, i.

6. Emil Fackenheim, *God's Presence in History: Jewish Affirmations and Philosophical Reflections* (New York: New York University Press, 1970), 20.

7. Elie Wiesel, "We are All Witnesses: An Interview with Elie Wiesel," *Parabola* 10 (May 1985): 32.

8. Wiesel, "Jewish Values in the Post-Holocaust Future: A Symposium," *Judaism* 16 (1967): 285.

9. Wiesel, *Kingdom*, 19

10. Primo Levi, *Survival in Auschwitz/The Reawakening: Two Memoirs*, trans. Stuart Woolf (New York: Summit Books, 1986), 65–66.

11. Elie Wiesel, *And the Sea Is Never Full: Memoirs, 1969–*, trans. Marion Wiesel (New York: Knopf, 1999), 21.

12. Elie Wiesel, *Messengers of God: Biblical Portraits and Legends*, trans. Marion Wiesel (New York: Summit Books, 1976), 69.

13. Elie Wiesel and Philippe-Michael De Saint-Cheron, *Evil and Exile*, trans. Jon Rothschild (Notre Dame: University of Notre Dame Press, 1990), 172.

14. Wiesel, *Messengers*, 97.

15. Ibid., 95.

16. Elie Wiesel, *Night*, trans. Stella Rodway (New York: Bantam Books, 1960), 30.

17. Ibid., 30.

18. Wiesel, *Messengers*, 72.

19. Wiesel, *Night*, 71.

20. Elie Wiesel (words) and Darius Milhaud (music), *Ani Ma'amin: A Song Lost and Found Again*, trans. Marion Wiesel (New York: Random House, 1973), 42.

21. Ibid., 43.

22. Andre Neher, *Exile of the Word: From the Silence in the Bible to the Silence of Auschwitz*, trans. David Maisel (Philadelphia: Jewish Publication Society of America, 5741/1981), 217.

23. Wiesel, *Night*, 82. Ellipsis in text.

24. Wiesel, *Messengers*, 81. Emphasis in text.

25. Ibid., 88–89.

26. Wiesel and Milhaud, *Ani Ma'amin*, 55.

27. Wiesel and De Saint-Cheron, *Evil and Exile*, 52.

28. Wiesel, *Night*, 64.

29. Elie Wiesel, "Art and Culture After the Holocaust," in *Auschwitz: Beginning of a New Era? Reflections on the Holocaust*, ed. Eva Fleischner (New York: Ktav, 1974), 413.

30. Ibid., 413.

31. Alfred H. Rosenfeld, "Reflections on Isaac," *Holocaust and Genocide Studies* 1 (1986): 245.

32. Neher, *Exile and Evil*, 217.

33. Wiesel, *Art*, 403.

34. Harry James Cargas, *Conversations with Elie Wiesel* (South Bend, Ind.: Justice Books, 1992), 85.

35. Ibid., 85.

36. Ibid., 86.

37. Wiesel, *Messengers*, 70.

38. Elie Wiesel, *All Rivers Run to the Sea: Memoirs*, trans. Marion Wiesel (New York: Knopf, 1995), 319.

39. Wiesel, *Messengers*, 5.

40. Ibid., 73.

41. Wiesel, *All Rivers*, 337.

42. Wiesel, *Kingdom*, 18.

43. Ibid., 18–19.

44. Ibid., 19.

45. Elie Wiesel and Richard D. Heffner, *Conversations with Elie Wiesel*, ed. Thomas J. Vinciguerra (New York: Schocken Books, 2001), 154.

The *Maggid* of Sighet: Jewish Contexts for Wiesel's Storytelling

DAVID PATTERSON

Elie Wiesel ends *Somewhere a Master*, a volume of tales about the hasidic masters, by saying, "In retelling these tales, I realize once more that I owe them much. Consciously or not, I have incorporated a song, an echo, a word of theirs in my own legends and fables. I have remained, in a vanquished kingdom, a child who loves to listen."[1] For the Hasid Elie Wiesel, the tales of the hasidic masters are far more than legend, folklore, or "literary influences"—they are manifestations of Torah, modes of prayer, and ways of connecting with the Holy One. Wiesel makes it clear that he sees his storytelling as a form of prayer when he refers to a teaching from the thirteenth-century Hebrew poet Eleazar Rokeah, who maintained that God is not silent—He is Silence. "It is to this silence that I would like to direct my words," says Wiesel.[2] And: "I have tried to link [my work] to ... the silence of Sinai."[3] Buried in the silence of Sinai is Aggadah—the Talmud, Midrash, and Kabbalah that incorporate the tales of the sacred Jewish tradition. And among those tales are the hasidic tales.

Wiesel gives us an indication of how hasidic tradition views storytelling in the tale that serves as an epigraph to his novel *The Gates of the Forest*. According to the story, when the Baal Shem Tov, founder of Hasidism, faced some calamity threatening the Jewish community, he knew just what to do. He would slip off into the forest to a special place, where he would light a fire in a particular manner and say a prayer that he kept for just such emergencies. Having completed this ritual, the miracle of deliverance was accomplished, and the community was saved.

A generation later, the task of petitioning the Holy One for the miracle of deliverance fell to the Baal Shem's disciple, Rabbi Dov Ber, the Maggid of Mezeritch. Like the Baal Shem before him, the Maggid would go off to a certain place in the forest, where he would cry out, "Oh, Lord, King of the Universe, hear me! Though I know the place in the forest, I do not know how to light the fire. Nevertheless my teacher taught me the prayer. And this must be sufficient!" And so it was: the miracle of deliverance was accomplished, and the community of Israel was saved.

After the great Maggid had gone to join his fathers, Rabbi Moshe Leib of Sassov was entrusted with the task of intercession. Whenever catastrophe threatened the Jews, he would seek out the very same place in the forest where his masters before him had uttered their prayers. "Oh, Lord, King of the Universe, hear me!" he would cry out. "I cannot kindle the fire of the Baal Shem, and I never learned the prayer that he and the Great Maggid offered up to You. But, as You can see, I do know the secret place in the forest. And this must be sufficient." And so it was: for with these words the miracle of deliverance was accomplished, and the Jews were saved once more.

Finally the responsibility for seeking deliverance fell to Rabbi Yisrael of Rizhin. And yet, even as the breath of destruction was about to sweep over the community, Rabbi Yisrael stood in his study as though paralyzed, his head buried in his hands. In his despair he did not cry out but spoke hardly above a whisper, saying, "Oh, Lord, King of the Universe, have mercy! The secret of the Baal Shem's ritual of fire and his prayer for salvation are long forgotten. Here I stand before You, unable even to find the place in the forest. All I can do is tell the story. And this must be sufficient." And so it was: having told the tale of the fire and the prayer and the place in the forest, Rabbi Yisrael found the salvation he sought for the sake of the community.

More than a tale about four hasidic masters, this is a story about a distinctively Jewish view of storytelling. It tells us that a Jewish story is much more than a story told by a Jew or a story about Jews. A Jewish story is about God's relation to the Jewish people, their relation to God, and what those two relationships have to do with the way people relate to one another. It is about handing down a teaching and assuming a responsibility. Therefore it is about a tradition that conveys what Jews hold dear, what Jews live for, and what Jews have to answer for. In this tale we see the importance of being in the right place at the right time, the importance of establishing a presence before the God who is known as *Hamakom,* "the Place"—through tales. We see what is at stake in kindling a fire, in bringing light into the darkness of the world. Indeed, the first utterance of Creation is "Let there be light," and in that utterance lies the meaning of all creation: we are born into the world to transform darkness into light—through tales. And the prayer? In this tale it is spoken not for the sake of the self but for the sake of others. That is what makes it a Jewish prayer. That is what makes this story about presence and light and prayer a Jewish story. And that is what makes the story itself enough, even when the rites and rituals are forgotten.

If, as Wiesel suggests, the hasidic tales form the contexts for his storytelling, the hasidic tales have their own Jewish contexts in the aggadic, midrashic, and kabbalistic traditions, which form part of the Oral Torah. Those traditions, too, provide the Jewish contexts for Wiesel's storytelling; they, too, are among the echoes that may be heard throughout his tales.[4] "Novelists should not speak," says Wiesel. "Their mission consists in listening to other voices."[5] Trying to understand Wiesel without the "other voices" of the sacred tradition is like trying to understand Dante or Milton or Dostoevsky without the Bible. Images and motifs from Midrash, Kabbalah, and Aggadah hover between the words and float in the margins of every line he writes. They are what make Wiesel a Jewish writer. And Wiesel is above all a *Jewish* writer. To approach him as anything else would amount to more than failing to understand him: it would be a betrayal of the murdered Jews whose muted outcry also abides between the words and in the margins of his every line.

The point to be made is not only that certain tales find their way into Wiesel's stories; certain figures and motifs from the aggadic tradition show up in Wiesel's tales as well. His allusions to Avraham Avinu, Moshe Rabbenu, and Rabbi Akiba—indeed, his entire volumes of *Messengers of God, Five Biblical Portraits*, and *Sages and Dreamers*—are themselves vessels of Aggadah. Before examining some of the ways in which Wiesel draws the aggadic tradition into his tales, then, let us briefly consider the significance of storytelling in the Jewish tradition, so that we may acquire a better sense of the Jewishness of this Jewish storyteller.

Storytelling in the Jewish Tradition

Jewish tradition teaches that the Torah is the blueprint, the soul, and substance of all creation: fours times, says Rabbi Shimon bar Yochai, the Holy One looked into the Torah before beginning His work of Creation (*Zohar* I, 5a; see also *Bereshit Rabbah* 1:1; *Tanchuma Bereshit* 1). Unlike a blueprint, however, the Torah is itself the *stuff* of Creation. This teaching from the Zohar and the Midrash is central to the ancient mystical teachings found, for example, in the *Sefer Yetzirah*, the *Book of Creation*, where it is written that Hashem "created His universe with three books [*sefarim*]: with text [*sefer*], with numbering [*sefar*], and with storytelling [*sipur*]" (1:1). Judah Halevi explains these concepts by saying, "*Sefar* means calculation and weighing of the created bodies.... *Sipur* signifies the language, or rather the divine language, 'the voice of the words of the living God.' This produced the existence of the form which this language assumed in the words: 'Let there be light,' 'let there be a firmament.' The word was hardly spoken, when the thing came into existence. This is also *sefer*, by which writing is meant, the writing of God means His creatures, the speech of God is His writing, the will of God is His speech" (*Kitav al khazari* 4:25). The People of the Book — the People of the *Sefer* — are the people of the tale: that is what it means to be the People of the Covenant of Torah. For, as we see from the *Sefer Yetzirah*, in the beginning was the tale — the *sipur* — and the tale is made of Torah, as much as the Torah is made of the tale. "In the beginning there was the word," Wiesel states it. "The word was the tale of man; and man is the tale of God."[6] Both man and God are made of the tale that is Torah.

"Prophets transmit the word of God," says Wiesel. "Just Men conceived it. Often in the form of tales. Every word is a tale, they said in Bratzlav [Breslov]. Example: Torah. Or Talmud. Or Zohar. The tale of the Law is as important as the Law. And it is more profound than the commentaries"[7] — where the tale of the Law is the tale of the Torah, that is, the tale in the Torah and the Torah in the tale. The Torah begins not with a catalogue of commandments but with the tale of creation: as part of Torah, *creation itself is made of the tale of creation.* Thus the Torah includes the tale of the Torah in the Torah itself, in the Book of Deuteronomy: the teaching is not complete without the tale of the teaching. Because Moses relates the tale of the Torah to the Israelites, they are able to bear the Torah into the Land. It is a tale, moreover, not just for the Jews but for all the nations. Hence, according to the Midrash, when Moses related the tale of the Torah just before the Israelites entered the Holy Land, he taught them not only in the holy tongue but also in all the seventy languages of the nations (*Tanchuma Devarim* 2). That is what the Jews are chosen for: to tell the nations the tale of the Torah — that is the light unto the nations: the *tale*. That is the meaning of the Covenant.

Jewishly understood, then, the Covenant is more than a partnership or an agreement; like marriage, it is an intimate relation. To be sure, the Midrash teaches that a marriage was performed at Mount Sinai, with the two tablets signifying Israel and God, the bride and the groom (*Shemot Rabbah* 41:6; *Tanchuma Ki Tisa* 16). Hence Martin Buber's assertion that "in the beginning is the relation."[8] Significantly, the verb *siper* means not just to "tell a tale" but also to "*relate* a tale." It is precisely through relating a tale to another human being that we enter more profoundly into a relation with that person. Simply stated, to know someone is to know his or her story. That is where the soul is transmitted from one person to another; that is where life is transmitted from God to humanity. Just as the soul is made of Torah, as it is written (see, for example, Talmud Bavli, *Makkot* 24a; *Zohar* II, 165b), so is it made of tales: when God breathed the breath of life into Adam, He breathed tales into him.

Recall in this connection the teaching from the Zohar, were it is written that there are three kinds of speech: speaking, saying, and relating (*Zohar* I, 234a). Rabbi Menachem Mendel Schneerson, the late Lubavitcher Rebbe, explains: "Speaking and saying come from the surface, not from the depth of the soul. The mouth can sometimes speak what the heart does not feel. Even what the *heart* says can be at odds with what the man truly wills in his soul.... But 'relating' comes from the depths of a man's being."[9] Relating a tale is a calling of deep unto deep. To transmit a tale is to transmit a portion of one's soul. If, in the words of Emmanuel Levinas, the soul is "the other in me,"[10] the soul is the tale in me. God breathes into Adam the breath, the *neshimah*, of life, which is the *nishmat kol chai*, the breath of all life. Thus tales are transmitted not mouth to ear but mouth to mouth. To receive a tale, as Wiesel has said, is "to become part of the tale,"[11] which happens when we transmit the tale in turn: to receive a tale is to become a storyteller. Created in the image and likeness of the Holy One, the human being not only *speaks*, as Maimonides suggests (*Moreh Nevuchim* 1:51) — he tells tales.

Thus, in his comments on the depths of relating, Rabbi Schneerson goes on to note a teaching from the *Sifre* on Deuteronomy 11:22: "You wish to recognize the One who spoke and brought the world into being? Learn Aggadah for in Aggadah you will find God."[12] Why? Because, according to the fourteenth-century sage Rabbi Yitzchak Abohav, Aggadah is concerned with "the description of the true nature of the universe and the ideals toward which one should strive. It speaks allusively of mysteries and mysticism. It speaks of ethics and character and human nature. It speaks of purification of the body and sublimation of the soul. These are absolute truths."[13] And these absolute truths bespeak an absolute Good. In the light of that absolute Good — and contrary to postmodern proclivities — Wiesel engages in his aggadic endeavor. And where lies the absolute Good? In the task of creating a dwelling place — for God and humanity. That Good, Buber states it, lies in "the movement in the direction of home."[14] It is not for nothing, therefore, that Elie Wiesel, the Maggid of Sighet, keeps a picture of his home in Sighet over the desk where he pens his tales. Before him stands the vanquished kingdom, where he remains a child who loves to listen — after the Nazis' radical assault on the child.

Which leads us to one more point that must be made about storytelling in the Jewish tradition, particularly in the contexts of Wiesel's tales: it concerns the significance of the child in the Jewish tradition. Anyone who has small children knows that they love nothing more than hearing stories: a *child* who loves to listen, Wiesel describes himself. This is not an accident. Fresh from the hands of the Creator, children love to hear the tales of the past and the teachings of the tradition that give them a sense of meaning and future. Therefore the children were among the first whom the Nazis targeted for extermination, not only to annihilate the Jewish future that they represented but also to destroy the Jewish tradition that they sustained: it is they to whom we first tell our tells. Says Wiesel, "It was as though the Nazi killers knew precisely what children represent to us. According to our tradition, the entire world subsists thanks to them."[15] To be sure, many texts from the aggadic tradition attest to the importance of the child both to the life of the tradition and to the Holy One Himself, whose presence is revealed through the tradition.

In the Midrash, for example, it is written, "Rabbi Yehudah said: Come and see how beloved are the children by the Holy One, blessed be He. The Sanhedrin were exiled but the *Shekhinah* did not go into exile with them. When, however, the children were exiled, the *Shekhinah* went into exile with them" (*Eichah Rabbah* 1:6:33). Similarly, the Talmud teaches that all of Creation is sustained by the breath of little school children (*Shabbat* 119b), and not by the pillars of power, as invoked by the Greek image of Atlas holding up the world on his shoulders: it is not might but holiness that keeps the world from slipping into the abyss. And so in the Zohar we read, "Who is it that upholds the world and causes the patriarchs to appear? It is the voice of tender children studying the Torah; and for their sake the world is saved" (*Zohar* I, 1b). One can see that the murder of the child is central to the Nazi assault on the Holy One. And in the death of the child we see Him in the throes of death.

Wiesel drives home this point with devastating pathos in *Night*, where the reader collides with one of the most dreadful of all the memories that haunt this Jewish storyteller: the hanging of a child. In the assembly of prisoners forced to witness the hanging the young Eliezer hears a Jew next to him asking, "Where is God? Where is He now?" And from within his soul comes the terrifying reply: "Where is He? Here He is — He is hanging here on these gallows."[16] Then there is Issachar's wife, the woman in Wiesel's *A Jew Today* who sees dead children everywhere. "They are God's memory," she repeated over and over.[17] That is to say, they are God's memory of us, as well as our memory of God. If, as it is written in the *Tikunei Zohar*, children are "the face of the Shekhinah,"[18] it is because that is the face that turns to us, full of intense anticipation, as we sit down to relate the tale of God's memory. "God of Auschwitz," we recall Elhanan's prayer in Wiesel's *The Forgotten*, "know that I must remember Auschwitz. And that I must remind You of it.... Remember that only memory leads man back to the source of his longing for You."[19] And only tales lead us back to the source of memory itself.

Elie Wiesel is a teller of tales not because of any "literary" aspiration or even any "artistic" endeavor. In his own words, he tells tales "in order not to go mad. Or, on the contrary, to touch the bottom of madness."[20] And what lies at the bottom of madness? The *alef* that precedes the *beit* of *bereshit*, the word with which the Torah and all its tales begin, the *alef* that is silent or absent or present *as* silence, the *alef* that harbors the secret of the Divine Name itself, which is the memory of God. How, then, are Wiesel's tales situated in these contexts of Jewish storytelling?

Wiesel's Tales
in the Contexts of Jewish Storytelling

Of all the survivors to write their tales in response to the *Shoah*, Wiesel draws most upon the distinctively Jewish tradition of storytelling. Not only does he weave elements of Midrash and Aggadah into his own tales, as we shall see, but he has written his own versions and commentaries on the Jewish tales themselves. His retelling of the story of the Golem is a good example. It is based on a legend about the great sixteenth-century mystic Rabbi Yehudah Loeve, the Maharal of Prague. At a time when the Jewish community came under the threat of danger, he created a humanoid being, a Golem, to protect the Jews of Prague.[21] It is said that somewhere in Prague, hidden away in an attic, the Golem still sleeps. If so, he slept through the slaughter of the Jews of Prague. Or had we simply forgotten the esoteric learning that would bring him to life?

Another tale from the aggadic tradition that appears among Wiesel's works is more than a tale or a legend — it is the Haggadah, a prayer in the form of a tale that we tell and retell at the Passover Seder. In his commentary on the Haggadah Wiesel writes, "To listen to a story is no less important than to tell it. Sometimes it is even more important."[22] To listen to this liturgical tale of liberation is especially important in the post–Holocaust era, as Jews face new contexts for returning from exile to the Holy Land. If the Nazis' war against the Jews was a war against memory, as Wiesel maintains,[23] it is a war against the Jewish memory of Jewish teaching and tradition; it is a war against the Jews' memory of who they are. In the post–Holocaust era, more than ever, listening to the tale is part of remembering who we are. And part of who we are lies in the tale that is also a prayer, the tale of our movement from slavery to liberation, from death to life: the Haggadah.

Wiesel's engagement with the Haggadah extends into his fiction, particularly to his novel, *The Fifth Son*. In the Haggadah there are four sons who ask four questions.[24] The wise son asks, "What are all these testimonies, laws, and rulings that Hashem our God commanded you?" The wicked son asks, "What is the purpose of all this to you?" The simple son asks, "What is this?" And then there is the son who does not even know how to ask the question. Our capacity for returning from death to life rests upon our ability to remember the testimonies, laws, and rulings given to us by God. It also rests upon our ability to ask the question — not for the sake of ourselves, as the wicked son implies, but for the sake of God and humanity. As for the son who did not know how to ask, Wiesel notes that Rabbi Levi Yitzhak of Berditchev identified with him, as he would cry out to God, demanding an explanation for the suffering of the Jews.[25] Perhaps that silenced outcry is what belongs to the fifth son. Wiesel also points out that Rabbi Samson Raphael Hirsch read the four sons as four successive generations.[26] Perhaps the fifth son signifies the generation that was murdered. In *The Fifth Son* he is simply gone; Wiesel says no more about how he fits in with the four sons of the Haggadah.

Just as the aggadic tales assume the form of prayer, so do Wiesel's tales often appear in the form of prayers. *The Town Beyond the Wall*, for instance, is divided into prayers, not into chapters. In it Michael endures the torture of standing at a wall in order to save the life of his friend Pedro, just as Jews stand at the Western Wall to pray. In *Against Silence*, Wiesel tells us where his own hometown now resides: "Not here, but up there, in a Jerusalem of fire, hanging onto eternal memories of night."[27] Thus in this novel we see a parallel. The town beyond the wall is Michael's hometown beyond the Iron Curtain, where, with Pedro's help, he returned to confront the Indifferent One, who stood by as the Jews were sent to the murder camps. The town beyond the Western Wall is the Heavenly Jerusalem, where God dwells, awaiting the hour when we shall make it possible for Him to enter the earthly Jerusalem (can *He* be the Indifferent One?).[28] In both cases "God is imprisoned," as Michael says.[29] To explain the nature of God's imprisonment, Wiesel ends the novel with a tale from Jewish folklore. According to the story, a man once proposed to God that, in order to better understand each other, he and God should trade places, just for a second. God agreed, and in an instant God and man exchanged places.

A second went by and then two, and God, who was now a man, said, "You asked for a second, and You have had two. It is time to change back."

But the man, who was now God and therefore all-powerful, refused. Since that terrifying moment, many years, perhaps centuries, have gone by. Humanity's past and God's present — the past for the God who became man and the present for the man who become God — have become too much for either of them to bear. The liberation of one is now tied to the liberation of the other. Now, in the post–Holocaust era, their ancient dialogue has been renewed, charged with despair and dizziness, with anger and frustration, and above all with infinite longing.[30] The nature of that longing we discover in *The Gates of the Forest*, where Gavriel's father tells him, "God's final victory, my son, lies in man's inability to reject Him. You think you're cursing Him, but your curse is praise; you think you're fighting Him, but all you do is open yourself to Him; you think you're crying out your hatred and rebellion, but all you're doing is telling Him how much you need His support and forgiveness."[31] The tale that assumes the form of a prayer is just such an outcry.

If, for Wiesel, telling tales is akin to praying, then as he tells his tales, he faces Jerusalem. "The gate of heaven," says the Midrash, "is in Jerusalem" (*Midrash Tehillim* 4:91:7). In Jerusalem, therefore, stands the gate of prayer, which, for the Jewish storyteller, is the gate of tales. Nowhere is this more the case than in *A Beggar in Jerusalem*, a tale set in the time of the Six Day War.[32] There the Hasid Wiesel recalls a remark from the Storyteller of Hasidism, Rabbi Nachman of Breslov, who said that "no matter where he walked, his steps turned toward Jerusalem."[33] So it is with Wiesel: no matter what the tale he relates, his words are turned toward Jerusalem. To be sure, in the Talmud it is written, "Rabbi Shmuel bar Nachmani said in the name of Rabbi Yochanan: 'Three are called by the Name of the Holy One, blessed be He, and they are the righteous, the Messiah, and Jerusalem'" (*Bava Batra* 75b). Jerusalem, then, represents precisely what the Nazis attempted to destroy at Auschwitz: the Commanding Voice of the Divine Presence as She dwells in the world.

Just as the *Shekhinah* or Divine Presence is identified with Jerusalem, so is She associated with the community of Israel (see *Zohar* II, 98a); the assault on the body of Israel, then, entails an assault on the *Shekhinah* and her dwelling place Jerusalem. These are the aggadic teachings that must be kept in mind when in Wiesel's novel we read, "Jerusalem: the face visible yet hidden, the sap and the blood of all that makes us live or renounce life. The spark flashing in the darkness.... A name, a secret. For the exiled, a prayer. For all others, a promise.... Jerusalem: the city which miraculously transforms man into pilgrim; no one can enter it and go away unchanged."[34] As the site where the Temple stood, Jerusalem signifies the presence of Torah in the world, and Torah signifies sanctity in the world. To be sure, the Midrash teaches that the windows of the Temple were designed not to let light in but to allow the light of Torah to radiate into the world (*Tanchuma Tetsaveh* 6). It is no accident, therefore, that Wiesel compares the annihilation of the Jews in the Holocaust to the burning of the Temple.[35] At Auschwitz the Temple was itself placed upon the altar.

Insisting upon the sanctity of every human being, as well as the connectedness of each to the other, Jewish teaching maintains that every human being is tied to the holiness of the Holy City. In the *Tanna debe Eliyyahu*, for instance, it is written that the site where the altar stood in Jerusalem is "the place whence Adam's dust was taken."[36] The one through whom each human being is bound to the other, Adam is made not only of dust but also of the light of the Holy One. As Adam is created in the image and likeness of the Holy, so is Jerusalem. Therefore in our prayers and our tales we sometimes refer to God as the *Shokhen Yerushalayim*, "the One who dwells in Jerusalem" (see, for example, Psalms 135:21). The Jews make no claim to Jerusalem; rather, Jerusalem lays claim to the Jews. That is why Jerusalem signifies the light of the world.

This association between Jerusalem and all of humanity Wiesel articulates in *A Beggar in Jerusalem* by relating a tale from Nachman of Breslov. It is the story of a city that contains all cities. In that city there is a street that contains all streets, and on that street stands a house that contains all houses. Inside the house is a room that contains all rooms, and inside the room sits a man who contains all men. And that man is laughing.[37] Why laughing? Because, says Wiesel, "revolt is not a solution, neither is submission. Remains laughter, metaphysical laughter."[38] What is metaphysical laughter? It is the laughter couched in the name of Isaac, who, like the children of Israel, was laid upon the altar. Thus the God of Isaac is known as the Fear of Isaac (see, for example, Genesis 31:53). That Fear is transmitted — but with a twist — in the post–Holocaust tales of the Maggid of Sighet.

The aim of his storytelling, however, is not to paralyze us with fear but to enable us to live — by transforming us into messengers, as it happens in his novel *The Oath*. In this tale of the destruction of a Jewish community an old man saves a young man bent on suicide by relating to him a tale and thus turning him into a messenger: "I'll transmit my experience to him and he, in turn, will be compelled to do the same. He in turn will become a messenger. And once a messenger, he has no alternative. He must stay alive until he has transmitted his message."[39] And so Wiesel transforms all of us into messengers, that is, into storytellers. That, indeed, is the task of every human being: to become a storyteller, a witness, "a messenger, a link between God and man, between man and man."[40] That link is the portion of the Messiah in every human being. Indeed, Rabbi Yitzchak Ginsburgh points out that, according to the aggadic tradition, every soul harbors a portion of the soul of the Messiah.[41] While Wiesel has said that the Messiah is present in all of his writings,[42] this teaching from the Aggadah is explicitly stated in *The Oath*: "The Messiah. We seek him, we pursue him. We think he is in heaven; we don't know that he likes to come down as a child. And yet, every man's childhood is messianic in essence. Except that today it has become a game to kill childhood."[43] The evidence? Today, in the age of postmodernist fashions and fads, it has become a game to silence the tales of the Aggadah — or rather to get rid of the silence within those tales by deconstructing it into a blank. Indeed, nothing is more antithetical to the postmodernist stance than the pursuit of this figure that appears in all of Wiesel's works: the Messiah.

In *The Testament,* Wiesel invokes another aggadic teaching concerning the Messiah: among the seven things that preceded Creation is the name of the Messiah (see, for example, Talmud Bavli, *Pesachim* 54a).[44] Because every human being harbors a trace of the Messiah, only the human being can manifest the name of the Messiah — by telling tales. From a Jewish standpoint, to tell tales is to affirm what Wiesel affirms in the title of one of his books: *Ani maamin beemunah shlemah beviat ha-Mashiach; veaf al pi sheyimanmean, im kol zeh achakeh lo bekol yom sheyavo*: "I believe with complete faith in the coming of the Messiah; even if he may tarry, no matter what, I shall await his coming every day."[45]

Sometimes this task of anticipation is performed silently, as in *The Testament,* a novel about the Soviet persecution of the Russian Jewish poet Paltiel Kossover. In order to protect his father's words, Paltiel's son Grisha gives himself over to a muteness that shouts louder than any word. If for his father silence was a prison, for Grisha silence was a sanctuary over which he kept a most stern vigil: in order to protect his father's words when the KGB wanted him to "talk," Grisha bit off his own tongue.[46] Thus he becomes a poet, "not like his father. In place of his father."[47] In so doing, he becomes not only a poet but also a messenger, like Wiesel, in the aggadic tradition. For his father Paltiel notes that, according to Aggadah, as long as King David was "composing his Psalms," "the Angel of Death could not approach him" (see Talmud Bavli, *Shabbat* 30a–30b).[48] Weaving his tales and composing his psalms, Wiesel shows us how to stave off the Angel of Death, who ruled over the Kingdom of Night and who lurks in the twilight of our own age.

Thus we abide in the twilight that Wiesel explores in his novel by that name. *Twilight* is about a Holocaust survivor and scholar of Jewish mysticism named Raphael and his encounters at a sanatorium that specializes in patients who take themselves to be biblical characters. Here too we have an aggadic teaching concerning the Angel of Death, this one from the hasidic master Nachman of Breslov. When we die, the legend teaches, we lie in the grave and wait for the Angel of Death to come to us, so that he might bring us into the presence of the Holy One, blessed be He. There is, of course, a catch: in order to draw nigh unto the Divine Presence, we must correctly answer a certain question. The question is the same for all, but for each the answer is different. And so, with his thousand eyes gazing upon us, the Angel poses the fearsome question: "What is your name?"[49] Just so, among the patients whom Raphael meets is one known as "the dead man," who is afraid that when the Angel of Death approaches him to ask him his name, he won't remember.[50]

It seems so simple at first glance; who, after all, does not know his own name? But how, indeed, do we determine our name, the utterance that articulates the essence of who we are? We say we know our name like the back of our hand, perhaps because our hand has done the deeds that define our name. What, then, does it mean to know our name? It will be of no avail to explain to the Angel, "I am the one who owns this company, who bears that title, and who has made these conquests." No, to know our name is to know the names of those who confer a name upon us, the names of our mother and father. It means knowing the tradition borne by those who have borne our names; it means knowing a teaching that harbors our future and our mission in life, as inscribed in our name; it means recognizing that we are called by name and answering to that call. Hence Rabbi Chayim ben Attar teaches that one who knowingly violates God's commandment forfeits his name (*Or HaChayim* on Genesis 3:30). Asking our name, the Angel tries to establish something about our being that is intimately tied to our doing: knowing our name means knowing what must be done. Which is to say: our *doing* is at the heart of our *being*.

Here too we find a midrashic connection in Wiesel's novel. For in the sanatorium Raphael also meets Cain, the one whom God asked, "Where is your brother?" (Genesis 4:9) and "What have you done?" (Genesis 4:10). Murdering his brother, Cain murdered his own name, and with it the Holy Name. Echoing the Midrash (see *Bereshit Rabbah* 1:11), Cain says to Raphael, "When I killed my brother, it was really Him I wanted to kill. And He knows it. Any fool knows that whoever kills, kills God."[51] It is worth noting that the same line appears in *A Beggar in Jerusalem*, where, as they are about to be murdered, a Jewish father say to his son, "Whoever kills, becomes God. Whoever kills, kills God. Each murder is a suicide, with the Eternal eternally the victim."[52] Perhaps that is why the patient who believes he is God asks Raphael to weep for him.[53] Perhaps there lies the immortality of the Immortal One: He can be murdered a million — even six million — times over. If children are God's memory, as Issachar's wife maintained,[54] perhaps that is what must be remembered. How? Through Aggadah.

Memory, in fact, is the defining theme of Wiesel's next novel, *The Forgotten*. It is about a Holocaust survivor name Elhanan, who, in the throes of Alzheimer's disease, must transmit his memory to his child Malkiel before it escapes him. There Wiesel writes, "It is memory that connects [a Jew] to Abraham, Moses, and Rabbi Akiba."[55] Wiesel maintains that connection by weaving Midrash and Aggadah — the tales of Abraham, Moses, and Rabbi Akiba — into his own tales. In this novel he compares Elhanan's effort to remember to a scribe copying Torah.[56] Just so, Wiesel himself struggles to remember, a word at a time, by drawing the tales that are themselves Torah into his own tales. When Elhanan's son Malkiel asks the caretaker Ephraim what he takes care of, Ephraim answers, "What people throw away, what history rejects, what memory denies. The smile of a starving child, the tears of its dying mother, the silent prayers of the condemned man and the cries of his friend. I gather them up and preserve them."[57] Just so, Wiesel gathers them up by gathering the aggadic memory of Abraham, Moses, and Rabbi Akiba into this memory, to preserve what Jews must not forget, if they are to remain Jews — especially in the post–Holocaust era: not only the cries of the murdered Jews but the tales of the murdered tradition.

If the Jews fall under a judgment after Auschwitz, it is a judgment as to whether they know their name, as to whether they remember Aggadah. And so we come to one more novel: *The Judges*, where the Judge, like the Angel of Death, asks the main character Razziel whether he knows his true name. And Razziel answers, "No."[58] Like Wiesel, Razziel is versed in Written and Oral Torah. Like Wiesel, he has many judges who gauge his every word. "When I write," Wiesel has said, "I feel my invisible teachers looking over my shoulders, reading my words and judging their veracity."[59] In the novel the one person referred to as "the Judge" judges five "hostages" caught in a storm en route to Tel-Aviv. The aggadic tradition here lies in the very name of the main character, Razziel, whose name is taken from one of the most ancient of the kabbalistic texts *Razziel Hamalakh*, or *The Angel Razziel*. To be sure, Kabbalah, with its variations in hasidism, is one of the main sources of Aggadah in this novel. The novel contains tales and allusions to tales of the Maharal of Prague,[60] Levi Yitzhak of Berditchev,[61] Moshe Leib of Sassov,[62] and Moshe Rabbenu.[63] And, like all kabbalistic Aggadah — indeed, like all of Wiesel's novels — this tale is laden with messianic allusions. It demonstrates that, like his character Razziel, Wiesel belongs "to a tradition that holds that everything that concerns the activities of men and their destinies can be found in the Talmud"[64] — that is, in the oral tradition: in Aggadah.

Concluding Reflections

If Elie Wiesel's tales are situated within a distinctively aggadic tradition, then, in a very important sense, they fall within the opposite of what we normally think of as a literary tradition. Whereas literature may draw upon themes and motifs from Torah, Aggadah *is* Torah. And — at least from a hasidic standpoint — Torah is not literature: it is what makes literature possible. In it lurks the question from on high, the question put to the first human being and to every human being, which literature struggles to answer: Where are you? Weaving the Aggadah of Oral Torah into his stories, Wiesel sets those stories apart from literature, making them, in a sense, a part of Aggadah itself. "Do you know," says Katriel in *A Beggar in Jerusalem*, "that it is given to us to enrich a legend simply by listening to it? It belongs as much to the listener as to the teller."[65] And so it is with Aggadah: the one who tells the aggadic tale simply transmits what has been received. Thus the storyteller himself enters into Aggadah, a messenger who entrusts the listener with a message to deliver and a truth to attest to. If "all revelation is a calling and a mission," as Buber maintains,[66] and if Wiesel's tales call us to a mission we cannot refuse, then in these tale lies a remnant of revelation. Precisely that remnant is the stuff of Aggadah. That is why Wiesel is more than a storyteller: he is a Maggid.

Through his tales he transmits a summons that comes from beyond the tales. Where is that "beyond?" It is couched in the texts and in the prayers of the aggadic tradition, which is itself a source of revelation, as Jewish thinkers such as Saadia Gaon have maintained.[67] We have seen that the sacred texts that form much of the sacred tradition are an explicit part of Wiesel's tales. Even Primo Levi, who turned his face from God in the face of Auschwitz, suggests that the tales of the *Shoah* might themselves be viewed as the tales of a new Bible.[68] If this is the case, then there must be a definitive link between the stories of the "new Bible" and the texts of *the* Bible. For the Jews living in a post–Holocaust world, Emil Fackenheim maintains, an encounter with the biblical text has become a necessity, if the Jews are indeed to live as Jews.[69] It is a key to any recovery of the tradition that has nurtured Jewish life for centuries. This existential necessity confronting the Jew lies in the nature of the Jewish relation to being. If being has meaning for the Jew, it is, in the words of Levinas, "to realize the Torah. The world is here so that the ethical order has the possibility of being fulfilled. The act by which the Israelites accept the Torah is the act which gives meaning to reality. To refuse the Torah is to bring being back to nothingness."[70] Either Torah or Auschwitz: that is the existential necessity confronting the Jew and underlying the recovery of Jewish life in the world. And neither the messenger nor the one who receives his message can avoid this either/or.

If the storyteller is such a messenger, as Wiesel has said,[71] then, as a messenger operating within the aggadic tradition, he is a messenger from Mount Sinai — who has been plunged into a mountain of ashes. "Let him who wants fervor not seek it on the mountain peaks," the Maggid of Sighet quotes the Maggid of Mezerich. "Rather let him stoop and search among the ashes."[72] And yet there is no *stooping* to search among these ashes. For they have ascended into the heavens to transform the sky into a cemetery. And so Wiesel ascends in order to search. Like the title character in his play *Zalman or The Madness of God*, he falls — upwards.[73] He searches not through "literary devices" or through "literary imagination" but with all the extra-literary sources of the sacred tradition at his disposal. And so we may better understand Wiesel's striking statement: "Now a few words about the literature of the Holocaust or about literary inspiration. There is no such thing, not with Auschwitz in the equation.... A novel about Treblinka is either not a novel or not about Treblinka. A novel about Majdanek is about blasphemy. *Is* blasphemy."[74] It is blasphemy, not due to any insensitivity, but because it robs this event in the sacred history of the Jewish people of its sacred contexts. If God showed His face at Auschwitz, as Wiesel has suggested,[75] then one means — perhaps the only means — of approaching that face is through Aggadah, the very thing that came under assault in the Nazi assault on the Holy One. After Auschwitz, however, this aggadic testimony requires sounding the depths of a certain madness, as Wiesel has said.

What sort of madness Fackenheim may help us to understand. "Midrash," he says, "was meant for every kind of imperfect world," but "it was not meant for Planet Auschwitz, the anti-world."[76] If the Midrash subjected to the Nazi assault is to find its way from the anti-world into the world — if the Jews are to recover the Jewish presence that the Nazis deemed an ontological crime — then what is needed is a kind of midrashic madness, a madness that finds an opening for holiness to return to a realm where holiness has been vanquished. For midrashic madness, Fackenheim explains, "is the Word spoken in the anti-world which ought not to be but is. The existence it points to acts to restore a world which ought to be but is not, and this is *its* madness. After Planet Auschwitz, there can be no health without *this* madness.... Without this madness, a Jew cannot do — with God or without Him — what a Voice from Sinai bids him do: choose life."[77] And so, through his character Zalman, Wiesel cries out, "One has to be mad today to believe in God and in man — one has to be mad to believe. One has to be mad to want to remain human."[78] One has to be mad, as the Maggid of Sighet is mad, to tell these tales.

"In the beginning," says Dr. Benedictus in *Twilight*, "there was madness."[79] In the new beginning there is midrashic madness. With this midrashic madness, a Jew must choose life *as a Jew*, bearing Jewish children into the world, despite the fact that the identity that gives him life my well threaten his life. For in the Holocaust, Fackenheim points out, Jews were slaughtered not because they abandoned the Torah but because their grandparents adhered to it.[80] That is why a Jewish response to the *Shoah* cannot oppose the silent indifference of the Muselmann — of the Jew transformed into the nothingness of the *Shoah* itself — without a dose of midrashic madness: after Auschwitz, the Jewish storyteller must seek the Word which ought not to be but is. Which is to say: the mending of the world requires the mending of the word — through the tales of the Torah that constitutes the world itself. For the world is in the word, not the other way around. And for a Jew, the world made of Torah is rooted in the aggadic word of Torah.

How, then, shall we understand this midrashic madness with regard to the tales of the Maggid of Sighet? A tale from the Midrash itself may provide a key to this question. It is about the night when Jacob wrestled his identity as a Jew — as Yisrael — from the Angel of Death. As the Angel wrestled with Jacob, it is written, "he put his finger to the earth, whereupon the earth began spurting fire. Said Jacob to him: 'Would you terrify me with that? Why, I am altogether of that stuff!' Thus it is written, 'And the house of Jacob shall be a fire' (Obadiah 1:18)" (*Bereshit Rabbah* 77:2). In the post–Holocaust era these words of Torah ring with new and terrifying depths of meaning. And Wiesel helps us to sound those depths. In the time of the *Shoah*, says Wiesel, "fire was the dominant image."[81] And so the Maggid of Sighet answers fire with fire — the fire of *Shoah* with the black fire on white fire of Torah (see *Tanchuma Bereshit* 1; see also *Devarim Rabbah* 3:12), with the fire that is the stuff of the soul itself. To be sure, "the ultimate mystery of the Holocaust," he has said, "is that whatever happened took place in the soul."[82] And with Wiesel, what takes place afterward transpires in the soul as well. Thus he relates a vision in which the Baal Shem appeared to his son Rebbe Hersh. Rebbe Hersh asked his father, "How shall I serve the Creator?" And, erupting into a myriad of flames, the Baal Shem answered, "Like this."[83] Wiesel, too, follows the teaching of the Besht. That is why to read Wiesel is to burn with him.

With Wiesel, however, we burn with the fire that issues not only from the word of creation and revelation but also from the silence of annihilation and nothingness. Above all, we burn with the longing for redemption. As for any mystic — indeed, for any Jew[84] — Wiesel's aim is to hasten the coming of the Messiah. He provides a hint of this aim in his volume of aggadic tales, *Sages and Dreamers*. "In mystical terms," he writes, "man must seek out the lost sparks, gather them, and deliver them to their sacred source. Everywhere there are souls waiting to be called. Everywhere, and especially beneath the ashes, sparks exist only for this call. What is required is for man to find these souls and save them; when all have been 'restored,' the divine flame will become the messianic light."[85] The soul on fire is one who seeks the lost sparks, especially beneath the ashes. And no soul burns more intensely than Elie Wiesel.

Notes

1. Elie Wiesel, *Somewhere a Master: Further Hasidic Portraits and Legends*, trans. Marion Wiesel (New York: Summit Books, 1982), 205.

2. Elie Wiesel, *Against Silence: The Voice and Vision of Elie Wiesel*, Vol. 2, ed. Irving Abrahamson (New York: Holocaust Library, 1985), 60.

3. Elie Wiesel, *Against Silence: The Voice and Vision of Elie Wiesel*, Vol. 1, ed. Irving Abrahamson (New York: Holocaust Library, 1985), 273.

4. Other scholars have noted Wiesel's "midrashic manner," but I do not know of any who have explored the midrashic and aggadic contexts of his writing as I am doing here. See, for example, Sidra DeKoven Ezrahi, *By Words Alone: The Holocaust in Literature* (Chicago: University of Chicago Press, 1980), 120.

5. Wiesel, *Against Silence*, Vol. 2, 249.

6. Elie Wiesel, *A Beggar in Jerusalem*, trans. Lily Edelman and Elie Wiesel (New York: Random House, 1970), 135.

7. Elie Wiesel, *Souls on Fire: Portraits and Legends of Hasidic Masters*, trans. Marion Wiesel (New York: Vintage, 1973), 187. Elsewhere he writes that, with Rabbi Akiba, "the tale of the law becomes part of the law itself"; see Elie Wiesel, *Sages and Dreamers*, trans. Marion Wiesel (New York: Summit Books, 1991), 234.

8. Martin Buber, *I and Thou*, trans. Walter Kaufmann (New York: Charles Scribner's Sons, 1970), 69.

9. Menachem Mendel Schneerson, *Torah Studies*, adapted by Jonathan Sacks (London: Lubavitch Foundation, 1986), 74.

10. Emmanuel Levinas, *Otherwise than Being or Beyond Essence*, trans. Alphonso Lingis (The Hague: Martinus Nijhoff, 1981), 69.

11. Elie Wiesel, *Against Silence*, Vol. 1, 187.

12. Schneerson, *Torah Studies*, 74–75.

13. Yitzchak Abohav, *Menoras Hamaor: The Light of Contentment*, trans. Y. Y. Reinman (Lakewood, N.J.: Torascript, 1982), 246.

14. Martin Buber, *Between Man and Man*, trans. Ronald Gregor Smith (New York: Macmillan, 1965), 78.

15. Elie Wiesel, *A Jew Today*, trans. Marion Wiesel (New York: Random House, 1978), 178–79.

16. Elie Wiesel, *Night*, trans. Stella Rodway (New York: Hill & Wang, 1960), 71.

17. Wiesel, *A Jew Today*, 81.

18. Cited in Nehemia Polen, *The Holy Fire: The Teachings of Rabbi Kalonymus Kalman Shapira* (Northvale, N.J.: Jason Aronson, Inc., 1999), 102.

19. Elie Wiesel, *The Forgotten*, trans. Marion Wiesel (New York: Summit Books, 1992), 11–12.

20. Elie Wiesel, *From the Kingdom of Memory: Reminiscences* (New York: Summit Books, 1990), 13.

21. See Elie Wiesel, *The Golem: The Story of a Legend*, trans. Anne Borchardt (New York: Summit Books, 1983).

22. Elie Wiesel, commentary in *A Passover Haggadah*, ed. Marion Wiesel (New York: Simon and Schuster, 1993), 67.

23. See Elie Wiesel, *Evil and Exile*, trans. Jon Rothschild (Notre Dame: University of Notre Dame Press, 1990), 155.

24. Elie Wiesel, commentary in *A Passover Haggadah*, ed. Marion Wiesel (New York: Simon and Schuster, 1993), 32–33.

25. Ibid., 35.

26. Ibid., 34.

27. Wiesel, *Against Silence*, Vol. 3, 1.

28. As the talmudic sage Rabbi Yochanan taught, "The Holy One, blessed be He, said: 'I will not enter the heavenly Jerusalem until I can enter the earthly Jerusalem'" (*Taanit* 5a).

29. Elie Wiesel, *The Town Beyond the Wall*, trans. Stephen Becker (New York: Holt, Rinehart and Winston, 1964), 10.

30. Ibid., 179.

31. Elie Wiesel, *The Gates of the Forest*, trans. Frances Frenaye (New York: Holt, Rinehart and Winston, 1966), 33.

32. "I had a psychosomatic experience while writing *A Beggar in Jerusalem*," says Wiesel. "I lost my voice. Everything had gone into the book"; see Wiesel, *Against Silence*, Vol. 3, 281.

33. Wiesel, *A Beggar in Jerusalem*, 12.

34. Ibid., 11.

35. See Elie Wiesel, *Ani Ma'amin: A Song Lost and Found Again*, trans. Marion Wiesel (New York: Random House, 1973), 27.

36. *Tanna debe Eliyyahu: The Lore of the School of Elijah*, trans. William G. Braude and Israel J. Kapstein (Philadelphia: Jewish Publication Society, 1981), p. 411; see also *Bereshit Rabbah* 14:8; *Pirke de-Rabbi Eliezer* 11.

37. Wiesel, *A Beggar in Jerusalem*, 30. Wiesel also relates this tale in *Souls on Fire*, 199–200.

38. Wiesel, *Souls on Fire*, 199.

39. Elie Wiesel, *The Oath*, trans. Marion Wiesel (New York: Avon, 1973), 42.

40. Wiesel, *Against Silence*, Vol. 2, 82.

41. Yitzchak Ginsburgh, *The Alef-Beit: Jewish Thought Revealed through the Hebrew Letters* (Northvale, N.J.: Jason Aronson, Inc., 1991), 7.

42. Wiesel, *Against Silence*, Vol. 3, 288.

43. Wiesel, *The Oath*, 132.

44. Elie Wiesel, *The Testament*, trans. Marion Wiesel (New York: Summit Books, 1981), 160.

45. The word referred to here is *Ani Ma'amin*; the affirmation of faith in the coming of the Messiah is the twelfth of Maimonides' Thirteen Principles of Faith.

46. Wiesel, *The Testament*, 304–05.

47. Ibid., 17.

48. Ibid., 30.

49. This teaching is from Nachman of Breslov, *Tikkun*, trans. Avraham Greenbaum (Jerusalem: Breslov Research Institute, 1984), 102; see also Rabbi Nathan of Nemirov, *Rabbi Nachman's Wisdom: Shevachay HaRan and Sichos HaRan*, trans. Aryeh Kaplan and ed. Aryeh Rosenfeld (New York: A. Kaplan, 1973), 148. The tradition that the Angel of Death is covered with eyes is from the Talmud (*Avodah Zarah* 20b). Sometimes, as in the case of Wiesel, the Angel comes to us not to take us but to leave us with new eyes.

50. Elie Wiesel, *Twilight*, trans. Marion Wiesel (New York: Summit Books, 1998), 141.

51. Wiesel, *Twilight*, 58.

52. Wiesel, *A Beggar in Jerusalem*, 208.

53. Wiesel, *Twilight*, 213.

54. Wiesel, *A Jew Today*, 81.

55. Wiesel, *The Forgotten*, 71.

56. Ibid., 159.

57. Ibid., 192.

58. Elie Wiesel, *The Judges* (New York: Alfred E. Knopf, 2002), 42.

59. Wiesel, *From the Kingdom of Memory*, 173.

60. Wiesel, *The Judges*, 71.

61. Ibid., 137–38.

62. Ibid., 149.

63. Ibid., 183.

64. Ibid., 43.

65. Wiesel, *A Beggar in Jerusalem*, 107.

66. Buber, *I and Thou*, 164.

67. See Saadia Gaon, *The Book of Belief and Opinions*, trans. Samuel Rosenblatt (New Haven: Yale University Press, 1976), 336.

68. See Primo Levi, *Survival in Auschwitz*, trans. Stuart Wolf (New York: Macmillan, 1961), 59.

69. Emil L. Fackenheim, *To Mend the World: Foundations of Post-Holocaust Jewish Thought* (New York: Schocken Books, 1989), 18.

70. Emmanuel Levinas, *Nine Talmudic Readings*, trans. Annette Aronowicz (Bloomington: Indiana University Press, 1990), 41.

71. Wiesel, *Against Silence*, Vol. 2, 57.

72. Wiesel, *Souls on Fire*, 71.

73. Elie Wiesel, *Zalman or The Madness of God*, adapted for the stage by Marion Wiesel (New York: Random House, 1974), 88.

74. Elie Wiesel, "The Holocaust as Literary Inspiration," in *Dimensions of the Holocaust* (Evanston: Northwestern University Press, 1977), 7. Elsewhere Wiesel writes, "There is no such thing as Holocaust literature — this cannot be. Auschwitz negates all literature"; see Wiesel, *A Jew Today*, 197.

75. Wiesel, *Against Silence*, Vol. 3, 309.

76. Emil L. Fackenheim, *The Jewish Return into History* (New York: Schocken Books, 1978), 265.

77. Ibid., 269.

78. Wiesel, *Zalman*, 79.

79. Wiesel, *Twilight*, 37.

80. Emil L. Fackenheim, *God's Presence in History: Jewish Affirmations and Philosophical Reflections* (New York: Harper & Row, 1970), 73.

81. Wiesel, *Evil and Exile*, 39.

82. Wiesel, *Against Silence*, Vol. 1, 239.

83. See Wiesel, *Souls on Fire*, 52; see also *Tsvat HaRibash* (Ashdod, 1999), 63–64.

84. "To be Jewish," Wiesel correctly states it, "is to link one's fate to that of the Messiah"; see Wiesel, *Somewhere a Master*, 23.

85. Wiesel, *Sages and Dreamers*, 353–54. This idea is based on a teaching from the Talmud, where it is written, "Know that there exists on high a substance called 'body' [*guf*] in which are found all the souls destined for life. The son of David will not come before all the souls which are in the *guf* have completed their descent to the earth" (*Yevamot* 63b; *Avodah Zarah* 5a; *Niddah* 13b; see also *Zohar* I, 119a).

Laughter and the Limits of Holocaust Storytelling: Wiesel's *The Gates of the Forest*

Jacqueline Bussie

I'm listening to the war and I'm laughing.—Gavriel, in Elie Wiesel's *The Gates of the Forest*

He [Rebbe Nachman] thought that he would take his wife and go live in some far-off place, hidden from the public. Sometimes he would go out to the market to have a look at the world—and to laugh at it.—Hayyey II 2:19

People say that stories are good for putting one to sleep. But I say that through stories, peoples can be woken from their sleep.—Rebbe Nachman of Bratzlav

God created man because he loves stories.—Elie Wiesel

Anyone who reads one of Elie Wiesel's novels comes quickly to the following realization: a master storyteller weaves the tale found within these pages. Author of dozens of novels, essays, and short stories, Wiesel is an artist whose primary medium is the word, particularly the written word. Winner of the Nobel Peace Prize, Wiesel obviously has mastered the art of communication through language. Ironically, however, Wiesel's fiction and non-fiction writing each testify to the inexpediency of words.

In a well-known essay on so-called Holocaust art, Wiesel makes the cryptic claim: "Now he [the post–Holocaust artist] has to remember the past, knowing all the while that what he has to say will never be told. What he hopes to transmit can never be transmitted. All he can possibly hope to achieve is to communicate the impossibility of communication."[1] How does Wiesel witness simultaneously to the necessity of communication and the impossibility of communication, to the necessity of words and the worthlessness of words? To put it another way, how does Wiesel resolve the double-bind of post–Holocaust existence and use language to communicate the inadequacy of language? How does he both speak of the Holocaust and not speak of it?

My answer: through hasidic stories replete with laughter, the strange laughter that runs rampant throughout the pages of any Wiesel novel or tale, laughter that goes virtually ignored in the critical literature. How has critical discussion of Wiesel's work neglected to interpret the fact that in Wiesel's novel *The Gates of the Forest*, the word laughter and its derivatives occur a record 292 times for 226 pages of text? What can such laughter mean? We expect malicious laughter from the executioners, but what to make of the fact that in *Gates*, the vast majority of the laughter in the text comes from the novel's persecuted hasidic protagonist, Gavriel, a man with no ostensible cause for laughter? Wiesel writes: "The sadder the stories, the more Gavriel laughed."[2] How are we to understand such paradoxical Jewish laughter, laughter that is related to tragedy and not comedy? How could anyone laugh at the Holocaust? Should we even venture to 'explain' such risibility?

The hermeneutical task is so daunting, almost all have feared to tread. The exception is Joe Friedemann, whose text *Le Rire dans l'Univers Tragique d'Elie Wiesel* is the only work devoted uniquely to laughter in Wiesel. Tellingly, Friedemann's book remains untranslated from the original French. Moreover, Friedemann does not address the religious significance of this laughter or attempt to understand the laughter in Wiesel's tales in its natural context of Hasidism and hasidic storytelling. My essay, however, addresses this inexplicable *aporia* within Wiesel scholarship.

I propose that Wiesel sustains the inexpressibility of the world-shattering, language-rupturing experience of the *Shoah* through hasidic storytelling itself— particularly Bratzlavian storytelling, a tradition which incorporates paradox and *ab intra* acknowledges the limits of human understanding and language and through the incorporation of the trope

of laughter into his hasidic stories. Most criticism of Wiesel analyzes his
work devoid of an understanding of Hasidism. Once contextualized, the
otherwise incomprehensible laughter within Wiesel's hasidic tales emerges
as testimony to the limitations of Holocaust storytelling. In particular,
Wiesel's *The Gates of the Forest* and the laughter found in its pages begs
to come into dialogue with the thought and life of the greatest hasidic
storyteller, Rebbe Nachman of Bratzlav.[3]

Storytelling has always been important in the Jewish tradition. Rabbinic commentary devotes considerable ink to the significance of the fact
that the Torah begins with narratives, or stories, rather than with the laws.
But scholars agree that Hasidism, and in particular Rebbe Nachman of
Bratzlav, radicalized the role of storytelling in the lives of the Jewish faithful. Hasidism, a Jewish sect devoted to mysticism and lay piety and
opposed to secular studies and rationalism, was founded in Poland in 1750
by the Baal Shem Tov (Rabbi Israel ben Eliezer). Yitzhak Buxbaum explains
that Hasidism moved storytelling from the periphery of Judaism to its very
center, and thereby raised the art to an unprecedented level of intensity
and purpose. Rebbes not only vigorously encouraged storytelling, but also
reinterpreted storytelling as a *mitzvah* [divine commandment] and a spiritual practice. A hasid writes: "Therefore it is a very great and important
mitzvah to tell stories praising the *tzaddikim* and their service of God,
blessed be He."[4] Hasidic thinkers often legitimate this *mitzvah* by citing
the Kabbalah, which states that "God, blessed be He, created the world
with the scroll, the scribe, and the story."[5] Every hasid, then, is called to
participate in the listening to and telling of tales, particularly those about
rebbes and *tzaddikim* [righteous and holy persons].

Elie Wiesel grew up within this tradition of stories, listening to tales
and dreaming of one day becoming a rebbe himself. Wiesel, in the text
Four Hasidic Masters in which he retells numerous hasidic tales, writes of
his hasidic grandfather: "A fabulous storyteller, he knew how to captivate
an audience. He would say: 'Listen attentively, and above all, remember
that true tales are meant to be transmitted.... My very first Hasidic tales I
learned from him. He made me enter the universe of the Baal Shem, where
facts became subservient to imagination and beauty."[6] Wiesel explains that
he continues the storytelling legacy of his grandfather and forebears:

> Repetition is part of the Hasidic tradition. In the school of Bratzlav, for
> example, disciples and their students tell the tales of Rebbe Nahman a

thousand times, and each time they discover some new meaning.... So do we. In retelling these tales, I realize once more that I owe them much. Consciously or not, I have incorporated a song, an echo, a word of theirs in my own legends and fables. I have remained, in a vanished kingdom, a child who loves to listen."[7]

Wiesel's prolificacy reveals that he too takes the *mitzvah* of storytelling to heart. Wiesel in particular emphasizes his own sense of indebtedness to Nachman: "I remember reading these [Rebbe Nachman's] stories as a child and, spellbound, thinking that I had understood them. Now I reread them, and though I am still under their spell, I no longer understand them.... I shall not live his adventures, though I may sometimes claim those of his heroes and their victims as my own."[8] Wiesel's debt to Nachman and his tradition of hasidic storytelling begs further exploration.

What does storytelling mean to Hasidism? This question is best answered by looking to the figure of Rebbe Nachman of Bratzlav, "the first Jewish religious figure to place storytelling at the center of his creative life ... [he] invented a new form of Jewish self-expression."[9] Tradition also credits Nachman for articulating a mini-theology of storytelling's multiple functions, four of which prove to be of primary importance for Nachman and his successor Wiesel.

First, the tales are told to inspire others to action and to a longing for God and for joy. Often, hasidic stories are told about *tzaddikim*—righteous persons who are on a path of seeking God. Rebbe Nachman, who himself was drawn to God and Hasidism through story-hearing, stated: "Stories of the *tzaddikim* inspire a person, awakening his heart and setting it on fire, arousing him to turn to God with an intense and overpowering craving."[10] Wiesel, who entitles one of his best-selling books *Souls on Fire*, obviously agrees that hasidic tales achieve this end. Hasidic stories thus help others achieve a much-needed spiritual awakening. Said Rebbe Nachman: "People say that stories are good for putting one to sleep. But I say that through stories, peoples can be woken from their sleep."[11] In light of the Holocaust and the millions of bystanders who sat idly by why millions of Jews were murdered, Wiesel too doubtless feels that the world is in need of a spiritual wake-up call. Wiesel has often said that the opposite of love is not hate, but indifference. Wiesel and Nachman each understand the hasidic tale to combat the indifference of the spiritually asleep.

Second, hasidic tales serve to mend and restore broken lines of communication, between God and humanity, and between human beings when faith and traditional religious means fail. Rebbe Nachman explained to his followers: "The Baal Shem Tov, may the memory of a *Zaddik* be blessed ... when he saw the lines of communication with heaven were broken and it was impossible to mend them with prayer, he used to mend them and restore them by telling a tale."[12] Hasidism arose within a cruel period of anti–Semitic persecution and oppression of Eastern European Jews, who predominantly felt powerless, egregiously marginalized, and abandoned by God. Wiesel explains: "God is not indifferent and man is not his enemy — that was the substance of the hasidic message. It was a message against despair, against resignation.... It taught him that hope must be derived from his own history and joy from within his own condition."[13] In the face of persecution and the perceived absence of God, the 18th century hasidim like Nachman tell stories to invoke God's presence and to teach that in spite of everything, redemption is possible through human action. In the face of the Holocaust, 21st century hasidim like Wiesel continue to tell stories for the same purpose. For Wiesel, however, the need to mend the lines of communication between God and humanity is even more urgent, because Wiesel understands that the covenant itself, the foundational commitment of God to his people, was ruptured by the *Shoah*. In a world where the absence of God is so poignant as to be palpable, Wiesel, still a faithful hasid to this day, through his stories attempts to sustain the tenuous divine-human relationship.

Third, storytelling is a form of indirect, intuitive, and imaginative communication that steps in where discursive thought fails. Hasidic storytelling underscores the limits of rationality and discursive thought. Rebbe Nachman only began to tell stories in the last four years of his life. His disciple Nathan reports: "When Rebbe Nachman began telling stories, he said clearly, 'I will start telling stories.' His meaning was that since he hadn't succeeded in bring people close to God with his lessons, he had to do so with stories."[14] Scholars and even Wiesel himself note that Nachman's switch to storytelling occurs after his failure to extend his teachings to a larger following and after the tragic death of his son. Wiesel remarks: "As a Master, founder of a school, he transmits his vision of the world by telling tales, masterworks of their kind, rather than by enunciating theories."[15] Owing to these events in his life which defied rational explanation, Rebbe Nachman became strongly anti-rationalist and began to tell imaginative stories rather than teach in a traditional manner. Because

Nachman understood the *medammeh*— the imagination — to be 'the main locus of faith,' Nachman chose to speak of the life of faith not directly, but indirectly through the medium of his imagination, that is, his stories.[16] Wiesel chooses the same path.

Hasidic storytelling for Nachman is a form of communication that acknowledges its own limits by incorporating those limits into the story. Scholarship unanimously agrees that Rebbe Nachman's tales are filled with strange gaps. Rebbe Nachman eschews the continuities demanded by discursive thought, and this is one of the most striking aspects of his stories. Explains one scholar: "Born in a moment of despair, his [Rebbe Nachman's] tales have a tragic urgency. The hoped-for act of restoration, which is the goal of every seeker in every tale, is deadlocked, deferred, and only sometimes fully realized. These are stories of a world in crisis, of faith under siege. The present evil is ubiquitous.... Reb Nahman turned to storytelling when all else failed."[17] Another scholar characterizes Reb Nachman's stories as having a "strange sense of incompleteness."[18] Wiesel offers his own analysis:

> Continuity? He [Rebbe Nachman] prefers unbridled ... fantasy disdainful of frontiers, all frontiers; those of the mind as well as those of lands inhabited though cursed.... Impossible to know who is playing what role and for how long. The episodes arbitrarily fit into one another ... becoming inextricably tangled. And then, just as arbitrarily, they reach an abrupt ending.... One easily loses the thread.... One ends up forgetting the main, subterranean plot. Like Nahman's heroes, the reader–listener no longer has any notion where he is or what might be awaiting him at the next step; he is helpless, lost in a strange land.[19]

Rebbe Nachman's tale *The Lost Princess*, for example, ends with an "ending" that should be more accurately called a pseudoending: "And how he saved her is not told." Similarly, Rebbe Nachman leaves one of his most famous thirteen tales, *The Seven Beggars*, without an ending of any kind — the seventh beggar never reappears at the wedding celebration. One of Wiesel's tales, *The Forgotten*, in a strikingly similar fashion, ends in midsentence like a typographical error, stopping the reader cold: "And I who speak to you cannot say more, for."[20] Wiesel, commenting on *The Seven Beggars*, argues that Rebbe Nachman intentionally incorporates the limits of storytelling into his stories:

> He was too skilled a craftsman to botch a tale.... But then, how could he neglect the framework and underestimate the importance of the work's

very structure? Why did he leave so many gaps? Threads leading in too many directions at once; action ten times suspended — and seven times resumed? Have they a purpose? The answer is contained in the question. The same failings — or apparent failings — may be found in all his tales, in everything he created; therefore they must be deliberate.[21]

Hasidic storytelling presents questions without answers, paradoxes without explanations, and contradictions without resolutions. Storytelling, a la Rebbe Nachman, does not aim at conclusiveness. Nachman's life's work suggests that when a hasid speaks of subjects about which conclusiveness is not possible — God, death, evil, meaning — storytelling is the mode of communication most suited for such an impossible task. Elie Wiesel, similarly, has stated on innumerable occasions that there can be no answer or explanation given for the Holocaust. Nachman's model of inconclusive storytelling as a mode of faithfulness no doubt contributes to Wiesel's repeated claim that the only possible faith for himself as a Jew and Holocaust survivor is Hasidism. Tradition has paved a way for Wiesel to be able to tell his tales of life *in extremis*— hasidic stories can be told with gaps and without endings.

Fourth, the hasidic tale sanctifies. Hasidic tales are holy, life-giving stories, offering Hasidim who tell and listen to them a means of *devekut*, or cleaving to God. Rabbi Israel of Rizhin has said that you give a Jew life by telling stories.[22] Because Hasidism believes all daily activities of life are potentially sanctifying, however, the content of hasidic tales is usually prosaic. Scholars note that the unprecedented secular content of Rebbe Nachman's tales often shocked listeners. Yaffa Eliach remarks that after Nachman, the hasidic tradition places no restrictions on its tale-tellers. Writes Eliach: "This supreme, unquestioned literary freedom of the Hasidic tale enables and encourages the teller to probe dangerous, problematic, and otherwise forbidden topics."[23] In the case of Rebbe Nachman, his tales repeatedly touch on the problems of doubt, evil, and the absence of God. In the case of Wiesel, Holocaust stories must also speak of these same unspeakable issues.

The similarities between Rebbe Nachman and Elie Wiesel, with regard to biography as well as thought, are striking and revealing, though surprisingly unexplored. Reb Nachman's authoritative biography reads: "An acute awareness of his own mortality, a sense of aloneness and isolation both from man and from God, a rich imagination fired by early study of the mythic imagery of the kabbalah, and a deep well of inner pain and longing — these were the legacies of childhood that Nachman was to carry with him into his adult life."[24] If we did not know that these words were written about Nachman, we could assume that they were written about Wiesel, who inherited a similar legacy by living his childhood in Auschwitz. The same goes for this passage: "This life was one of constant struggle, or constant rise and fall in relationship to God, a life alternating between periods of bleak depression leading him to the brink of utter despair, and redoubled efforts to try once more to come close to God.... There seemed to be hardly a day in his life when he did not touch the borders of both heaven and hell."[25]

Each man turned to storytelling in his latter years, in the wake of life's tragedies for which they could find no rational answer. Nachman lived with persecution and opposition and in the latter years of his life, with illness, much personal suffering, and a heightened awareness of his own mortality. In 1805, the rebbe witnessed the death of his young son. The next year, his wife died of tuberculosis, and in the same year, when he was thirty-five, Nachman himself came down with the dreaded fatal illness. In Auschwitz, the young Wiesel too tragically encountered the radical negativity of illness, the death of his family, and the failure of the messiah to appear.

With regard to theology, it would seem that in the 18th century work of Nachman, Wiesel discovers a surprising resource for post–*Shoah* Jewish faith and thought. In particular, Bratzlavian thought provides Wiesel with the needed groundwork for three theological concepts that are fundamental to each man's thought and storytelling: an awareness of the limitations of language and discursive thought, an understanding of faith and doubt as a dialectic, and an understanding of faith as a paradox of conflicting narratives. Wiesel, though drawing heavily from the Bratzlav well by conveying these theological concepts through storytelling, nonetheless puts his unique watermark on the tales by using laughter to communicate the importance of all three of these characteristics for post–Holocaust faith and expression. Through the inclusion of laughter, Wiesel continues the legacy and *mitzvah* of storytelling he inherits from his hasidic forbears, while adapting it to his own unique post–*Shoah* purposes.

The Failure and Limits of Language and Discursive Thought

First, as is well-documented, Rebbe Nachman was often overcome with the limits of language and rational, discursive thought. To his disciples, he often commented that there were "no words." When afflicted with periods of spiritual "dryness," Nachman would tell his students that he was unworthy and unable to teach or say anything.[26] As a Holocaust survivor, Wiesel's experience is an exponential echo of Nachman's. To the careful reader, Wiesel struggles in all of his work to convey to his audience that the radical negativity of the *Shoah* irreparably ruptures language, rendering discursive thought woefully inexpedient. To convey a very real sense of this crisis of representation and interpretation, Wiesel in his essays often uses the direct means of stating in no uncertain terms that words fail in post–Holocaust discourse. In the storytelling, Wiesel with great frequency puts such comments in the mouth of the narrator or protagonist. In *The Gates of the Forest*, for example, the narrator notes that "at this hour ... neither words nor wrath made any sense."[27] Similarly, in the novel *A Beggar in Jerusalem*, the protagonist Katriel states: "I don't like words! They destroy what they aim to describe, they alter what they try to emphasize. By enveloping the truth, they end up taking its place."[28]

Wiesel describes this phenomenon as the "double-bind" of the post–Auschwitz world: "How can we speak of it ... how can we not speak of it?"[29] For Wiesel, to speak of the *sui generis* event of the Holocaust is to betray it because words cannot begin to adequately circumscribe the experience; however, not to speak of the event is also a betrayal — a betrayal of the memory of the dead and the injustices perpetrated against them. Wiesel feels that on the one hand he must tell the stories of the dead, since they cannot tell us their own stories. Wiesel acknowledges that he received this imperative to tell the dead's stories from his hasidic grandfather: "A fabulous storyteller, he knew how to captivate an audience. He would say: 'Listen attentively, and remember above all that true tales are meant to be transmitted — to keep them to oneself is to betray them."[30] On the other hand, however, Wiesel feels that no one can fully speak for the dead except the dead themselves, who remain silent: "Sometimes, thinking of the dead whose memory I have sworn to preserve, I told myself, To write this story you'd already have to be dead; only the dead can properly write their story."[31] The grandfather's admonition to the child Elie presents the adult

Wiesel, a Holocaust survivor, with the seemingly impossible charge of telling the stories of six million murder victims. Writes Wiesel:

> Language ... no longer serves as a vehicle to transmit knowledge or experience. It has become an obstacle rather than a mirror. As a writer hoping to communicate the incommunicable I feel it personally. It is not because I cannot explain that you won't understand; it is because you won't understand that I can't explain.[32]

In this understanding of the limits and inadequacy of words, Wiesel echoes not only Nachman's experience but also the experience of his Jewish contemporaries. Jewish thought today almost unanimously acknowledges that the *Shoah* ruptures language, resulting in a crisis of representation. During the last fifty years, Jewish thinkers and survivors have each made this point in their own distinct manner, with differing opinions on the gravity and or reversibility of this crisis. George Steiner, for example, says that silence is the only possible answer to the Holocaust, because the world of Auschwitz lies outside speech and reason. Theodor Adorno once said that no poetry could be written after Auschwitz, and then later retracted the statement.

We know, however, that poetry has been written, and the poems of Holocaust survivors Paul Celan and Nelly Sachs, to name only two, could serve as evidence against Adorno's claim. However, there is an equal amount of evidence that Celan and Sachs might paradoxically agree with Adorno's statement in spite of the fact that they each wrote Holocaust poetry. The life and work of these two poets has lent an odd credibility to Adorno's statement. Nelly Sachs, for example, succumbed at least temporarily to insanity, losing language as a mode of communication. One of Paul Celan's poems states: "A word — you know:/ a corpse."[33] As for Paul Celan the survivor, he eventually took his own life, leaving the question regarding poetry's possibility as tragically suspended. Contemplating the fate of Celan and Sachs, Wiesel comments:

> Just as readers would commit suicide in the 19th century, writers did in ours, because they felt impotent. They realized that once you have penetrated the kingdom of night you have reached the end.... There is nothing else to say. There is nothing else to do. You remain a prisoner forever. So they felt inadequate and guilty. They thought they had said something. No, they had said nothing. It was simply too much for the survivor.[34]

Wiesel understands the double-bind of the survivor's situation because, of course, it is his own. He says something, yet like Celan and Sachs, feels that he says nothing. Wiesel's own life mirrors this struggle between speaking and non-speaking, an exaggerated version of the struggle that was once Nachman's. Many readers forget that Wiesel kept himself to a strict vow of silence about what he had endured for ten years after the war ended. During that decade, Wiesel did not speak or write about his experience at Auschwitz. Since then, however, he has become prolific, publishing over forty full-length works. Does Wiesel contradict himself? How can he rationally talk all the time about the impossibility of telling, while he goes on telling — publishing, teaching, and touring on the lecture circuit? Susan Shapiro answers this question by citing Wiesel's odd claim to write "not with words but against words":

> How can one express or convey the experience of a radically negating event that shatters the very conventions of speech and discourse without employing those conventions and, thereby, already domesticating that radical negativity? ... One hermeneutical strategy employed differently by various poets and novelists was to "not write with, but against words," so as to testify in this way to the impossibility of fully, actually telling.[35]

Shapiro, however, does not explain in practical terms what it means to write with words against words. Interestingly, Rebbe Nachman, one hundred and fifty years earlier, anticipated this need of the Jewish faithful to use words against words and acknowledge the limits of telling as well as of rationality. Said the rebbe: "The end of knowledge is the realization that we do not know."[36] The rebbe's advice on this matter appears to have helped Wiesel in his struggle to live in such tension. For Rebbe Nachman too insisted on teaching and the publication of his stories, yet he frequently insisted that what he wanted to communicate could not be communicated:

> The greatness of God is something that no one can communicate to his fellowman, or even to himself from one day to the next. That which is brilliantly clear to him on one day is something that he cannot communicate to himself on the day that follows. That is why he [King David] said: "For I know [that the Lord is great]" — because this cannot be told at all.[37]

For Nachman, God cannot be spoken of because the Almighty alternates between being overwhelmingly present and holy, and being overwhelmingly absent and incomprehensible. For on another occasion, Rebbe Nachman taught his disciples:

> Creation came about through the word.... Language defines all things. But in the void which surrounds all the worlds and is completely empty, there is no language.... For thus it is in the highest thought, that which is beyond language ... there are no words to resolve it. The same is true of all these questions which come from the void, where there exists neither mind nor language. As they are silent, so must one confront them by silent faith alone.[38]

How does one speak of the necessity of silence? How does one teach the knowledge that that we cannot know? To live into this tension rather than resolve it and to communicate the limits of rational discourse, Nachman turned to storytelling. Imagination is more important than reason in the Hasidic life; therefore storytelling takes precedence over discursive thought.[39]

Wiesel heightens his readers' (and perhaps his own) awareness of this paradox of the necessity and impossibility of post–Holocaust storytelling in three main ways, two of which occur to the knowledgeable reader before she even delves even into the first page of any of his stories. First, to this day, and to the surprise of audiences around the world, Wiesel makes the strange assertion that his fictional books are "*not* about the Holocaust." Lest we forget the dangers and limitations of storytelling, it seems this is Wiesel's way of reminding those of us who will listen that the story of the Holocaust can never fully be told, but instead is constantly elusive. We must never deceive ourselves into thinking that we are getting "the whole story," or the final and definitive telling of the event.

Second and similarly, Wiesel, like many survivors, never writes his stories in his native tongue, Yiddish, or even his third language of everyday life, English. Instead, he writes in French, the language he adopted as an orphaned refugee living in Paris after the war. Nachman was able to tell stories in the religious tongue of traditional Judaism, but living in a post–Holocaust world, Wiesel rejects this luxury. For Wiesel, speaking only in an adopted tongue and refusing to tell the story in his mother tongue testifies to the careful observer that the language of faith is ruptured by radical negativity. A new language must be adopted, even though it too is imperfect. In keeping with the biblical tradition of Genesis and the tower of Babel, Wiesel understands language to be corrupted and confused (*babel* in Hebrew). "The Lord came down to see the city and the tower, which mortals had built. And the Lord said ... 'Come, let us go down, and confuse their language there, so that they will not understand one another's speech'" (Gen 11:5–7). Telling the story of the Holocaust in Hebrew for Wiesel would be adopting God's own language to tell a human story. Likewise, writing in the language of German, for example, would mean adopting the language of the oppressor. Wiesel avoids the radically profane and radically sacred languages, opting for the relatively neutral ground of French. In the face of linguistic corruption, Wiesel faces an incredible challenge. He must attempt to express the inexpressible.

Third, once the reader begins the journey into Wiesel's world of storytelling, Wiesel unveils the trope of laughter as his most innovative means of addressing the need to acknowledge the limits of storytelling within the confines of the story itself. Laughter is perhaps his most important tool, as it is universally accessible and perceptible even to those readers who know nothing about Wiesel's biography or commentary. Fascinatingly, while Wiesel denies that any of his stories are about the Holocaust, he does concede that they are all about laughter. Again, the critical literature ignores this hermeneutical key that Wiesel himself offers about his own work. Wiesel in a recent interview makes the cryptic statement: "In my own way, I speak of Isaac constantly, in all my writings. In fact, I speak of almost nothing else."[40]

What is the significance of Isaac for Wiesel? The name Isaac in Hebrew means "he who laughs." For Wiesel, Isaac is the quintessential survivor in Jewish history: "Why was the most tragic of our ancestors named Isaac, a name which evokes and signifies laughter? Here is why. As the first survivor, he had to teach us, the future survivors of Jewish history, that it is possible to suffer and despair an entire lifetime and still not give up the art of laughter."[41] In another radio interview, Wiesel elaborates:

> I find that laughter belongs to Jewish history. It takes part in Jewish mystery. Example: Isaac, the second patriarch, is after all called Isaac. Why Isaac, he who will laugh? Why does he laugh? The most tragic figure in Jewish history after all is Isaac, the son of Abraham, almost killed by his father, for his Father. I believe therein lies the secret of Jewish existence, because Isaac for me is the first survivor, the first survivor of the first Holocaust. Now, normally Isaac, after this horrible experience, should

have become numb, bitter, angry, should have committed suicide, should have sent to the devil all his brothers, all his prayers, all his dreams. However, he was a dreamer, a poet.... And in spite of everything, Isaac, in spite of everything, was capable of laughter. It's that laughter that I try in my books, my tales, to capture, and to transmit.[42]

Isaac therefore is a paradigm for the Jewish people because he survived the first holocaust — *ola*, meaning burnt offering — requested by God of Abraham, and all Jews alive today have also survived the Holocaust of World War II. Isaac's dilemma, that of reconciling his faith in a benevolent, omnipotent God with the world's negativity which negates God's benevolence and omnipotence, is therefore a universal dilemma facing all post–Holocaust Jews. Wiesel suggests through these statements that his work is more about surviving the Holocaust and the paradox of post–Holocaust faith and existence, rather than the Holocaust per se. After all, hasidic tales are told not only to teach but also to inspire the hearer to emulation. Given this logic, the last thing Wiesel would want to do as a hasidic storyteller is to tell stories "about the Holocaust"; such tales of evil would fill listeners with sheer terror.

The Gates of the Forest is therefore more properly understood not as a story about the Holocaust, but as a story about Gavriel, the laughing Isaac character of the book. The epigraph to *Gates of the Forest* reads: "God made man because he loves stories." Turning to the first page, the very first five sentences of the story signal that this story is about a man who laughs in the midst of linguistic rupture:

> He had no name, so he gave him his own. As a loan, as a gift, what did it matter? In time of war every word is as good as the next. A man possesses only what he gives away. Gregor loved and hated his laugh, which was like no other, which did not even resemble itself ... the laugh of the man who saved his life.[43]

Wiesel thus discloses the plot: Gavriel saves Gregor's life by teaching him how to laugh. The two characters are the twin protagonists of the novel; indeed, some interpreters hypothesize that the two characters constitute one composite character. Gregor, a hasidic Jew and lone survivor of his family, lives during the Holocaust. At the story's beginning, a stranger visits Gregor, who has sought refuge in a cave in a Transylvanian forest. Gregor bestows his real name Gavriel, meaning "man of God," upon the stranger, and gives himself the new, non–Jewish name Gregor. But Gregor quickly discovers that the stranger, a fellow hasid, exhibits a most unusual behavior: he laughs. Gregor describes his laughter as "not the laughter of one man but of a hundred, of seven times seven hundreds."[44] Heretofore paralyzed by fear and in hiding for over six days, Gregor is so stunned by Gavriel's incongruous laughter that he emerges from the cave, whereupon he shouts, "Stop! Stop laughing! ... I'm alone and the war is still raging. It will go on and on, and I shall be more and more alone. Be quiet, will you? Listen to the war and you won't laugh any longer!"[45] In keeping with the biblical Isaac, Gavriel laughs and explains to Gregor, "I thought I was the only one left, the last survivor. That gave me the right to laugh didn't it?"[46] Gavriel, like Isaac, survives by laughter.

Gregor, like most of us, considers the rational, appropriate physiological responses to the war and its suffering to be tears or cries of anguish, and so he quickly labels Gavriel's laughter as obscene and unfounded. Gavriel, however, retorts that for him the exact opposite is the case: "I'm listening to the war and I'm laughing."[47] Indeed, as Gregor talks to his new acquaintance he discovers that on the contrary, the deeper the darkness, the more strident Gavriel's laughter becomes: "The sadder the stories, the more Gavriel laughed. Sometimes he laughed without saying a word, and Gregor realized that the event was so heavy with horror, experienced or anticipated, that words could really not contain it."[48] In these lines, Wiesel suggests that laughter becomes an expedient form of extra-linguistic expression in the post–Holocaust world precisely because language has become lamentably so inexpedient. Here again, the echoes of Nachman are heard.

Laughter for Gavriel, then, is a choice, an act of the will that not only interrupts our traditional conception of laughter as mere physiological response but also our parochial understanding of weeping as the only appropriate response to a tragic situation. Gavriel's choice of laughter is inherently paradoxical, as laughter usually manifests joy, pleasure, or satisfaction, none of which Gavriel experiences in the moment. Wiesel expects that the reader will share Gregor's first response to Gavriel's unusual laughter, and at least initially, find it reprehensible if not incomprehensible. Gavriel states: "You think I'm mad, don't you?"[49] However, in the tale Gavriel emerges as a hero, not a madman — Gregor spends the entire story trying to learn to laugh like Gavriel. Again here, understanding Bratzlavian theosophy provides an interpretive clue, for Rebbe Nachman once said: "One may even have to do things that seem like madness for the sake of serving God."[50] Laughing at the Holocaust is holy madness.

In all probability, Rebbe Nachman is in part the real-life *tzaddik* inspiration behind the fictional character of Gavriel. In *Souls on Fire*, Wiesel quotes an odd characterization of Rebbe Nachman from Hayyey II 2:19 that undoubtedly lies hidden behind Gavriel's character: "He [Rebbe Nachman] thought that he would take his wife and go live in some far-off place, hidden from the public. Sometimes he would go out to the market to have a look at the world — and to laugh at it."[51] The *badkhan*, or holy jester who summons God's presence through incongruous behavior, is a popular figure within Hasidic tradition and one that fascinates Wiesel.[52] At times Rebbe Nachman played the fool, or *badkhan*, in public. His disciples describe that on his trip to Israel: "He acted in all sorts of childish ways, going about barefoot, without a belt, or without a top hat. He would go about [in the street] in his indoor clothing, running around the market like a child. There he would play war games, as children do."[53]

Interestingly, Wiesel parts ways with hasidic tradition, by refusing to write off Nachman's foolish behavior as a mere ruse to deceive Satan of his true identity. Writes Wiesel:

> Why was the Rebbe posing as a madman? ... I lean toward an explanation that places the accent on his laughter. Laughter occupies an astonishingly important place in his work. Here and there, one meets a man who laughs and does nothing else.... Laughter that springs from lucid and desperate awareness, a mirthless laughter, a laughter of protest against the absurdities of existence, a laughter of revolt against a universe where man, whatever he may do, is condemned in advance.... How then can a man take himself seriously? Revolt is not a solution, neither is submission. Remains laughter, metaphysical laughter.[54]

Readings these lines, it should not surprise the reader-listener that in Wiesel's Holocaust tales, hasidic protagonists like Gavriel emulate the real-life rebbe, and laugh in protest while the hell of war rages on.

Faith and Doubt as Dialectic

The second way in which Nachman functions as theological resource and inspiration for Wiesel's post–Holocaust thought is in his revolutionary understanding of the complex interrelationship between faith and doubt. Rebbe Nachman was a man who even from his childhood was plagued with radical doubts about God, including His existence, goodness, justice, and omnipotence. Rebbe Nachman understood the source of doubt to be the universal experience of the absence of God in the midst of negativity, an experience all true believers must confess that "every man is filled with suffering."[55] The cornerstone of Nachman's unique religious thought is his acute sense of the absence of God and a subsequent search and longing for God's ever elusive presence. Nachman's disciple Nathan describes Nachman's own struggle this way:

> He would often speak to God in heartfelt supplications and pleas ... but nevertheless he felt he wasn't being noticed or heard at all.... Days and years passed by, and still he was far from Him; he had not attained any sense of nearness at all.... Despite all this, he would fortify himself and refuse to leave his place. At times he would become depressed.... At such times he would cease his private prayers for a number of days. Then he would catch himself and be overcome with shame for having called the goodness of God into question.... All of this happened to him any number of times."[56]

We cannot help but draw immediate parallels here with Wiesel, whose own autobiography *Night* reverberates with the unanswered question asked from within the barbed-wire of Auschwitz: "Where is God now?" Wiesel consistently portrays the distance between God and humanity as an infinite well of suffering. Wiesel, in his stories, frequently puts God on trial and questions God's goodness and justice. The protagonist of *The Gates of the Forest*, to name only one example, declares: "Oh God, you have set yourself on the side of the torturer, you are guilty; you are the ruler of the universe, but you are guilty."[57] Nachman's radical doubts could only have seemed blasphemous to many who had never before encountered them in a rebbe and man of faith. Wiesel reports that the opponents of Nachman in his own day were myriad. Relatedly, it is my experience as a professor that new, inexperienced readers of Wiesel simplistically assume that he is an atheist or a heretic because of the constant accusations of guilt he hurls at God either in the first person or via the mouths of his protagonists. One of the greatest obstacles of teaching Wiesel, in my mind, is explaining to students that for Wiesel, faith and doubt are not opposites. In Wiesel as in all of Bratzlav Hasidism, faith is an *antidote* to despair and doubt, and not merely an *antinomy*. Doubt is an essential element of faith. Rebbe Nachman revolutionized the way his followers understood faith and doubt: faith and doubt constitute a dialectic.

The most revolutionary aspect of Bratzlavian thought therefore is that doubt is the sign of a genuine faith, rather than a flawed one. The saying, "A person can be a *zaddiq* even if he doesn't have complete trust (in God)" is a thought completely original to Nachman.[58] Wiesel takes this lesson of the rebbe's to heart, as is evident when he states while reflecting on the Holocaust: "In our epoch, I would say, there is nothing so whole as broken faith. Faith must be tested. But ... without faith we could not survive."[59] Nachman's biographer writes: "Man lives in a world where God cannot be 'seen'; given this reality, doubt is an inevitable part of the life of every religious human being.... Nahman interprets the rabbinic dictum: "know what to answer the heretic" to refer to the heretic ... inside the heart of every would-be believer."[60] Nachman is his own best heretic and God's toughest critic; the same must be said of Wiesel and in my classroom, it often is.

With some impressive hermeneutical maneuvering, Nachman ultimately elevated doubt to the status of a spiritual virtue. Given that faith never can or should be rational, Nachman positively reinterpreted doubt as an impetus toward faith because it fills believers with a great longing for God. *Razon we-kissufim* [desire and longing] is a concept that Nachman added to the Hasidic vocabulary because he felt such yearning to lie at the heart of a sincere faith.[61] Nachman classified doubt as well as questions about God as "*azut di-qedushah*," or holy audacity. Explained Nachman:

> With regard to these objections to God he liked to say: Of course there have to be questions about Him; this is only fitting to his exalted state. For it is of the very nature of His greatness that He be beyond our minds' grasp. It is impossible that we understand His conduct with our intellect. There must be objections raised to Him ... for if He conducted Himself as our minds dictate, our minds would indeed be equal to His own![62]

Doubt, in other words, suggests the very real existence of God because if God does exist, we cannot ever fully understand Him. Those who doubt are those who come closest to God, because they accurately perceive God's genuine transcendence.

Gavriel's laughter, understood in this theological context, is a form of holy audacity. Gavriel (and eventually Gregor) with his laughter protests God's absence, but protests this to God Himself. Gavriel laughs because he both believes and disbelieves in the divine existence, goodness, justice, and promise. Gavriel is in spiritual crisis, which induces a crisis of representation. How can it be said that one both believes and does not believe in God? Discursive thought forces Gavriel to choose between faith and doubt. For rationality the situation is either/or. For faith, however, particularly in the Bratzlavian tradition, no choice is necessary given that faith and doubt constitute a dialectic. Faith adopts a 'both-and' stance instead of an either/or. In the Talmud, at times no concrete decision is made between competing authoritative claims, and the dialectical tension is merely allowed to stand unresolved. A rabbinic saying addresses such cases: "Both these and those are the words of the living God."[63] Nachman, intrigued by this saying, comments, "Let someone give me an answer! ... For really there is no answer at all.... How could the intellect possibly comprehend that both are true, if one says the opposite of the other? ... He who looks into them ... sees that his answer is nothing and that the question remains.... One must rely on faith alone."[64] Gavriel, too refuses to choose, and his laughter expresses his protesting faith, characterized as it is by doubt. Reflecting on the Messiah, Gavriel laments: "I think of nothing else. That's the way we're made, I guess, to be blinded by presence and haunted by absence. I think of him all the time and I laugh."[65]

Doubt, then, is not a rejection of God, but a rebuttal. Nachman reconceived of doubt as an articulation of the believer's anger at God's absence. While Hasidism understands God's presence or *Shekhinah* as going into exile in the world in order for creation to happen, Nachman added to tradition the notion that that God's *zimzum* [withdrawal] from the world causes the believer great suffering and doubt. In life, Nachman realized, believers encounter many obstacles to faith that engender suspicion of God's absence — the main obstacles being negativity and suffering. Nachman uses the term *meni'ah* to refer to these obstacles, and the term *maqqif* to the questions or challenges to faith engendered by the *meni'ot*, which the mind cannot resolve and thus trigger doubt. The spiritual life is an endless series of *maqqifin*, and for Wiesel, the Holocaust is the ultimate *maqqif* and *meni'ah*. In Bratzlavian thought, struggling through each *maqqif* even without resolution brings the believer closer to God. Doubt, for those who ascribe to Rebbe Nachman's theosophy, is constructive. In

Gavriel's words: "God's finally victory, my son, lies in man's inability to reject Him. You think you're cursing Him, but your curse is praise; you think you're fighting Him, but all you do is open yourself to Him; you think you're crying out your hatred and rebellion, but all you're doing is telling Him how much you need His support and forgiveness."[66] Faith and doubt, hope and tragedy are not mutually exclusive: this is Gavriel's message to all who hear his story.

Bratzlavian theosophy understands faith to be nurtured by question-asking, even if answers do not arrive. The religious life therefore moves not from answer to answer but from question to question. Nachman envisions "a faith growing in paradoxical complexity as it seeks to incorporate those very challenges that had sought to destroy it. A religious life that thrives on challenge does not want to provide 'answers' to the eternal questions, but seeks rather to raise the level of struggle to an ever-higher pitch."[67] Such line of thinking could only serve as a comfort to Wiesel, who argues that with regard to the devastation of the Holocaust that answers are not only undesirable but impossible: "This tragedy defies and exceeds all answers. If anyone claims to have found an answer; it can only be a false one. So much mourning, so much agony, so many deaths on one side, and a single answer on the other? One cannot understand Auschwitz either without God or with God."[68] Wiesel here resonates with Nachman, who often told his disciples that his statement 'I don't know' was the highest of all his teachings, and who said, "I wanted to be answered by a voice from heaven.... Any answer that was not from man would be acceptable — but [I] had not yet received it."[69]

Nachman, an anti-rationalist, understood faith to be absurd, contrary to reason and logic. Nachman wrote: "This is the root of faith: that the faithful one realize that he has no understanding at all.... True faith is belief in God without any sign, proof, or reason. This is the complete faith."[70] Because faith is absurd without empirical grounding, it is courageous, even miraculous. Wiesel too understands faith as miraculous; Gregor says: "No one has a right not to believe in miracles just because it's a time of war or to make fun of those who believe in them, because their faith is in itself a miracle."[71] Faith is a struggle, a seeking after God that one does not give up in spite of not finding. Faith in God for a hasid, then, is at all times a struggle, as it is constantly endangered by the empirical reality that contradicts faith and induces doubt. In keeping with this line of Bratzlavian thought, *Gates of the Forest* ends with Gregor telling his wife Clara: "Let's resume the struggle.... It is because it is too late that we are commanded to hope."[72]

While Jewish tradition usually counters doubt with theodicy, or a defense of God, Nachman's work arguably suggested that theodicy — a verbal articulation of God's innocence — cannot be achieved. Nachman said to his disciples: "The problem of why the righteous suffer and the wicked prosper ... this appears to be a perversion of justice, God forbid, and even Moses was not able to fathom it while he was alive.... By loving God so much that you cast yourself into the mud for Him, worshipping him with the love of an ordinary servant, you may grasp that which Moses in his lifetimes, and the mind when it is operating, cannot understand: the problem of theodicy."[73] Theodicy, that is the problem of reconciling a just and omnipotent God with the undeniable existence of evil in the world, exposes the limits of language and discursive thought for Nachman. In the stories, therefore, Nachman counters theodicy with silence, much as his successor Wiesel counters it with laughter — both extralinguistic means of underscoring the inexpediency of language. As we recall, Nachman's tales contain extensive details, page after page, of conflict, only to move to a hasty and disproportionately short one-sentence ending, what many consider a pseudo-ending and form of silence. Nachman's narrative suggests that no defense of God can be given, but stories can be told that leave the case as well as the verdict in perpetual suspense.

I argue that Nachman did this purposefully, with the theological aim of leaving the reader dissatisfied. Nachman's failure to satisfy by means of a denouement is an intentional method of making manifest theodicy's failure to satisfy. Nachman wanted to tell the story, but also to show his reader-listeners the impossibility of fully telling. Nachman wants the reader to leave the tale with questions in mind such as: can the world's pain and suffering ever really be resolved? Even if conflict is overcome, is conflict ever negated or should it remain in our memory? How can we speak of redemption in a world that appears so unredeemed? I believe Nachman here takes his cue not from the explanatory rabbinic tradition but from biblical storytelling, in particular the story of Job.

In Job, thirty-seven chapters are dedicated to the laments and suffering of Job, and then Yahweh speaks from the whirlwind for four chapters. In response, in only six short verses, Job immediately repeals his previous position of defiance and questioning. For readers like Wiesel, the story of Job fails to satisfy, and Wiesel suggests this may be its indirect spiritual lesson. Wiesel considers Job's final acceptance of the divine will to be a "hasty abdication," commenting: "I was offended by his [Job's] surrender in the text.... He should've continued to protest."[74] To the question of theodicy, Rebbe Nachman, unlike Job, fails to supply the facile traditional answer of divine inscrutability. In a post–Holocaust world, Wiesel as storyteller feels compelled to follow suit. Gavriel refuses to offer a theodicy, but instead laughs as he swings precariously on the pendulum of faith and doubt.

Faith as Paradox and Collision of Narratives

Once faith and doubt are understood as a dialectic, faith takes on a paradoxical character in Bratzlavian thought. Faith is a form of defiance and resistance to despair and empirical reality. Explains one Bratzlavian scholar: "Faith and hope are needed precisely because life entails discrepancies, irrational uncertainties, and questions for which no rational answers may be found — Rabbi Nachman constructed his systematic dialectic-dialogue theory of the paradox, which puts the hypothesis, or the question, in the center of the world."[75] Wiesel too desires to testify to such a paradox, as he states in the aptly titled *Hope Against Hope*: "I deliberately use paradoxical language when it comes to the question of faith after Auschwitz.... The paradox in this is that despite everything and in defiance of everything we must have faith. Even if we find no faith we must raise it up in the hope that one day we will understand why, and that one day we will be able to give a reason for believing."[76]

For Bratzlavian thought, the main paradox of faith is that faith entails simultaneously a belief in the absence and presence of God. Nachman, drawing on kabbalistic sources, taught that the world was formed in a void. God had to withdraw himself from this void in order for creation to occur:

> Now this void was essential for the Creation.... At the same time, God's withdrawal (*zimzum*) in forming the void remains incomprehensible until the end of time. Two contradictory things must be said of it: the void comes about through *zimzum*, the withdrawal of God. There is, as it were, no God there, for if divinity were present in it, it would not be a void ... and there would be no room for Creation. Yet in a deeper sense, surely there is divinity there nevertheless.[77]

In these lines, Nachman argues that given that Creation is inherently paradoxical, faith must naturally be paradoxical as well. Hence the popular saying of the Seer of Lublin: "A Hasid, like a child, should cry and laugh at the same time."[78]

Nachman thus effectively described faith as a conflict of narratives, a resource that proves invaluable to Wiesel as post–Holocaust storyteller who desires to remain within his hasidic tradition. For, as Kenneth Surin explains, at the heart of Wiesel's *Gates of the Forest* lie two divergent narratives, which seemingly negate one another yet coexist:

> The narrative of faith collides with the narrative of its negation, but neither achieves an ascendancy over the other. At the level of belief, Auschwitz gives one reason both to believe and to disbelieve: the testimony of its witnesses speaks for both these seemingly irreconcilable moments, moments which must nevertheless be simultaneously affirmed.... To safeguard the possibility of truth it is necessary to hold the one moment as the necessary dialectical negation or counterpoise of the other. The testimony of affirmation needs to be "ruptured" by its counterpart testimony of negation, and vice versa.[79]

In other words, in the event of the Holocaust, the meaningful narrative of faith possessed by Gavriel and the Jews collides incommensurably with the meaningless narrative of empirical radical evil and tragic-suffering. In order to tell the story truthfully, Wiesel has to balance every theological affirmation that stems from Jewish tradition and scripture with its negation — the empirical reality of the Holocaust. Wiesel sustains this hermeneutic of rupture in *Gates of the Forest* in two ways.

First, Wiesel's protagonists utter affirmations and then in the next breath negate these affirmations. In *Gates* we read: "Every death leaves a scar, and every time a child laughs it starts healing.... What then is man? Hope turned to dust. But whenever Gregor thinks of the remote village in Transylvania he knows that the opposite is equally true. What is man? Dust turned to hope."[80] Second, Wiesel figuratively portrays this collision of narratives by conceiving of God as on trial during and after the *Shoah*, with both the defense and the prosecution presenting their respective 'narratives.' As in any trial, the narratives negate one another. Can both sides be telling the truth? Can any judgment be reached? Gregor tells of a rabbi during the Holocaust who put God on trial, "I intend to convict God of murder, for he is destroying his people.... The trial proceeded in due legal form, with witnesses for both sides with pleas and deliberations.' Concludes Gregor paradoxically, as he grants the veracity of the defense and the prosecution: "I tell you this: if their death has no meaning, then it's an insult, and if it does have a meaning, it's even more so."[81]

In post–Holocaust stories like *Gates*, Wiesel struggles to tell the tale of divine promise of blessing and life and the tale of divine absence and death. In the midst of this dialectic, Wiesel agrees with Adorno who avows:

> If thinking is to be true — if it is to be true today, in any case — it must also be a thinking against itself. If thought is not measured by the extremity that eludes the concept, it is from the outset in the nature of the musical accompaniment with which the SS liked to drown out the screams of its victims.... One who believes in God cannot believe in God.... To a thinking that tries to remove the contradiction, untruth threatens here and there.[82]

Gavriel himself incarnates this paradox: "There was a trace of irony in his voice. It seemed to affirm and deny the conclusion: everything is true and everything is a lie. Men love and kill one another, God bids them pray and yet their prayers change nothing."[83] This paradox motif recurs when Gregor shouts accusingly at the Rebbe: "After what happened to us, how can you believe in God?" the Rebbe answers with a smile and the retort: "How can you *not* believe in God after what has happened?"[84] Belief stands counterpoised by disbelief, irreconcilable in post–Holocaust story.

Wiesel's second means of sustaining this hermeneutic of rupture is through Gavriel's laughter. For Gavriel, as for his real-life antecedent Rebbe Nachman, this collision of coexistent yet irreconcilable narratives constitutes the life-story he yearns to tell. The collision of narratives ignites the sparks of Gavriel's promethean laughter, a laughter born of conflict yet transcending it. Gavriel's story begins this way:

> Imagine a life and death struggle between two angels, the angel of love and the angel of wrath, the angel of promise and the angel of evil. Imagine that they both attain their ends, each one victorious. Imagine the laugh that would rise above their corpses as if to say, your death has given me birth; I am the soul of your conflict, its fulfillment as well.[85]

The angel of promise — Gavriel's faith narrative — and the angel of evil — Gavriel's Holocaust narrative — are locked in combative embrace in Gavriel's psyche and spirit. However, just as Surin predicts, neither narrative achieves ascendancy over the other because each effectively negates the other. Wiesel makes the same assertion by stating metaphorically that if both angels are "victorious," this would mean that both narratives are equally dead, each canceling the other out and creating a "corpse." Caught in the collision of incommensurable narratives, Gavriel faces the supreme challenge of not only enduring but also *expressing* this inexpressible paradox. His faith remains, but in nuanced, broken, and ruptured form. He laughs to express the paradox that is his faith.

In order to be true to experience and to communicate the truth of this lived paradox to others, Gavriel must confess that his testimony of affirmation (faith) and his testimony of negation (doubt) coexist and reciprocally rupture one another. Gavriel yearns to find a means to simultaneously honor both testimonies. To let either go from his standpoint is to "allow untruth to threaten here and there." As a character much like Wiesel himself who sustains his faith through the event of the Holocaust, Gavriel understands all to well the interminability of this struggle and the ensuing spiritual anguish of being unwilling to allow either narrative to eclipse the other. Nonetheless, Gavriel refuses to relinquish the equal yet opposite claim either narrative makes on his existence, faith, and worldview.

For Wiesel, post–Holocaust faith is absurd and contra-rational because in confronting the Holocaust, Jewish theology encounters a radical dissonance between the scriptural divine promises for the Jews as Yahweh's chosen people and the tragic-suffering and catastrophe that historically befell the elect during the *Shoah*. Wiesel comments: "One cannot understand Auschwitz either without God or with God."[86] Emil Fackenheim best encapsulates the conflict of narratives burdening Yahweh's people in his statement: "At Treblinka, Jews were singled out for death as inexorably as at Sinai they had once been singled out for life."[87] In short, the problematic: Gavriel believes fervently in two narratives — Sinai and Treblinka — that logic and rationality dictate negate one another. Here we need only call to mind Irving Greenberg's touchstone for post–Holocaust theological statements: nothing can be said that is not credible in the presence of burning children. Wiesel adopts this same touchstone for his post–Holocaust storytelling. How can two reciprocally negating stories be told? What can be said of God and faith in the presence of burning children? How can one communicate to the reader an ontological dissonance so severe that language cannot circumscribe it?

Paradox, by befuddling discursive thought, usually results in silence.

However, the philosophical incongruity theory of laughter argues that paradox also may evoke laughter:

> The source of the ludicrous is always the paradoxical.... Accordingly the phenomenon of laughter always signifies the sudden apprehension of an incongruity between such a conception and the real object thought under it, thus between the abstract and concrete object of perception. The greater and more unexpected, in the apprehension of the laugher, the incongruity is, the more violent will be his laughter.[88]

A greater incongruity than exists between Sinai and Treblinka cannot be imagined. Wiesel understands from his hasidic forebears that silence alone is a reprehensible response to paradox; silence betrays the dead because their stories must be told. Rebbe Nachman acknowledged this problematic by incorporating silence into his stories; Wiesel acknowledges it by incorporating both silence and laughter into his. Says Gregor to Gavriel: "You saved my life at the risk of your own; you taught me the value of silence, of laughter."[89]

Wiesel uses laughter to communicate incongruity and convey the limits of his own storytelling within the story itself. Through Gavriel's laughter, Wiesel signals to the reader ruptures in understanding as well as ruptures of language. As Holocaust survivors attest, a paradoxical belief in the truth of both Sinai and Treblinka cannot be expressed in words. Language, therefore, precisely because it has been ruptured by this collision of narratives, does not and cannot safeguard the "possibility of truth" noted by Surin. Not language but laughter, which Surin fails even to mention, serves precisely this function in *Gates* as it allows Wiesel to tell Gavriel's "true" story — riddled as it is with contradiction. Faced with the theological contradiction posed by simultaneously engaging both Sinai and Treblinka, Gavriel laughs where discursive thought fails. Language cannot express the dialectic of presence and absence, horror and promise, faith and bewilderment in which Gavriel and his people are enmeshed, but his laughter attests to the reality that both radical negativity and faith remain, challenged, and ruptured by each other. Two contradictory narratives impel Gavriel to simultaneously hope through faith and to abandon hope — a disjunction Wiesel wonderfully portrays in the following passage: "I no longer believe in the coming of the Messiah.... No, Gregor, there can be no more hope.... But until the last minute Gavriel did not give up hoping."[90]

Gavriel's laughter, then, results because he desires to communicate an absurd contradiction created by the *Shoah* that words cannot grasp. Precisely because Gavriel refuses to relinquish either his belief in Yahweh's promises to his chosen people or his wartime horror experience, the Holocaust becomes for him a haunting experience which resists thought. To put it simply, Gavriel's laughter attests that *both* God is good *and* life is horror. Life is shit and life is beautiful, sometimes both at the very same time. Gavriel both believes in God and cannot believe. He both loves God and despises him. He is utterly skeptical, yet he dares to hope. Linguistically, this is all nonsense. Rationally, this is incoherent. Nonetheless, the "both-and" quality of Gavriel's fragmented faith represents the truth for Gavriel at the level of lived experience. His story, a reflection of Wiesel's and Nachman's, is a "both-and" tale. Says another character in *Gates* regarding Gavriel: "You don't know yet that a man can laugh while he suffers."[91]

Gavriel's laughter manifests his paradoxical, language-crippling struggle to hold both narratives of faith and negativity, neither of which can be willingly jettisoned, in tensive relationship. We recall that when rational, discursive thought failed Rebbe Nachman, he abandoned it, turning instead to communication not through logic but through the imaginative medium of storytelling. Similarly, Gavriel tells his multivalent stories to Gregor and laughs at points of collision between these stories. Whereas discursive and theological language strive toward systematic clarity and thus reductively force thought into "either/or" distinctions, laughter allows Gavriel to escape the either/or choice between the narratives. The Holocaust, Wiesel believes, enshrouds all thought in radical ambiguity, precluding facile either/or distinctions: "Ambiguity is the name of our sickness, of everybody's sickness. What are we looking for in life, in existence, in history, in our own being? For the One to do away with ambiguity."[92] The trope of laughter provides Wiesel a means to communicate ambiguity. Wiesel uses such laughter as a stopgap in his storytelling, a reminder that contradictions still await redemption. In the words of Martin Buber: "Central to Hasidism is faithfully to endure the contradiction and thus to redeem the contradiction itself."[93]

Wiesel uses the trope of the laughter of the oppressed in *Gates* to sustain the broken, paradoxical, and contradictory character of post–Holocaust faith. Fortunately, Rebbe Nachman already in the 18th century understood a collision of narratives to be central to hasidic faith, thus providing Wiesel with an available avenue of continuity, and not contradiction, with his hasidic heritage. On a personal level, Wiesel states the paradox of Holocaust survival in this way: "Because I remember I despair. Because I remember, I have the duty to reject despair."[94] At the narrative level, Gavriel explains to Gregor:

> You mustn't forget laughter either. Do you know what laughter is? I'll tell you, it's God's mistake. When God made man in order to bend him to his wishes he carelessly gave him the gift of laughter. Little did he know that later that earthworm would use it as a weapon of vengeance. When he found out, there was nothing he could do; it was too late to take back the gift. And yet he tried his best. He drove man out of paradise, invented an infinite variety of sins and punishments, and made him conscious of his own nothingness, all in order to prevent him from laughing.... God made a mistake before man made his.[95]

According to Gavriel, then, laughter is paradoxically both gift and weapon, a holy and audacious thing much like hasidic song, which according to the tale's rebbe represents both joy and dagger. Gavriel portrays laughter as a 'weapon of vengeance' not only against those who oppress but also against Godself. Wiesel says that Rebbe Nachman "complained to God about God."[96] Angry with Moshe the Beadle for not hastening redemption, Gavriel laughs and then screams in protest: "If this is God's will, then deny it! The time has come for you to impose your will upon His, to pin Him to the wall.... You'll be damned? So what."[97] Gavriel and his laughter personify what Wiesel describes as "supreme defiance" and "supreme faith against faith."[98]

Gavriel's risibility is a weapon in that it angrily accuses God of injustice in the midst of tragic-suffering and expresses resistance to the absurd horror that appears to have overtaken God's creation. Like the biblical Sarah, Gavriel with his laughter challenges God to faithfulness and fulfillment of God's incongruous promises. Gavriel's laughter, like Sarah's, emerges out of an incongruous collision of narratives and summons the divine to divine faithfulness. Laughter is a "mistake" because it allows human beings to hold God accountable to God's creation; it allows us to criticize God and in particular, God's absence. Nonetheless, laughter is the link that keeps the divine-human relationship alive. Proclaims Gavriel: "God likes those who stand up to him."[99]

In the Jewish tradition, in the holy books the divine name is written as a string of consonants, absent the vowels — YHWH, often referred to as the Tetragrammaton. The Tetragrammaton signifies the extent of divine holiness; YHWH is so holy the divine name can never be spoken or fully written. The incompleteness of the divine name in Hebrew further symbolizes the great distance between the human and the holy, between humanity and G-d (the word holy literally means separate or set apart). The inconclusive, gapped spelling of the divine name suggests that the divine story and perspective can never fully be understood by humanity. But for the hasidim like Wiesel and Nachman, human stories possess a holiness of their own. They too symbolize the chasm between G-d and human beings, yet from the reverse perspective, from below. Nachman and Wiesel's stories audaciously suggest that human stories of despair and suffering elude divine comprehension. The divine and hasidic stories each have gaps that as yet remain unfilled, not fully grasped by the respective covenant partner. The hasidim tenaciously hold out hope that their stories will mend the world. Their storytelling aims to bring all of these stories together into one, as they were in the beginning before the *Shekhinah* went into exile during Creation.

Through the Torah, then, YHWH tells his stories from the divine perspective. Through hasidic storytelling, YHWH's people including Elie Wiesel give their stories from the human perspective back to YHWH. Wiesel's stories, like the laughter found within their pages, are both gift and weapon. The culture of Bratzlavian storytelling demands that they must also be weapon, because the relationship between Yahweh and his people is in perennial crisis. In a world filled with doubt, despair, suffering, and the experience of a seemingly godless universe, the full story of the divine-human covenant cannot be told without both sides represented. Relatedly, each human story is incomplete without everyone else's. Wiesel tells his stories to remind us that no one human story taken alone tells the "whole story." Wiesel tells stories also to remind G-d of the extraordinary pain of human suffering over G-d's absence as well as of the equally extraordinary yearning of our hope for His redemption and presence. Until such time as the world is redeemed and this paradox is resolved, I suspect that Wiesel will continue to tell stories with laughing characters. Wiesel the storyteller begs us to hear their laughter and to join in Gavriel's summons to G-d to be G-d and actualize a much-awaited redemption: "I think of nothing else. That's the way we're made, I guess, to be blinded by presence and haunted by absence. I think of him all the time and I laugh."[100]

In conclusion, laughter is Wiesel the storyteller's means of pointing out to both G-d and listener that the divine story is a story with incomprehensible gaps. Laughter functions within the tale as a stopgap — a supralinguistic sign which acknowledges that language, and even the story itself, fail to fill the gaps in our theological understanding. G-d alone can ultimately remove them and until God does so, storytelling remains a *mitzvah* for the hasidim and for every Jew at the Passover *seder*. The human story cannot be fully told, just as the Torah can never be fully understood or its stories told enough times. No telling is exhaustive or definitive. This is the strength and beauty of stories, as well as their limitation and anguish. Rather than jettison belief in G-d and relationship with G-d, Wiesel, like Rebbe Nachman, tells stories that sustain the relationship with G-d when prayer and logic have failed to achieve this end. The story is the crucial but tenuous link that holds the divine and human together. Though it is never enough, it must be enough. To remind us of this truth, we end where Wiesel's story begins, with the final words of the hasidic tale, which serve as an epigraph to *The Gates of the Forest:*

> Then it fell to Rabbi Israel of Rizyn to overcome misfortune. Sitting in his armchair, his head in his hands, he spoke to God: "I am unable to light the fire and I do not know the prayer; I cannot even find the place in the forest. All I can do is to tell the story, and this must be sufficient. And it was sufficient."

Notes

1. Elie Wiesel, et al., *Dimensions of the Holocaust: Lectures at Northwestern University* (Evanston: Northwestern University, 1977), 8.

2. Elie Wiesel, *The Gates of the Forest*, trans. Frances Frenaye (New York: Schocken Books, 1996), 34.

3. *Gates of the Forest* is the best choice for our analysis because the word laughter and its derivatives occur in this text more times than in any other of Wiesel's work.

4. Yitzhak Buxbaum, *Storytelling and Spirituality in Judaism* (Northvale, N.J.: Jason Aronson, Inc., 1994), 7; 49; 89.

5. Ibid., 215.

6. Elie Wiesel, *Souls on Fire: Portraits and Legends of Hasidic Masters*, trans. Marion Wiesel (New York: Random House, 1972), 7.

7. Elie Wiesel, *Four Hasidic Masters and Their Struggle Against Melancholy* (Notre Dame: University of Notre Dame Press, 1978), 123. Note that two variant, acceptable spellings of Nachman and Bratzlav exist in the literature — Nachman or Nahman

and Bratslav or Bratzlav. These terms are used interchangeably and account for the different spellings found in this chapter.

8. Wiesel, *Souls on Fire*, 180.

9. David G. Roskies, "The Master of Prayer Rabbi Nahman of Bratslav," in *God's Voice from the Void: Old and New Studies in Bratslav Hasidism*, ed. Shaul Magid (Albany: State University of New York Press, 2002), 71; 96.

10. Buxbaum, *Storytelling and Spirituality*, 11.

11. Y. David Shulman, *The Chambers of the Palace: Teachings of Rabbi Nachman of Bratslav* (Northvale, New Jersey: Jason Aronson, Inc., 1993), 74.

12. Yaffa Eliach, *Hasidic Tales of the Holocaust* (New York: Vintage Books, 1982), xix–xx.

13. Wiesel, *Four Hasidic Masters*, 13; 15.

14. Shulman, *The Chambers of the Palace*, 74.

15. Wiesel, *Souls on Fire*, 175.

16. For Nachman's comments on the role of imagination, see Arthur Green, *Tormented Master: The Life and Spiritual Quest of Rabbi Nahman of Bratslav* (Woodstock, Vt.: Jewish Lights Publishing, 1992), 342.

17. Roskies, "The Master of Prayer Rabbi Nahman of Bratslav," 71.

18. Ora W. Elper, *Tradition and Fantasy in the Tales of Reb Nahman of Bratslav* (Albany: State University of New York Press, 1998), 49.

19. Wiesel, *Souls on Fire*, 181.

20. Elie Wiesel, *The Forgotten*, trans. Stephen Becker (New York: Summit Books, 1992), 237.

21. Wiesel, *Souls on Fire*, 182.

22. Buxbaum, *Storytelling and Spirituality*, 52.

23. Eliach, *Hasidic Tales of the Holocaust*, xxi.

24. Green, *Tormented Master*, 33.

25. Ibid., 40.

26. Ibid., 80–81.

27. Wiesel, *The Gates of the Forest*, 48.

28. Wiesel, *A Beggar in Jerusalem*, 162.

29. Alvin H. Rosenfeld and Irving Greenberg, ed., *Confronting the Holocaust: The Impact of Elie Wiesel* (Bloomington: Indiana University Press, 1978), xii.

30. Wiesel, *Souls on Fire*, 7.

31. Wiesel, *The Forgotten*, 113.

32. Elie Wiesel, *Ethics and Memory* (New York: Walter de Gruyter, 1997), 13.

33. Lawrence Langer, ed., *Art from the Ashes: A Holocaust Anthology* (New York: Oxford University Press, 1995), 605.

34. Wiesel, *Dimensions of the Holocaust*, 8.

35. Susan Shapiro, "Hearing the Testimony of Radical Negation," *Concilium*, 175 (1984): 6.

36. Green, *Tormented Master*, 294.

37. Ibid., 300.

38. Ibid., 316.

39. In a sermon in 1809, Nachman reinterpreted Gen 1:26, "Let us make man in our image," as "Let us make man endowed with an imagination." See Green, *Tormented Master*, 341.

40. Elie Wiesel and Michael de Saint Cheron, *Evil and Exile*, trans. Jon Rothschild (Notre Dame: University of Notre Dame Press, 1990), 172.

41. Elie Wiesel, *Messengers of God: Biblical Portraits and Legends*, trans. Marion Wiesel (New York: Random House, 1976), 97.

42. Quoted in Joe Friedemann, *Le Rire dans l'Univers Tragique d'Elie Wiesel* (Paris: A.-G. Nizet, 1981), 28. My translation.

43. Wiesel, *The Gates of the Forest*, 3.

44. Ibid., 7.

45. Ibid., 7.

46. Ibid., 8.

47. Ibid., 7.

48. Ibid., 34.

49. Ibid., 13.

50. Quoted in Green, *Tormented Master*, 305.

51. Quoted in Green, *Tormented Master*, 58 and in Wiesel, *Souls on Fire*, 190.

52. The *badkhan* character is found in numerous hasidic tales, particularly in those that Wiesel chooses to retell in *Four Hasidic Masters*. See on page 101, the tale about Rebbe Naphtali, in which the Maggid exclaims, "Naphthali, Naphthali, are you aware of your own strength? What I cannot accomplish with my tears, you accomplish with laughter!"

53. Green, *Tormented Master*, 68.

54. Wiesel, *Souls on Fire*, 198–199.

55. Green, *Tormented Master*, 287.

56. Ibid., 27.

57. Wiesel, *The Gates of the Forest*, 198.

58. Green, *Tormented Master*, 52.

59. Wiesel and de Saint Cheron, *Evil and Exile*, 11.

60. Green, *Tormented Master*, 291.

61. See Green, *Tormented Master*, 54.

62. Green, *Tormented Master*, 108.

63. Quoted in Green, *Tormented Master*, 298.

64. Ibid.

65. Wiesel, *The Gates of the Forest*, 48.

66. Ibid., 33.

67. Green, *Tormented Master*, 297.

68. Elie Wiesel, *From the Kingdom of Memory* (New York: Summit Books, 1990), 183.

69. Quoted in Green, *Tormented Master*, 262; 329.

70. Ibid., 306.

71. Wiesel, *The Gates of the Forest*, 170.

72. Ibid., 225.

73. Green, *Tormented Master*, 305.

74. Wiesel, *Messengers of God*, 234.

75. Mordechai Rotenberg, *Dialogue With Deviance: The Hasidic Ethic and The Theory of Social Contraction* (Philadelphia: Institute for the Study of Human Issues, 1983), 183.

76. Ekkehard Schuster and Reinhold Boscher-Kimmig, *Hope Against Hope: Johann Baptist Metz and Elie Wiesel Speak Out on the Holocaust*, trans. J. Matthew Ashley (New York: Paulist Press, 1962), 95.

77. Quoted in Green, *Tormented Master*, 311.

78. Wiesel, *Four Hasidic Masters*, 91.

79. Kenneth Surin, "Taking Suffering Seriously," in *The Problem of Evil: Selected Readings,* ed. Michael L. Peterson (Notre Dame: University of Notre Dame Press, 1992), 344.

80. Wiesel, *The Gates of the Forest,* 87.

81. Ibid., 197.

82. Theodor Adorno, *Negative Dialectics,* trans. E. B. Ashton (New York: Continuum, 1966), 401–402.

83. Wiesel, *The Gates of the Forest,* 9.

84. Ibid., 194.

85. Ibid., 3.

86. Wiesel, *From the Kingdom of Memory,* 183.

87. Emil Fackenheim, "Midrashic Existence after the Holocaust: Reflections Occasioned by the Work of Elie Wiesel," in *Confronting the Holocaust: The Impact of Elie Wiesel,* ed., Alvin H. Rosenfeld and Irving Greenberg (Bloomington: Indiana University Press, 1978), 99.

88. John Morreall, ed., *The Philosophy of Laughter and Humor* (Albany: State University of New York Press, 1986), 54–55.

89. Wiesel, *The Gates of the Forest,* 204.

90. Ibid., 47.

91. Ibid., 174.

92. Harry James Cargas, *Harry James Cargas in Conversation with Elie Wiesel* (New York: Paulist Press, 1976), 18.

93. Martin Buber, *The Origin and the Meaning of Hasidism,* trans. Maurice Friedman (New York: Harper and Row, 1966), 178.

94. Wiesel, *From the Kingdom of Memory,* 248.

95. Wiesel, *The Gates of the Forest,* 21.

96. Wiesel, *Souls on Fire,* 176.

97. Wiesel, *The Gates of the Forest,* 48.

98. Cargas, *Cargas in Conversation with Elie Wiesel,* 111.

99. Wiesel, *The Gates of the Forest,* 31.

100. Ibid., 48.

Transfiguration

GRAHAM B. WALKER JR.

In the Fall of 1998, I was privileged to attend the Andrew W. Mellon Lecture Series at Boston University. This is the annual lecture series given by Elie Wiesel. The invitation was given by Wiesel himself in response to a book I wrote some ten years earlier identifying various theological challenges presented by his writing. The morning of the first lecture I was given the opportunity to interview Wiesel. As usual, one meets such moments with a sense of awe and stupor in one's life. Yet, I managed to articulate a few questions about which I sought clarification concerning his writing. One event, however, I did not anticipate was the correction I received when I referred to *Night* as a novel. Almost in midsentence, Elie Wiesel corrected my categorical error and referred to *Night* as autobiographical history. I am sure we discussed other matters that morning, but that simple correction has haunted my perception of his self-identification as a writer for years. Where does Wiesel's writing stand on the line between history and fiction? What is the role between the two? Is there a way these two modes of narration converge with respect to what we know today as the Holocaust? In large measure, this essay proposes a response to these questions.

When it comes to *Night*, the issue of categorization was not mine alone. Daniel R. Schwarz writes:

> I am interested not in indicting Wiesel for transforming his nominalistic memoir into novelistic form, but in how, in response to publishing circumstances and perhaps his own transformation, he reconfigured an existential novel about the descent into moral night into a somewhat affirmative reemergence to life. While the narrator is a fifteen-year-old

boy, Wiesel was born in 1928 and would have been sixteen for most of the 1944–45 period. Is not this age discrepancy one reason why we ought to think of *Night* as a novel as well as memoir?[1]

Naomi Seidman has traced the significant changes in the text that was to become *Night*. The Yiddish text was submitted in 1954, yet in 1956 it appeared as volume 117 of a series on Polish Jews entitled *Dos Poylishe Yidntum* [*Polish Jewry*]. Wiesel's Yiddish title is better known as *Un di Velt Hot Geshvign* [*And the World Remained Silent*]. Seidman notes that the Yiddish documentary testimony was edited in the translation process to the French *La Nuit* with the effect of positioning the memoir within a different literary genre. She writes, "Wiesel and his French publishing house fashioned something closer to mythopoetic narrative."[2]

It is precisely what Seidman calls the "mythopoetic narrative" that I believe provides the crucial interface between history and fiction for Wiesel. The paradigm for this convergence may be found in Aristotle's discussion of the linkage between mythos and mimesis in *Poetics*. Nelson Goodman describes this as the convergence of the two narrative poles by identifying the role of fiction as a reorganizing of the world in terms of works and the works in terms of the world.[3] The novel, for Wiesel, re-describes what conventional language has already attempted to describe. Wiesel's need to "redescribe the world" may help to explain the "reconfiguration" that Schwarz notes in *Night*. Wiesel's "somewhat affirmative reemergence to life" as noted by Schwarz is not so much a reconfiguration as a transfiguration with the intent of drawing together mythos and mimesis in human action.

Wiesel re-describes the world for a post–Holocaust generation in direct contradiction to a literary history that locates the protagonist on a continuum between the individual rebel and the obedient martyr. In Western culture, death is often portrayed as a stage toward salvation; it becomes a rite of passage from disorder and injustice to order and fulfillment. Sacrificial death is highly valued whereby one man or woman obedient to a given value system offers up his or her life for the community in order to preserve those values for the living. But a vision of salvation that depends upon ritual death seems woefully inadequate for contemporary emulation. As Wiesel says in an interview with the Christian novelist François Mauriac:

> Sir ... you speak of Christ. Christians love to speak of him. The passion of Christ, the agony of Christ, the death of Christ. In your religion, that is all you speak of. Well, I want you to know that ten years ago, not very far from here, I knew Jewish children every one of whom suffered a thousand times more, six million times more, than Christ on the cross. And we don't speak about them. Can you understand that, sir? We don't speak about them.[4]

The survivor is Wiesel's protagonist — humanity between the archetypes of rebellion and submission. The survivor is the meeting place where the ontological absurdity of the Holocaust meets with the transcendent hope for the future. Wiesel's survivor, the mythopoesis of continuance, the Wanderer, is one who cannot be contained within the archetypes so familiar to the Western literary tradition: Christ or Faust.

Christ or Faust

Harold Fisch outlines the archetypes of Faust as an image of rebellion and Christ as an image of submission in his book *A Remembered Future*.[5] In the Christ image, God chooses to be with man; in the Faust image, man strives to be God. These two images present two of the major responses to oppression and victimization in our world today. If one follows the archetype of the Christ, then one is obedient to the ideals for which one submits to the extreme abuses which the oppressor affords. However, if one chooses the path of Faust, then the lust for power and control are what will separate one from any would-be oppressor. The Christ figure is the portrait of integrity that conquers a violent world by refusing to participate in it and thus is not reduced to its level of violence. Christ willingly and painfully dies for the greater truth — and through death, he enters that truth. Faust, however, is the rebel who violently defies the authoritarian conqueror; and though he is eventually defeated by some force greater than his own, he does not submit without a fight. Faust makes his stand against the demonic by employing the demonic for his own services.

The submissive model of Christ is sometimes morbidly human. A strong sense of tragedy and the severe dread of death define two of the characteristics associated with those faithful who focus on the submissive Christ. The submissive Christ is the victim who satisfies the violent world's tortures, exchanging his pain for the faithful followers. This Christ is celebrated most during the Passion week, when the faithful reenact the step-by-step march to the cross. The faithful feel death in all its horror as they identify with the victim. This identification increases a sense of passion for life, dread of death, and thanksgiving because their immortality is bought at such a high price. The submissive vision of Christ, however, also produces that ancient rage as the faithful look for a scapegoat "to pay the price" for the victim's agonizing death. It is this by-product of the submissive Christ, the projection of the causes of suffering onto others (e.g. the Jews) that is most dangerous about this model.

Another characteristic of this submissive Christ is his docetic worldlessness. He is regarded as a purely supernatural being who is only veiled in humanity. The submissive Christ, therefore, offers immortality but no ethical vision of life here and now. This Christ is entirely "otherworldly." He is known, only by his death, as a passageway through life's sorrows and the means of entering into the afterlife.

The image of Faust was originally portrayed by Marlowe in *Doctor Faustus*. This Faust was a medieval scholar who turned to magic and the dark sciences to achieve power over political and religious empires. Faust used his magical powers to transcend ordinary humanity. Magic and alchemy are perfect symbols for Faust, who sought to transcend his fellow humanity; magic is a participation in the substance of the divine which allows one to exert control over all others. Faust sought the power of God. This was Faust's release from a violent world: He could control the very sources of violence. Magic was his ultimate freedom from solidarity with the world. He could be powerfully alone with himself. Faust's life is a marriage between heaven and hell; if he must live in this world, then he will live in it with power. The danger of this archetype is that it breeds annihilation. There is always someone stronger. There is always more magic. Finally, this archetype rejects solidarity with the rest of humanity and in the end this only denies a fundamental need of all humans: belongingness.

A New Archetype

Wiesel's protagonist offers a new way forward that participates in neither the Faust image nor the Christ image. Choosing neither the ambiguities of murderous power (Faust) nor active submission to victimization (Christ), Wiesel identifies a more suitable image than the traditional victim or rebel. In short, he suggests a conception of post–Holocaust humanity defined by "incessant motion" and teleology based on the voices of those forgotten in history. In short, the narrative conclusion is still becoming. This new humanity is pulled in two directions simultaneously: on the one hand by the memory of the victims, the absurdity of their death, and on the other by a transcendent hope for the future which has no foundation in the past. Because the absurdity of death cannot be forgotten, cannot be justified as meaningful in any system of thought, and because the past cannot be relived, the survivor is the meeting place of the living and the dead. The survivor's struggle is a form of "wandering" without resolution. He creates a hope for the future generation by warning from the past. The one link between these past realities and future possibilities is the survivor.

The submissive Christ and the Faust archetypes are necessarily static images. The submissive Christ suffers his agony on the cross to redeem humanity from living in this world, thereby justifying suffering and his eventual death as a necessary means for the greater good of the afterlife. Faust, meanwhile, exchanges his afterlife for a moment of defiant victory in life. Each and every moment in either the submissive Christ image or the Faust image is subservient to the fixed roles established by the mythic structure from which the images emerged. This structure tends to be ritualistic and circular. In each case, these archetypes accept death as a means toward a greater good. In the case of the survivor, however, suffering does not lead to saintliness or power. For the survivor, suffering and death are not the answers; suffering and death are only questions.

A predominant literary convention that Wiesel uses to unite his protagonists with the narrative voice of the survivor is "the Wanderer." This pilgrim structure is essential for Wiesel because of its creative potential in communicating both the story of pain and an impetus for hope. The wanderer is the bearer of a historical record that holds us as readers in suspense, in tension between a remembered past and the prospects of the future. Accordingly, certain "spots of time" come to us weighed with significance. These events, borne by the wanderer, break the harmony of historic analogy by their intrusion into our lives and their concreteness. These events discredit the circularity of time and our sense of wellbeing and wholeness. What we do with these memories is our responsibility; the vehicle is the wanderer.

Ultimately, this is Wiesel's most penetrating challenge. In the following hasidic story Wiesel metaphorically illustrates the predicament of language and the challenge for those of us who seek to live within it.

> And it came to pass that the traveler lost his way in the forest. He walked and walked day and night, all by himself, full of fear and crushed by fatigue. And suddenly he saw a castle and was overcome with joy. Then he saw that the castle was burning, and he was overcome with sadness. It must be an empty castle, thought the wanderer. But then he heard a voice crying, "Help me, help me. I am the owner of the castle." And the solitary Rebbe of Kotsk, who quoted this midrashic tale, pounded the table with his fist shouting, "the castle is ablaze, the wanderer is lost, the forest is burning, but the owner is calling for help. What does it mean? It means there is an owner." And for us [says Wiesel], we would paraphrase the story and say, "The castle is ablaze; the wanderer is lost; the forest is burning; the entire world is burning, and we are still inside, inside the burning castle."[6]

The Diviner of Silence

Wiesel's protagonist viator is constructed against the literary terrain of silence and Wiesel's struggle with silence begins in his book *Night*. The order of Wiesel's life prior to the Holocaust consisted of the unity of the world of words with the speaking of God in the Torah. The order of Wiesel's life in the small Hungarian town of Sighet was God-intoxicated, insulated, and protected from most of the outside world. The rural and unmolested life of Sighet created a sense of belongingness, security, and longing for the Messiah characteristic of a covenant people. In this world the Torah conveyed the very presence of God. The Torah, as the word of God, provided the framework wherein the interplay of God and humanity united in harmony. Lawrence Cunningham, however, expresses the inversion of Wiesel's world, a collapse into silence, which began in 1944:

> What has largely been overlooked is that Wiesel, writing some years after these events, frames the story of that inversion in terms of the oldest "biography" of his own people: the story of the Exodus. The life-giving biblical myth of election, liberation, covenant, and promise becomes the vehicle for telling the story of the unnatural order of death-domination. It is as if Wiesel, either consciously or unconsciously, felt constrained to

write a near parody of the Exodus story in order to give reality and urgency to the story that he feels is his vocation to tell and tell again.[7]

And just as the Exodus experience preceded the giving of the word in the Covenant, so also the "Anti-Exodus constitutes the experience which reduced the word to silence."[8] In *Night* there is a slow, progressive deconstruction of the word of tradition to the point that "God," the most secure and benevolent word of any tradition, hangs on a gallows, dying. The silencing power of the Holocaust world order begins to modulate in *Night* until it is the only reality which remains at the conclusion of the story. In Wiesel's subsequent novels the interplay between silence and the word forms a pronounced dichotomy focusing on the conflict of the mute survivor who must somehow live with the two worlds of Exodus and Anti-Exodus struggling for control.

The significance of the "God on the gallows" and the silencing of tradition is clearly articulated in *Night*. Cunningham again observes:

> Thus, the ancient dialogue between God and men now turned into a long and progressive silence in which the desert experience of Auschwitz and Buchenwald obscured and muted the presence of God.... The unfolding of this death becomes clearer in the novel if careful attention is paid to the parallel that Wiesel sets up between the death of his father and the death of his God.[9]

What Cunningham shows is the clear link in Wiesel's writing between God-talk and human experience. The radical questioning of a benevolent and unified world order is evident in the image of "God hanging on the gallows." The absence of a benevolent world order is not merely a privation of the good, rather, it indicates the raging presence of an ungovernable force which destroys the Holocaust survivor's sense of well-being and at-homeness. However this malevolent order is understood, it is experienced as indescribable terror.

Thematically, there are at least two kinds of silence in Wiesel's novels: the silence of possibility, community, and creativity; and the silence of chaos, solitude, and destruction.

> As a child I studied the Talmud, and also mysticism. My master was a mystic. And silence, in mysticism, is extremely important; it's the essential. What you don't say carries weight. For instance, I wondered many times: within our tradition we know what God said at Sinai. But there are

certain silences between word and word. How was this silence transmitted? This is the silence that I tried to put in my work, and I tried to link it to that silence, the silence of Sinai. There is a healthy silence, Sinai, and an unhealthy silence, that of chaos before creation.[10]

Night confirms the silence of nonbeing and chaos by tracing the protagonist, Eliezer, from security within his tradition to the silencing of the word in the death camps. Eliezer asks: "Why should I bless His [God's] name?" This is the outcry of the fifteen-year-old boy who cannot prevent the mass murder of children, family, and friends. He is a boy who laments the loss of creative, mystical silence, and the loss of the security of tradition. The security of the tradition has been supplanted by the silence of nonbeing in the death camps.

In the foreword to *Night,* François Mauriac says this outcry is "the death of God in the soul of child who suddenly discovers absolute evil."[11] As the story develops, it is on the eve of Rosh Hashanah that Eliezer, who had been a devout Jewish child until the death camps, cries out:

> Why, but why should I bless Him? In every fiber I rebelled. Because He has thousands of children burned in His pits? Because He kept six crematories working night and day, on Sundays and feast days? Because in His great might He had created Auschwitz, Birkenau, Buna, and so many factories of death? How could I say to him: "Blessed art Thou, Eternal, Master of the Universe, who chose us from among the races to be tortured day and night, to see our fathers, our mothers, our brothers, end in the crematory? Praised be Thy Holy Name, Thou Who hast chosen us to be butchered on Thine Altar?"[12]

After the Holocaust, Eliezer could no longer speak of God's unified goodness or his ultimate purpose. Eliezer, the student of the Talmud and Kabbalah, finds that these words of tradition could not contend with the oppressive silencing of the death camps.

Eliezer was transformed from a young boy with faith secure in the shelter of his image of God — the Protector, Redeemer, Law-giver — into an orphan old and theologically homeless before his time. He lost his father without tears; he lost his faith in God's goodness; and he lost hope in humanity's potential for doing good. With the justice of God, the restraints of twentieth century Judeo-Christian civilization, and the bonds of his family stripped away, Eliezer experienced the collapse of the word into silence — a dimension of silence previously unimaginable. At the conclusion of *Night* the young Jew Eliezer cannot even find the language to ask questions of the abysmal reality created by the Nazi world order.

Silence received new meaning because words usually assigned the task of creating community formed no community; rather, these same words were transformed into a chamber of horrors in the death camps — "chosen" now meant chosen to die. All that was left of the Holocaust victim and for the Holocaust survivor was silence — not the mystical silence of Eliezer's youth, but a polluted silence, because millions were "forgotten by God, forsaken by Him, they lived alone, suffered alone, fought alone."[13] Historical memory rendered those who entered the death camps voiceless, and for Wiesel the world's silence was matched only by the silence of God. In this silence all hope in world order and all linguistic promise were negated. What kinds of words could possibly communicate this event without continually legitimating it?

Language had been corrupted to the point that it must be invented anew, but this is an impossible task. Language had to be purified somehow: "This time we wrote not with words but against words," says Wiesel.[14]

By writing he only hopes to communicate the impossibility of communicating "total silence" because it is impossible to invent new language, new words. They must, therefore, be in tension with each other. Yet, does the inexpressible horror of the Holocaust, even inadequately communicated, act as a purifying agent for the reconstruction of a world of words?

Andre Neher suggests that Wiesel is a diviner of silence, and that a computer would doubtless inform us that no literary creation of the twentieth century evokes silence with such variety, intensity, and diversity as that of Elie Wiesel.[15] Terrence Des Pres concurs with Neher, suggesting that "silence, and the tension between silence and the need of the witness to speak, is the matrix of meaning on which Wiesel's accomplishment stands."[16] Neher offers at least two suggestive sources of silence in Wiesel's writing that require brief investigation: scenic and phenomenological silence.

Scenic Silence

Literary characters exist and move in a literary space, a setting, which exists prior to any activity of the protagonist or any other character. For

Wiesel, this literary space is characterized by scenic silence. Typologically, a clear polarity exists between the characters of the story and their setting. In this respect the chief function of the setting is to contribute to the mood of the narrative. *Night* introduces silence as the setting for all Wiesel's following novels. Typically, the setting is comprised of physical structures and events which "frame" the significance that grows out of the social, moral, and cultural action of the story. There is a shift of settings in *Night*—a reversal, to be accurate. The setting of *Night* begins in Wiesel's home in Sighet and shifts to the silence after the Holocaust. Instead of the action of the story becoming the focus, it is the shift of settings that takes center stage. The actions of the story are step-by-step illustrations of the metamorphosis that is occurring below the surface. The context of the world is changing as the story *Night* develops. The original setting creates the mood of peace and security, and the transformation of this setting shifts the mood of the story to terror and loss. The very fact that Wiesel does not focus on the death camps as the action of the story to be resolved shows that he has weighed the Holocaust ontologically; it becomes the ground of the life which Wiesel spends his life acting against.

The atmosphere of *Night* represents to a great extent what a story communicates to us as readers. When we travel through the various scenes of the text, we are left with nothing but Wiesel's experience by which to judge what has been communicated to us in the story. Inevitably we will experience an "absence," a gap, which exists between Wiesel and us because the worlds we do not share. This lack of identification, this vacuum between Wiesel and us, allows a wide variety of responses on our part to his works. Wiesel, however, focuses our vision by establishing concentric circles of discourse around the historicity of *Night*. He refers us to the event of the Holocaust to fill the gaps in our understanding.

Yet, Wiesel's reference to the historical events of the Holocaust only creates further gaps and dissonance because understanding of the Holocaust lacks any degree of the horror experienced there. Wiesel thematically uses "silence" as the structural basis for referring to the historical events. Wiesel struggles to draw some portrait of the death camps because of the enormous burden he carries to let the victims of this world speak to future generations. The silent members of the event must not go unnoticed.

Wiesel maintains this scenic silence as an almost sacred silence toward the events of the Holocaust. As far as he is concerned no referential code of words can encompass, contain, enclose, or solve the events to which he refers. Since a gap must remain between Wiesel and us that cannot be bridged, Wiesel's use of thematic silence makes this a conscious and structured gap. In this sense the structure of Wiesel's novels takes seriously Michael Wyschogrod's warning:

> Art takes the sting out of suffering. It transforms suffering into a catharsis for which people are willing to pay money to experience.... Any attempt to transform the holocaust into art demeans the holocaust and must result in poor art.[17]

The problem is that art denies what it seeks to accentuate — the dehumanization which was so focused in the Holocaust. Instead, art enshrines dehumanization. Art sets in motion a dilemma: To surrender the world of the Holocaust to silence is to reverence the horror of the event but also to run the risk of dismissing it, forgetting it, and denying that it was possible. To speak of the event, to portray it artistically, reduces it, giving it manageable boundaries, offering it form and beauty.

Nevertheless, Wiesel speaks against this backdrop and need for silence. Silence is maintained as an ontological setting for what happened in the Holocaust, but this same silence must be broached in order that history may record the voice of the voiceless. The traditional characters of history include the heroes of tradition and the enemies of tradition. These two opposing figures include the subtypes of tragic heroes and tragic figures. The tragic heroes are all those who "die for the cause"; they suffer for the ideal; they are willing to sacrifice their life for the future of others; they sanctify death. Their death is a noble death. On the other hand, the tragic figure personifies the portrait of "hubris," pride. The tragic figure rebels against the limitations of his finitude by denying his solidarity with the rest of humanity thereby maintaining his own life at whatever cost it may exact from others. His self-denial and hubris inevitably destroy him because his lust for power separates him from all others. He becomes isolated and inevitably stands alone with his finitude, without community.

Unlike either of these traditional characters in history, the Holocaust victim and survivor are not allowed to speak in history because they fit none of the normative patterns. They do not reinforce the group ideal, that is, the hero; they do not demonstrate personal sacrifice for the group ideal, that is, the tragic hero; they do not demonstrate corporate evil, that is, the enemy; and finally, they do not demonstrate personal arrogance and pride, that is, the tragic figure. Their story is suppressed and repressed because they represent neither the ideal nor its anti-type, and more often than not, historical records attempt to forget rather than remember victims and survivors. Thus they are *lost in history.*

Phenomenological Silence

Scenic silence establishes the ontological status of silence in Wiesel's writing, but Wiesel also uses the theme of silence phenomenologically as a subject of his stories. In his writing, silence moves from the unspeakable dimension of the setting to the foreground as the muted silence of the victim and the purging silence of the mystic, which cleanses language that has become *the* receptacle of nonbeing.

Wiesel's protagonists begin with an awareness of suffering so great that it draws them into a silence where no discourse is possible — *a mute silence. The* extremity of the external conditions has destroyed the very ability to speak. This is senseless suffering in which the people affected no longer have any possibility of determining a course of action, of learning from their experience, or taking measures that would change anything. They become examples of suffering so extreme that it leads to the abandonment of all hope except survival. They are reduced to endurance alone.

This pain is so intense that it isolates individuals from others, and they no longer can care for another. The block leader in *Night* tells Eliezer that even survival demands isolation.

> Listen to me, boy. Don't forget that you're in a concentration camp. Here every man has to fight for himself and not think of anyone else. Even of his father. Here, there are no fathers, no brothers, no friends. Everyone lives and dies for himself alone.[18]

Death becomes increasingly attractive. Everything recedes into the setting of scenic silence. This degree of suffering destroys a person's ability to communicate, making it impossible to say anything about the incurable destruction.

Night further demonstrates that language may lose its house of being. The vocabulary of election, of covenant, and of chosenness may alternatively mean chosen for the ovens. Speech is problematic, because any language may both reveal and conceal. Wiesel is more radical: The same language that approaches truth also approaches deception. Consequently, Wiesel uses silence as a strategy for purging and interrogating language and not just for the extension of a collapsed linguistic order — a *transcendent silence*. Therefore, the creative and purging characteristics of silence extend the depth of silence in Wiesel's works. He states:

> We say, for instance, that one way of purifying man is to purify his language, his word. How does one purify it? Through silence. What is prayer if not the exclusion of certain words, the protection of others, the creation of a certain zone of silence between one word and another.[19]

Wiesel declares even more specifically: "In the beginning there was the Holocaust. We must start all over again."[20] The tension between the tradition's at-homeness in words and explanations and Wiesel's experience of the silence between the words continues in *The Oath*.

A Dilemma of Word and Silence

The storyteller in Wiesel's *The Oath* was on the verge of suicide, but the old man Azriel tells the young man his painful story of the past in order to save the young man from self-destruction. Azriel, the old sage, tells the story of a bloody pogrom. The Gentile cycle of murdering the Jews was repeated in Kolvillag, and Azriel is now torn between two responses to the tragedy: Should he tell the chronicles of Kolvillag, chronicles of an endless history of murder, or should he keep his sworn oath of silence? Fifty years earlier, Moshe, a mystic and Azriel's teacher, persuaded the Jewish community to take an oath of silence: "our ancestors and forebears could not or dared not. We are going to impose the ultimate challenge, not by language but by the absence of language.... We shall testify no more."[21]

Everyone present took the oath: Whoever would survive would never speak of the town's last days and nights of terror, and anyone breaking the oath would be cursed. The one survivor, who escaped and who now struggles with the oath, is Azriel. Azriel's memories, now fifty years old, and the chronicles of Kolvillag preserved by Azriel's father, Shmuel, are all that he has left. Shmuel entrusted Azriel with the *Pinkas,* the book containing the deliberations of that community over the centuries. It is a symbolic gift of values, which includes memory, tradition, speech, and community. Yet the book entrusted to Azriel also doomed him to survive the pogrom, for whoever held the chronicles of the community in the past mysteriously survived the pogroms of the past. Azriel is bound by the same oath of silence. Azriel says:

> I will circle around the story, I will not plunge into it. I'll beat around the bush. I'll say everything but the essential. For you see, I am not free. My voice is a prisoner. And though at times words bend to my will, silence no longer obeys me: it has become my master. More powerful than the word, it draws its strength and secret from a savagely demented universe doomed by its wretched and deadly past.[22]

The burden of this oath is unbearable, and Azriel seeks release from its bounds; however, a *tsaddik*, a mystic religious leader, refuses his request, so Azriel endures in silence.

The logic of the oath was forged against a history where language had met its limits. Generations of chronicles detailing pogrom after pogrom did not stimulate repentance and compassion in the murderer's heart. Even the language of faith, God-language, did not stop the pogroms from coming. Therefore, Moshe had appealed to silence that transcends language and silenced the chronicles of Jewish death. The appeal to silence suggests that language is always ambiguous, because language clarifies and deceives. For fifty years after the destruction of Kolvillag, Azriel debates within himself the wisdom of silence as opposed to the wisdom of testimony. Azriel himself recalls a time in his life, prior to the pogrom, where he forgot the ambiguous character of language, persuading himself "that language was omnipotent as the link between man and his creator."[23] He believed language could mend anything, or at least trap one into believing that it could mend everything. Moshe the mystic led Kolvillag to abandon language for silence as the logical consequence of a man, a community, a tradition, devastated by a world that would not listen to the chronicles of injustice. Language seemed impotent to effect change. Thus, to speak of a suffering past seemed simply to provide the future the same possibilities. Moshe sought to transcend the world of words, not transform them. Ted Estess observes:

> While the encounter of Azriel and the young man [the suicidal youth] is the focal confrontation of the novel, the meeting of Moshe and Shmuel toward the end of the story is no less important. There in Moshe's prison

cell the spokesmen for history and silence, for memory and imagination, for the past and the future come face to face. For Moshe, history must cease: If suffering and the history of suffering were intrinsically linked, then the one could be abolished by attacking the other; by ceasing to refer to the events of the present, we could forestall ordeals in the future. Silence, then, is the way to "resolve the problem of Jewish suffering," "without the help of the Messiah."[24]

Moshe's oath of silence affords Azriel the ability of escaping the horrible memory, a martyr's tradition, and impotent speech in favor of living within the silent promise of the future.

Moshe's perspective describes a silence that purges a history of suffering. Consequently, silence is more than the negation of language: "When the Messiah will come ... man will be capable of understanding not only the words but also the blank spaces of the Torah. Yes, yes, they are important, those blank spaces."[25] Moshe argues for the superiority of silence on the basis that silence is the only weapon against the failure of words. Words did not act on either the conscience of the murderers or by a repeat of the Exodus. Moshe declares that

> rather than intervene and decide, He waits and judges only later. We do everything we can to attract His attention, to amuse or please Him. For centuries now we have given ourselves to Him by allowing ourselves to be led to the slaughterhouse. We think that we are pleasing Him by becoming illustrations of our own tales of martyrdom. There is always one storyteller, one survivor, one witness to revive the murderous past if not the victims.[26]

Moshe's strategy to break this cycle of suffering by silence is the last discernible option, because testimony from the past has only created a scenario of martyrdom for the victim and an impetus for the executioner.

Shmuel as the chronicler of the past and Moshe the mystic of silence have presented the only options available to Azriel: testimony or silence. Azriel, however, is bound by an oath to silence. But when Azriel encounters a child of Holocaust survivors, the storyteller, he risks the curse of breaking the oath. Why? Because the young Jew is contemplating suicide as a result of the deep despair he feels over the inability of his parents to found a world of purpose after the Holocaust. Azriel hears the two voices from his past: "Memory, insisted my father, everything is in memory silence, Moshe corrected him, everything is in silence."[27] Azriel, however, chooses to speak, and thus he breaks the oath of silence. He wonders:

"Have I lived and survived only for this encounter and this challenge? Only to defeat death in this particular case? Could I have been spared in Kolvillag so I could help a stranger?"[28] Azriel realizes language, especially storytelling, is one of the surest ties to and signs of life: "One does not commit suicide while speaking or listening."[29] The oath of silence, he realizes, is itself a type of suicide pact for the community; language, even with all its dangers and ambiguities, is the path to healing a relationship; and language provides not only the boundaries for human understanding, but also a bridge from one human to another. Azriel decides that if one life can be spared by telling his story, then so be it; Azriel will keep the young Jew alive by telling him the story of Kolvillag:

> Yes, that is the best method; it has been tested and proved. I'll transmit my experience to him and he, in turn will be compelled to do the same. He in turn will become a messenger. And once a messenger, he has no alternative. He must stay alive until he has transmitted his message. Azriel himself would not still be alive if his father the chronicler, his friends and his teacher Moshe the Madman had not made him the repository of their tragic and secret truth. By entrusting the book to him, his father doomed him to survival. So this is the example to follow, Azriel pondered. I shall hold him responsible for Kolvillag. But I shall be careful not to go afield, not to trespass. I shall have to watch myself more than before, to be certain that in speaking of the dead, I shall not betray them.[30]

Azriel's choice to break the oath does not signal an absolute refusal of silence, because he realizes what storytellers have to transmit has to do with silence as much as with words. He is not speaking to hear himself talk. It has been fifty years of silence which forms the context of his speech. But the silence of the storyteller is experienced only in the context of words and becomes present only when etched against words. For Wiesel the task of uniting one's words with one's silence is to move toward that place, perhaps unreachable, where one's speech does not betray that which one speaks. Speech can only be for the purpose of helping another.

The testimony of Azriel and the testimony of Wiesel each suggest that one should be careful with words; they are dangerous and can beget either the demonic or the divine. Nevertheless, the choice to speak is a choice for life, even if it saves only one life. In the novel *The Oath*, Wiesel recaptures the vision of a people who are the memory of the world: "Is oblivion not the worst of curses? A deed transmitted is a victory snatched from death. A witness who refuses to testify is a false witness."[31] At every moment the world, like the people of Kolvillag, lives on a precipice, and memory is the only anchor that keeps the world from falling into the abyss.

Yet where shall one begin this reconstruction of language and memory? Remembering Moshe's warning that chronicles of suffering often lead humanity down paths of divinely legitimated martyrdom, Azriel utters the first response into the silence: "Death, on all levels, is not a solution but a question, the most human question of all."[32] If death is the most human question of all, then Wiesel has carefully selected those words to begin all future discourse which questions human community at its fundamental level — telling the stories of the voiceless, the victims. So Wiesel writes:

> If the Greeks invented tragedy, the Romans the epistle, and the Renaissance the sonnet, our generation invented a new literature, that of testimony. We have all been witnesses and we all feel we have to bear testimony for the future. And that became an obsession, the single most powerful obsession that permeated all the lives, all the dreams, all the work of those people. One minute before they died they thought that was what they had to do.[33]

In *The Oath* more is at stake than the internal struggle of the child of survivors to find meaning in testimony or suicide; or for an old man to find purpose for a life of silence. The oppressive environment that silenced the parents of the suicidal youth remains, even though Azriel, the survivor of the Kolvillag pogrom, finds meaning in saving a life. The author, Elie Wiesel, challenges the overall silence imposed on survivor stories by society through Azriel's struggle against the conditions under which he will break his oath of silence.

The story of the survivor and of the victim is the story of a conceptually mixed dimension of humanity, because the tradition cannot make them heroes or enemies. The survivor is typically an historical figure out of place. He is the memory of pain. He or she is neither the role model of the traditional hero who conquers or who dies for the ideal, nor is he or she a tragic figure brought down by a personality flaw. History renders survivors and victims voiceless because of their inability to fit the normative patterns of order. They have no place or home in history. Wiesel constructs the narrative world of *The Oath* against this dilemma.

The Holocaust continues to impose a scenic backdrop for Wiesel's *The Oath.* The Holocaust remains the oppressive presence with ontological status that rivals the structure of the words themselves and perpetuates all four divisions of silence established in *Night.* The silence of *the event,* the Holocaust, permeates the narrative by way of the young Jew's conflict with his parents. The silence of *those lost in history* emanates every moment that Azriel ages without telling the story of Kolvillag. The *mute* silence of the suicidal youth reduces the young Jew's community to himself and Azriel. Finally, the *transcendent* silence championed by Moshe is observed by Azriel in the form of the oath. In *The Oath,* however, Wiesel cuts across all four divisions of silence when Azriel breaks the oath and begins to tell the story of the dead which questions all of humanity and even God.

In *Night,* Wiesel opened us up to a world of silent horror. In *The Oath,* Wiesel's characters struggle with the value of speech. Does anyone hear the stories of pain? Is silence the best response to a world gone awry? Azriel decided that if testifying saves one life then the story must be told. In the story of *The Fifth Son,* the son for whom the book refers remained unnamed and unidentified until the final pages. This ellipsis creates an overbearing absence in the plot, which constitutes the scenic silence of the setting and refers to the event of the Holocaust. In *The Oath,* Azriel insisted that death, on all levels, is the most human question of all; in *The Fifth Son,* the questioning of the living by the dead achieves its most explicit form. The Passover Haggadah, which speaks of four sons, frames the context for the fifth son: "Blessed is God who gave the Torah to His people Israel, blessed is He. The Torah speaks about four sons: one who is wise and one who is contrary; one who is simple and one who does not even know how to ask a question."[34] But in these days, since the Holocaust, there is now a fifth son. This son does not ask a question; rather, he is the question!

Once again the full range of Wiesel's use of silence is experienced in *The Fifth Son.* The protagonist, an unnamed narrator, is the son of Holocaust survivors. From his particular vantage point he is entangled in a family that says nothing concerning a missing child from the war years. The father, Reuven, is aloof, withdrawn, absorbed in pain, and muted by grief. The narrator's mother has been driven mad. Her silence has all but destroyed her. The narrator, therefore, suffers from an event which he has not even experienced.

When the narrator meets the muted silence of his parents, he turns outside the family circle to escape its silent disease. Bontchek, a friend of the narrator's parents from the death camp experience, appears, and from him the narrator gradually extracts his parents' story. The narrator is absorbed by Bontchek's story:

> Bontchek, who had become my friend, found in me a faithful and fervent audience. All that my father hides from me out of discretion, he will reveal to me. With him as my guide, I yearn to enter the ghetto and meet its quietly delirious inhabitants. I want to participate in their agony, to be one of them in their struggle.... I want to accompany the hungry, the sick, the sad-eyed, wide-eyed madmen, the mute old men, the despairing gravediggers, I want to remember every face, retrieve every tear and every silence, I want to live to relive my father's experience; without that knowledge, without that fragment of memory acquired after the fact, I can never get close to him, I feel that.[35]

The sequential descent into hell that the narrator's parents experience in the death camps was not uncommon for many of the victims of the Holocaust, but this particular descent was overseen by Gestapo officer Richard Lander, nicknamed "the Angel." Lander meticulously enforced the Jewish march of death, reminding Reuven: "From now on, your future will smell of the grave."[36] The narrator learns from Bontchek that few survived the Davarowsk ghetto, but he does not learn what silences his father and drives his mother mad. In an explosive confrontation between the narrator and his father the narrator declares: "You want me to be here? But why? To honor me with your silence?"[37] He continues:

> You claim to be a good Jew, you observe the laws of Shabbat, you claim to be my father, but isn't a father's duty to pass on his knowledge, his experience to his son? Am I not your son? What kind of father are you if you persist in living sealed off behind a wall?[38]

What Reuven couches in his silence is the forbidden knowledge, which he will not reveal to his son: that he had been president of the ghetto *Judenrat*; he had been in charge of administering Lander's policies against his fellow Jews; he had finally resigned in protest after a mass killing. And, because groups in the ghetto did not have the privilege of "resigning," the Angel executed half of the Jews by lottery to warn against insubordination by their successors. Although Reuven survived the lottery, he paid an even heavier price: He and his wife learn much later that their six-year-old son, whom they thought had been hidden from the Angel, was tortured and murdered.

Simha, another survivor, recounts for the narrator how Reuven and two other Jews vowed that, if they survived the war, they would hunt down Lander and murder him for his subsequent cruel actions. In the autumn of 1942, the Angel had demanded that over 200 Jews pray to him instead of God on the Day of Atonement or be shot. The Angel spoke: "I like Jewish prayers. It would please me to hear you recite them."[39] The S.S. officer continued: "Imagine that I am the Lord your God." And the scene concluded with the S.S. officer Richard Lander standing over the corpses, defying heaven and earth, shouting: "You see, I was right to proclaim it: I am Death and I am your God."[40] It was this gruesome experience that forced Reuven and others to make a pact to murder the Angel should anyone survive. In 1946, Reuven and Simha find the Angel, and they think they have fulfilled their pact of execution by planting a bomb near him.

Yet the narrator discovers later that Richard Lander, the Angel, is not dead; he is alive under the assumed name Wolfgang Berger. He holds a high position in German and European industry. The narrator told his father, Reuven, Simha, and Bontchek that they need not continue in their guilt over the death of Lander, whom they did not kill. Thus the narrator had to decide if the oath for revenge pledged by the four in the ghetto in the autumn of 1942 can be passed on to another generation. He decides that he must at least confront the Angel. As long as the Angel and killers of his kind exist, the world remains flawed. "They have killed eternity in man; they have no right to happiness."[41] Depriving the innocent of a future, they have stained history; and not to remind them of this stain is to insult the victims. "If Richard Lander is happy it means that happiness is forever corrupt. If the Angel can sleep peacefully somewhere, it means that the world has ceased to be a haven and has become a jail."[42]

The narrator struggles with the dilemma of vengeance: "The death of love and the birth of hate, of the desire for revenge."[43] He appeals to Rebbe Zvi-Hersh for guidance. He struggles further with whether or not there are times when events surpass the moral constraints of tradition and demand vengeance; so his dilemma is the same dilemma experienced by his father in 1942. The Rabbi responds: "To punish a guilty man, and to punish him with death, means linking yourself to him forever: is that what you wish?"[44] The meditated memory from parents and friends made it impossible for the narrator not to confront Lander. He is not free. The weight of the past exerts far more influence on his present than the future. Death negates the future tense, but not the past years or even hours that have elapsed for the narrator. Through him the dead are able to act again as the narrator confronts the Angel. Yet almost apologetically, he confesses that he will not carry out the murder of the Death Angel of the Davarowsk ghetto. Rather, in the tense moment of their encounter, the narrator, now assuming the name of his murdered brother, Ariel, tells the Angel the story—a story of suffering and war. It is also the unspoken story that shapes the lives of all the characters of the novel, and it now comes to word. In the face of the Angel the narrator cries out with clarity: "The words come to me easily as though they were seeking me."[45] He tells the Angel of a certain S.S. officer's bloody demand for worship and of the slaughter of an innocent six-year-old boy. And the narrator concludes his story with a question: "How?"

> How could you be present at so many executions, decree so much torture without giving up your sleep, your mind, your taste for lovemaking and wine, your memory? How could you inflict such suffering without it leaving its mark on your face? How could you perpetuate death and not endure it? You were Death, how did you succeed in staying alive? ... How could you inflict such pain on a small boy whom a thousand mouths were silently blessing, hoping to make him their messenger in heaven?[46]

At this the Angel asks him: "Who are you?" To which he responds: "Who am I? My name is Ariel. I am a child. A child of the ghetto of Davarowsk. Every Jew of the ghetto was my parent ... and every dead victim is my brother."[47] With the story told, Ariel has destroyed the comfort of the Angel's existence; the story renews Lander's memory. Ariel, the silent presence of this novel, has been given a voice in the life of his brother. And in telling the story the Angel is unmasked. The mute silence of so many people for so long a time is voiced. Accordingly, the narrator, now calling himself Ariel, concludes that justice must be human; it must pass through language and be justified by memory. And it is only through life that just words are translated into acts of justice.

In *The Fifth Son*, the word (the voice of the voiceless dead), silence, and the events of the Holocaust meet. Yet this meeting place is in no way conclusive, as the narrator states: "It would be too foolish to reduce an ontological Event to a word, a gesture, an impulse of hate."[48] Rather, the voices of the dead form questions for the living when they are heard; the voices of the dead destroy the comfort of the living. Thus, only in life are just words translated into acts of justice. The word regains its value in the questions that the dead place before the living. Wiesel articulates the path of critical memory, which leads to a creative response in the words of his narrator.

> I had observed in myself a gradual splitting into two: Ariel was and was not dead; I was and was not alive. Ariel lived inside me, through me; I talked to him to convince myself of his existence; I listened to him to persuade myself of mine. At first, it was: He, Ariel. Then: You, Ariel. And finally: I, Ariel.[49]

The memory of the innocent dead directly affects the narrator's sense of personal identity, and personal identity is a fundamental preoccupation with Wiesel. He explains:

> I'm convinced that when the first man, when Adam, opened his eyes and he saw God, he didn't say, "Who are you?" He said, "Who am I?" Who is the "I" in me? The "I" that speaks? The "I" that is spoken to? This dialogue, this quest of the real "I," which can never be solved, I try to transmit in my novels as well — in the form of my novels at least.[50]

Wiesel reveals through the voice of the narrator in *The Fifth Son* which words should be spoken against the backdrop of *Night:* The names of the dead are voiced to unite them with the living in order to unify history. History received its wholeness by binding the past to the present; this is the process of redemption. In *The Fifth Son*, the narrator reveals that the process of redemption begins by taking on another's identity, incorporating him into one's self, and becoming his voice.

Conclusion: The Voice of the Dead

In *The Fifth Son*, Wiesel establishes the analogy of anamnestic solidarity, or solidarity in memory with the dead and the conquered, as the most effective analogy of history. This solidarity with the dead is clearly seen in the movement of the protagonist from Ariel, "he," to Ariel, "you," and finally to Ariel, "I." This movement breaks the grip of history, pictured as a history of triumph and conquest.

Memory is no longer the case of nostalgia for some sort of paradise, because paradise has been transformed into the abyss of *Night*. Memory now becomes a source of questioning, as we see in *The Fifth Son*. In this sense, memory of the dead is always in the form of the interrogative for Wiesel. The memories of the dead are dangerous and unpredictable visitations from the past.

These are memories that must be taken into account because of their proleptic content: they foreshadow a potential movement in our history. Wiesel begins his universal rebellion against the order of death by the subversive power of remembering the particularity of suffering. Wiesel chooses stories as the vehicle for the memory of suffering. This vehicle is less argumentative in form than the formal systems of theologians. Ted Estess suggests that Wiesel's perspective affirms a narrative quality to human existence. But despite Wiesel's strong attachment to a narrative world view, he tells stories for a particular purpose. He writes:

> In days of old, a young Jew decided to go forth to see the world. His mother, a poor woman in ancient Palestine, had no parting gift except a pillow. "Take it my son," she said. "If you come to a strange city and find no bed at night, you can always go out to the fields and sleep on this pillow." So it came to pass: the young man arrived in Rome, and when evening fell, he went outside the city and cushioned his head on his mother's pillow. That very night the Temple in Jerusalem was burned and destroyed. And the pillow under the boy's head burst into flames. "I only write when the pillow burns," explains Wiesel.[51]

Wiesel resists the idea of history that screens out the importance of particular suffering for the sake of continuity and meaningfulness. As we saw earlier, history is often defined by those who prevail, the history of success and the established. The conquered are remembered as the examples of what will not endure, while the victims and survivors are forgotten or suppressed by history. A principle of selection prevails in history that creates the unacceptability of victims and survivors — a principle which flaws history by legitimating history's forgetfulness. The memory of suffering retrieves the vanquished and destroyed from the boundaries of history. The memory of suffering is a belief structure for the future that actively responds to human suffering. The reinvestment of the word with meaning begins with the story of the suffering: the dead, those already forgotten, have a meaning that is still unrealized. The potential meaning of history depends on the voice of these voiceless. Wiesel writes:

> When man, in his grief, falls silent, Goethe says, then God gives him the strength to sing of his sorrows. From that moment on, he may no longer choose not to sing, whether his son is heard or not. What matters is to struggle against silence with words, or through another form of silence. What matters is to gather a smile here and there, a word here and there, and thus justify the faith placed in you, a long time ago, by so many victims. Why I write? To wrench those victims from oblivion. To help the dead vanquish death.[52]

The memory of the suffering in the Holocaust brings a new moral imagination into political life; this memory brings a new vision of the suffering of others, which should mature into partisanship on behalf of the weak and dead in the same way that the protagonist in *The Fifth Son* becomes the voice of Ariel in the last scene. The once-silenced memory of a murdered six-year-old boy forty years later becomes a new question for the living.

The historian tries to retain from the past what deserves not to be forgotten; that is, what is memorable. And what is most worthy of safe keeping in our memories are the values that rule the individual actions, the life of institutions, and the social struggles of the past. Historians attempt to preserve this common treasure of humanity by suspending one's own condition; by bracketing one's desires. The historian imposes a dialectic between what is foreign and what is familiar and between what is near and what is far. This very dialectic is what brings history and fiction together because the recognition of the values of the past in their difference opens the real to the possible.

Elie Wiesel's protagonist, the Wanderer, the Survivor, against the backdrop of both deconstructive silence and reconstructive possibility, seeks not to "reconfigure" the world; rather, he seeks to transfigure the world precisely by means of "true" stories.

Notes

1. Daniel R. Schwarz, *Imagining the Holocaust* (New York: St Martin's Press, 1999), 50.

2. Naomi Seidman, "Elie Wiesel and the Scandal of Jewish Rage," *Jewish Social Studies,* 1, No. 3, (Fall 1996): 5.

3. Nelson Goodman, *Languages of Art: An Approach to a Theory of Symbols* (Indianapolis: Bobbs-Merrill, 1969), 241.

4. Elie Wiesel, *A Jew Today,* trans. Marion Wiesel (New York: Random House, 1978), 22.

5. Harold Fisch, *A Remembered Future* (Bloomington: Indiana University Press, 1984), 66–69.

6. Elie Wiesel, "The Holocaust as Literary Inspiration," in *Dimensions of the Holocaust: Lectures at Northwestern University* (Evanston, Ill.: Northwestern University Press, 1977), 19.

7. Lawrence S. Cunningham, "Elie Wiesel's Anti-Exodus," in *Responses to Elie Wiesel,* ed. Harry James Cargas (New York: Persea, 1978), 24.

8. Ibid., 24.

9. Cunningham, *Responses,* 26.

10. Wiesel responding to Harry James Cargas, in *Harry James Cargas in Conversation with Elie Wiesel* (New York: Paulist, 1976), 45–46.

11. Elie Wiesel, *Night,* trans. Stella Rodway (New York: Bantam Books, 1960), ix.

12. Ibid., 64.

13. Wiesel, "The Holocaust as Literary Inspiration," 7.

14. Ibid., 8.

15. Andre Neher, *The Exile of the Word,* trans. David Maisel (Philadelphia: Jewish Publication Society of America, 1981), 210.

16. Terrence Des Pres, "The Authority of Silence in Elie Wiesel's Art," in *Confronting the Holocaust,* ed. Alvin H. Rosenfeld and Irving Greenberg (Bloomington: Indiana University Press, 1978), 51.

17. Michael Wyschogrod, "Some Theological Reflections on the Holocaust," *Responses* 25 (1975): 68.

18. Wiesel, *Night,* 105.

19. Wiesel in *Harry James Cargas,* 48.

20. Elie Wiesel, "Jewish Values in the Post-Holocaust Future: A Symposium," *Judaism* 16 (1967): 285.

21. Elie Wiesel, *The Oath,* trans. Marion Wiesel (New York: Schocken Books, 1986), 239.

22. Ibid., 8.

23. Ibid., 51.

24. Ted L. Estess, "Choosing Life: An Interpretation of Elie Wiesel's *Oath,*" *Soundings* 61 (1978): 73. See also Wiesel, *The Oath,* 244.

25. Wiesel, *The Oath,* 154.

26. Ibid., 237.

27. Ibid., 280.

28. Ibid., 32.

29. Ibid., 14.

30. Ibid., 33.

31. Wiesel, *The Oath,* 187.

32. Ibid., 55.

33. Wiesel, *Dimensions,* 9.

34. Elie Wiesel, *The Fifth Son,* trans. Marion Wiesel (New York: Summit Books, 1985), 9.

35. Ibid., 92.

36. Ibid., 122. Richard Lander, nicknamed "the Angel," is an image of death and destruction, standing in stark contrast to the "sad-eyed angel" in Wiesel's first book, *Night*, 60–62. The use of "the angel" as a mirror image of divine character symbolizing vulnerability in *Night* and the divine legitimacy of violence in a society is seen in the character of Lander in *The Fifth Son*. This may simply be a coincidence in Wiesel's writing, which spans some 27 years; however, this coincidence provides a thought-provoking parallel structure for examining the "ambiguity of God."

37. Wiesel, *The Fifth Son*, 122.

38. Ibid., 131.

39. Ibid., 152.

40. Ibid., 154.

41. Ibid., 176.

42. Ibid., 176.

43. Ibid., 188.

44. Ibid., 190.

45. Ibid., 211.

46. Ibid., 212.

47. Ibid., 213.

48. Ibid., 208.

49. Ibid., 217.

50. Wiesel, *Harry James Cargas*, 109.

51. Wiesel, *Jewish Heritage,* 7 (Spring 1966): 27.

52. Wiesel, "Why I Write?" *Confronting,* 205–206.

The Artist as Witness, Prophet, and Encourager

CAROLE J. LAMBERT

Elie Wiesel sees himself as a messenger and a storyteller, two quite compatible vocations. Although awarded the Nobel Peace Prize in 1986, he confesses that "[a]ll my writing was born out of anger. In order to contain it, I had to write. If I had not written, I would have exploded."[1] This anger results from "[t]he magnitude of the catastrophe," the *Shoah*, which caused the murder of his beloved grandparents, parents, little sister, and many friends when he was only fifteen years old. He acknowledges that this trauma haunts all of his stories:

> The magnitude of the catastrophe, the absurdity of the tragedy, the silence of the world, the responsibility of the accomplices, the very fact that it could have happened, and the very fact that it could have been avoided — all these elements make it into a mystery, almost a religious mystery, with theological implications. This is really the story that we try to tell.[2]

My essay focuses on Wiesel's novels, for his fictional *Shoah*-haunted survivors can express their rage at God and others more freely than can the kind, dignified Nobel Laureate in his interviews, speeches, and essays. I shall emphasize Wiesel's fictional storytelling power in the following areas: the storyteller as witness to a Jewish past that risks being forgotten; the storyteller as prophet in the post–Holocaust era; and the storyteller as encourager of his readers.

The Storyteller as Witness

The Jewish past that Wiesel fears may be forgotten after he and other survivors have died includes both the *Shoah* and the eastern European Jewish life that the Nazi oppressors destroyed. He recreates this lost community when a survivor such as Michael in *The Town Beyond the Wall* returns to his home town, Szerencseváros, behind the Iron Curtain, only to discover that it is filled with strangers, some of whom have even hung a crucifix over his bed in what used to be his humble home.

Later Michael suffers several days of incarceration and torture by a new set of tormentors, the Communists, when he is betrayed by a neighbor, the same man who years before had watched indifferently from his window as Michael and his family were lined up and marched out of the synagogue courtyard to cattle cars deporting them to Auschwitz. Similarly, Eliezer in *The Accident* recalls being warmly embraced by Grandmother who was safe in the shtetl:

> One day my father slapped me. I had stolen some money from the store cash register in order to give it to a classmate. A sickly, poor little boy. They called him Haim the orphan. I always felt ill at ease in his presence. I knew I was happier than he was and this made me feel guilty. Guilty that my parents were alive. That's why I stole the money. But when my father asked me, trying to find out what I had done with it, I didn't tell him. After all, I couldn't tell my father that I felt guilty because he was alive! He slapped my face and I ran to Grandmother. I could tell her the whole truth. She didn't scold me. Sitting in the middle of the room, she lifted me onto her lap and began to sob. Her tears fell on my head, which she was holding against her bosom, and I discovered to my surprise that a grandmother's tears are so hot that they burn everything in their path.[3]

This is contrasted to the horrific image of the grandmother gasping for air in the "showers" of Auschwitz:

> Grandmother would have understood. It was hot in the airless, waterless chambers. It was hot in the room where her livid body was crushed by other livid bodies. Like me, she must have opened her mouth to drink air, to drink water. But there was no water where she was, there was no air. She was only drinking death, as you drink water or air, mouth open, eyes closed, fingers clenched.[4]

An important aspect of Wiesel's storytelling genius is his ability to recreate vividly a few poignant scenes like these which make a lasting impression upon his readers and thus fortify memory and defy forgetfulness. "My preoccupation," he explains, "is memory.... The first question is, How can I achieve a situation in which the victims, all the victims, can enter memory?"[5] A witness attests to the facts of certain events; memory is key to his endeavor.

Wiesel's goal of memorializing the victims in his fiction is achieved, however, only if his novels are read. *The Town Beyond the Wall* and *The Accident* each received the Prix Rivarol in France. In the United States, Wiesel is known as the author of his bestseller *Night,* his powerful memoir, much more than as a novelist. In fact, his novels often receive poor reviews such as Curt Schleier's condemnation of *The Judges*:

> Is it a parable? Is there some deeper allegorical significance buried in the text? Or is it just a wayward story idea from the Twilight Zone? Sadly, the last possibility seems most likely. Author Elie Wiesel survived the camps of the Holocaust, won the Nobel Peace Prize for his righteous efforts on behalf of the world's oppressed. He deserves a good review. "The Judges" does not.[6]

Negative reviews such as Schleier's do not trouble Wiesel because he does not read them.[7] He continues to be the messenger and storyteller he is, realizing that "each country receives my works differently."[8] He explains, "One must write out of one's own experience, out of one's own identity. One must cater to no one; one must remain truthful. If one is read, it's good; if one is not read, it's too bad. But that should not influence the writer."[9]

Actually, *The Judges* is far more than "a wayward story idea from the Twilight Zone." It presents a tense battle between the forces of good and evil, between a murderous, mentally disturbed Judge and a *Shoah* survivor become yeshiva teacher, Razziel Friedman. A reader educated in Wiesel's storytelling strategies will sort out the novel's complexities and understand its optimistic conclusion — the Judge dies and Razziel plus five others under the Judge's power survive — to be an ethical statement elevating love and justice.

One of the reasons why Wiesel's novels may not be well received by the American public is because they *always* incorporate ethical messages. He strongly believes that the possibility of "l'art pour l'art" disappeared with the *Shoah*. He recalls:

> These were men of culture, bearers of prestigious college degrees, possessing exquisite taste in music, literature, and the arts, possessing perfect manners and high "moral" standards — in their own Nazi context. All of which did not prevent them from throwing living children into the flames. I saw them, God, I saw them and I did not become blind.[10]

The belief that aesthetics and reason may foster ethical behavior has historically failed: "Now we know that beauty without an ethical dimension cannot exist."[11] Further, he affirms that "the purpose of literature is to correct injustice."[12] Elsewhere he writes:

> Literature is the art of correcting injustices. If there is nothing else I can do, I write a book. This is precisely the task of the witness today, of the modern storyteller, of the Jewish writer. We use words to try to alter the course of events, to save people from humiliation or death.[13]

Some literary critics may find Wiesel's approach to the novel to be too utilitarian, but it is indeed congruent with his vocation of storytelling messenger or witness to the atrocities he has experienced. This ethical bent may also cause him to sound like a modern prophet.

The Storyteller as Prophet

Anton Laytner notes that "it is the poet and the novelist who lead the people [in trying to understand the Holocaust], raising the questions that otherwise might remain unasked by the rabbi."[14] Jacob Jocz affirms, "An outstanding figure caught between faith and despair is Elie Wiesel. By reason of his personal experience of four concentration camps and by his great literary ability he occupies an almost prophetic position in the spiritual crisis of our age.... He has a perennial quarrel with God. Wiesel has been described as the Job of the twentieth century."[15] Wiesel, and his fictional protagonists, protests God's absence and indifference to His people of the covenant at the time of their greatest need. He provided no Moses to liberate them and no miracles to avenge their persecutors.

In addition to his commitment to memorialize the victims, Wiesel is also "preoccupied with God. Why the good are punished and the wicked rewarded...."[16] His interrogation of God follows the prophetic tradition established by Abraham, Moses, Job, Jeremiah, and other prominent

Tanakh figures. Wiesel believes that such protests against God are acceptable as long as they are made from *within* a faith community, not from outside of it. Thus he professes his ongoing belief in God:

> I have never renounced my faith in God. I have risen against His justice, protested His silence and sometimes His absence, but my anger rises up within faith and not outside it.... I have always aspired to follow in the footsteps of my father and those who went before him ... it is permissible for man to accuse God, provided it be done in the name of faith in God.[17]

More simply, he states: "It is because I still believe in God that I argue with Him."[18] Although he maintains belief in God, he never affirms his words to be directly inspired by Him in the traditional sense of the term "prophet"; rather, he is a secular prophet who speaks for the silenced voices of the *Shoah* in his challenges to God.

Wiesel's protesting prophetic stance is revealed in his enigmatic style, which may be a further stumbling block for some American readers. He purposefully writes *against words*: "To tell the tale, the writer must, after all, use words, but he writes against them, not with them; his goal is to convey 'not experience but at least a certain secret of the experience untouched by words.'"[19] He elaborates:

> I believe very much in the words you do not say. Sometimes I strike out a sentence if I believe in it too much; I am moving towards silence. The thirteenth century Hebrew poet Eleazar Rokeah says: "Some people complain that God is silent; they are wrong — God is not silent; God is Silence." It is to this silence that I would like to direct my words.[20]

Further, he believes that "[i]n literature the weight of silence determines the weight of art."[21] If Wiesel is really directing his words to the Silence that is God, then it becomes more understandable why he is unconcerned about negative reviews of his novels in the United States. Prophetic messages rarely are clear and welcomed; they represent communication between God and man and between man and God.

A Beggar in Jerusalem may be Wiesel's most prophetic novel to date. He describes his experience at the Wall in Jerusalem the day after Israel's astounding victory during the Six Day War involving Egypt, Syria, and Jordan in 1967, "what many at the time feared [would] be a new Holocaust."[22] He elaborates by writing:

I was there the day after the Old City was liberated. I saw so many people come and hug the Wall, kiss it, and cry that I felt the privilege of being alive during a historic or perhaps a trans-historic event. I felt that those Jews came to the Wall as beggars and as princes, that they belonged not only to our generation but to many centuries, that they had all helped our people win the war and survive — and helped keep the victory human, meaning pure of injustices, pure of vengeance. I had a fleeting sense of triumph that the victory had remained human and therefore Jewish. I remember I was standing next to the Wall, and I felt: This is it, what I see now I see not only for myself but for many other people, the witness must assume his responsibility and speak. And I remember that I heard then the words I was to write later. What I did later was nothing but transcribe them....[23]

A Beggar in Jerusalem was, indeed, written "in one great sweep ... as I was writing, my lips were moving.... Afterwards I was hoarse for a week."[24] Both the moments of viewing the newly liberated Wall and of writing about it appear to be mystical, prophetic, and yet humanistic. Wiesel has said, "I still believe that writing has a soul, and a writer is a prophet."[25]

A Beggar in Jerusalem presents eleven mystically mad storytelling beggars: Shlomo the Seer, an old and blind Hasid; Ezra ben Abraham, an old man from Morocco; Velvel, "the group's self-appointed clown"; Zadok, "the one-eyed dwarf," an emaciated Yemenite; Moshe the Madman and the Drunkard: "He becomes dangerous only in his fits of lucidity. Whenever he feels them coming on, he asks to be locked up."[26] Then there are Yakov the Timid; Zalmen, "au caractère mauvais"[27]; Menash, the "matchmaker" of the stars; Anshel who claims to have won the war because his "pockets are full of faces"; Dan, the Prince, "a psychotic, rogue, embezzler, vagabond and liar of considerable talent," and a latecomer, Itzik, not appearing until the third section of the novel.[28] Similar to the demented patients in *Twilight*'s Mountain Clinic — Adam, Cain, "the prophet," Abraham, Nadav (Aaron's son), a patient who claims to be a dead "friend," Boris the scapegoat, Joseph, Zelig, the Messiah, and God the Creator, among others — these characters speak bizarrely and enigmatically, yet there is a mystical coherence to their tales. For example, Anshel in *A Beggar in Jerusalem* explains:

"I've seen a lot of dead men," Anshel says, as if to excuse himself. "They all became children again. I saw them as children, yet I've trampled over some. War is war and is the same everywhere. I had no choice. I ran, I had to run. What else could I do? So, to make it easier for myself, after a while I stopped looking at the corpses below. After a while war had no face for me. For me, war was a beast which killed men by snatching their faces. Now the dead are taking revenge, and I'm seeing too many of those faces. They are everywhere."[29]

Wiesel offers a negative commentary on war through the crazy tale of Anshel and the faces that trouble him, a fascinating way to impress the reader without positing a pacifist slogan. Ultimately Anshel concludes his tale by exclaiming, "I've won the war! You don't believe me! You want proof? Look: faces, faces, my pockets are full of faces!" The reader's response may echo the narrator's: "So are mine."[30] Another madman who tells a strange tale is the mentally ill young man at Mountain Clinic in *Twilight*: "He is called Nadav, like the son of Aharon the High Priest (Ex. 10). Young and handsome, with nostrils flaring, hands clasping and unclasping, he acts like an animal ready to pounce. He threatens in a tone that brooks no appeal. One wrong word and Raphael will be struck down."[31] Nadav and his brother Avihu "offered strange fire before the LORD, which he commanded them not. And there went out fire from the LORD, and devoured them, and they died before the LORD" (Ex. 10:1b–2 KJV). Nadav explains:

> "You see me, right? You see my body, right? You are mistaken, my poor friend. I am nothing but a handful of ashes. My face is made of ashes. My chest is filled with ashes. And yet, the fire has never gone out. I feel it devouring me. I burn and burn, and the sea itself could not extinguish the flames that consume me.... I had always been wary of death and thus had seen it approaching. In fact, that's how I succeeded in outwitting the angel of death. I flew on its blazing wings, but I am still alive."[32]

Nadav's death by fire of course recalls the bodies burned in the concentration camps. His victory over death, however, frightens Raphael, the novel's protagonist, and Nadav's story leads into a mystical vision of heaven where "matter and spirit become one for the glory of the Creator." Below this mystical union the world, words, light, fear, and prayer "turn into faces." This story veers off the path of rationality into mysticism, and intertextually it is complicated even more by Wiesel's previous use of "faces" in Anshel's story. What both prophetic tales share is the faces of the dead, faces Wiesel insists must never be forgotten.

In "Nadab and Abihu: A Story of Fire and Silence," one of the essays in Wiesel's recent collection *Wise Men and Their Tales*, he discusses several interpretations of this tragic story and arrives at the following conclusions:

> "Woe to the generation in which parents bury their children," says the Talmud. Doesn't that evoke all wars? We link this tragedy of Nadab and Abihu to others equally overwhelming, personal and collective, and we read it on Yom Kippur to inspire repentance. Whoever weeps reading of the death of Aaron's two sons, says the Zohar, will not suffer the same fate; he will not see his children die young.[33]

Thus Wiesel's commentary, more rational than the mystical tale in *Twilight*, still emphasizes the horror of young, dead "faces."

Wiesel is careful to distinguish his novels' characters' mystical madness from clinical pathological madness: "Clinical madness is destructive or self-destructive. Mystical madness is redeeming. The difference between a mystical madman and a clinical madman is that a clinical madman isolates himself and others, while a mystical one wants to bring the Messiah."[34] He clarifies:

> I am for mystical madness, a madness that has only one obsession — redemption, only one concern — one's fellow man.... A mystic thinks of the Messiah and nothing else, not for himself but for everyone. One has to be mad, totally mad, to believe in such concepts — that we can redeem words, people; that we can save mankind; that we can help one another today. But I am for that madness.[35]

When asked by Lily Edelman why madness is such an important presence in his work, Wiesel replied, "For many reasons, but mainly because rationalism is a failure and betrayal."[36] He continues, "I like to think that my madmen are pure and beautiful, madmen who try to save the world and not to destroy it, to help, not to hurt. And because they were captured by the evil forces, I try to give them back to the pure forces."[37]

The two Pedros found in *The Town Beyond the Wall* and *Twilight* plus Paritus of *The Judges* are perhaps Wiesel's most impressive mystical madmen, although they exert their greatest influence on the novels' protagonists *in absentia*. While Michael in *The Town Beyond the Wall* is being tortured by the Communists after Pedro has helped him to return to his home town, he remembers vividly conversations he has had with Pedro during which Pedro often speaks in oxymorons: "*God, little brother, is the weakness of strong men and the strength of weak men.... Man is God's strength. Also His weakness.*"[38] An oxymoron, the combining of contradictory words, rhetorically tends to push the reader beyond the rational comprehension of language into the realm of irrational mysticism. A thoughtful reader is forced to pause when confronted with this rhetorical device in order to attempt to understand what Wiesel is communicating about God and man through this prophetic figure.

In *Twilight*, Pedro reappears, this time not as the Christian from Tangier in *The Town Beyond the Wall* but as a member of the Briha, "the clandestine Jewish organization established to help [Shoah] survivors."[39] Wiesel admits that both Pedros "are actually the same."[40] This second Pedro also speaks mystically: "*Remember that the misunderstood writer is often considered mad. The storyteller no one listens to is thought to have said nothing. The believer scorned by God is but a dangerous dreamer. And then, this too: a man without fear is a man without love.*"[41] Again, the reader must pause to figure out what Wiesel is communicating in such a complex passage. Even when one studies this citation in the full context of the whole novel, one cannot be certain of a definitive interpretation.

What is sure, however, is that both Pedros are benevolent characters. Pedro of *The Town Beyond the Wall* encourages Michael to rehabilitate his mute, psychologically broken cell mate: "*Save his soul. You can do it ... recreate the universe. Restore that boy's sanity. Cure him. He'll save you.*"[42] Pedro of *Twilight* affirms: "*to die while living is forbidden.*"[43] He encourages Raphael to return to the world of the sane rather than remain among the insane.

Paritus of *The Judges* also speaks mystically and is a positive influence on the novel's protagonist, Razziel Friedman, but he is a wise scholar, not the same as the two Pedros discussed above.[44] He has, however, done for Razziel what Pedro in *The Town Beyond the Wall* recommends that Michael do for his cell mate: restored him to psychological and emotional health after horrific torture by the Communists. Paritus is a storyteller, and Razziel recalls his tales while the Judge has locked him in a room with four other unfortunate survivors of a plane crash:

> Razziel remembered a question Paritus had put to him: "What becomes of the sound the wind makes when it shakes the tree?"
> "I don't know," Razziel had replied.
> "That's because you don't know how to listen. Know, then, that the sound remains within the tree. It will never leave it."

> Now Razziel paraphrased these words for Kali [his dying wife]. "Your life will remain within me. It will never leave me."[45]

Wiesel's mystical prophetic figures' messages strain the reader's comprehension as do the Biblical prophets' pronouncements, yet they are worth meditating upon, for they provide a wisdom beyond the rationalism that the *Shoah* proved to be a failure and they encourage sanity and life in a world still plagued by madness and murder.

The Storyteller as Encourager

An "encourager" is one who "impart[s] courage or confidence" to others; as witness, prophet, and professor, Wiesel is conscious of this aspect of his storytelling genius. "The tribe of Levi were the singers and composers, and I am a Levite, a descendant of that tribe."[46] Fortified by this ancestry, Wiesel tells tales that do indeed include beautiful madmen "who try to save the world."[47] He has also inherited a gift for storytelling from his beloved grandfather, Dodye Feig, the ever joyful hasid. He credits the itinerant beggars often entertained by his parents with a style and particular stories that he has passed on to his readers. Finally, he structures his tales like many famous hasidic storytellers such as Rebbe Nahman of Bratzlav:

> I try to write following the example of a very great Hasidic storyteller, Rebbe Nahman of Bratzlav. He is really my teacher. He lived some two hundred years ago and had direct influence on Kafka. Some of Kafka's stories sound almost plagiarized from Rebbe Nahman who writes in concentric circles. I try to write the same way. That means the "thématique" — as the structuralists would say — the basic themes, or as Malraux would say — the basic obsessions, remain the same: always injustice, always God, always death, always man's dialectical impossibility to understand and not to understand what is happening to him. Always the same. And basically it is: "How do I live with God, and how can I live without Him?"[48]

Although a gifted storyteller, Wiesel is not content with merely actualizing his talent; he wants to touch his readers profoundly and to encourage them to change for the better. His stories are particularly addressed to readers who share his "basic obsessions": "injustice ... God ... death ... man's dialectical impossibility to understand and not to understand what is happening to him." By reading about characters dealing with these issues, the recipients of his texts can discover who they are, what their own ethics include, and how they can reconstruct their own lives perhaps also shattered by unjust suffering.

For example, Beth, a young victim of horrific physical and sexual abuse, remarked, "So I read Wiesel and I try to understand how he still loves and trusts God after the holocaust. I think, in some ways, we are on the same journey."[49] When asked, "What would you like for your words to do?" Wiesel replied, "The first goal would be to shake readers out of their indifference. I would like the persons who read me not to be indifferent to their surroundings, to family and friends, to things in the world."[50] Indifference contributed to the *Shoah*; it can continue to foster contemporary tragedies. Words are Wiesel's weapon against indifference, "[f]or words in our tradition have their own power, their own mystery. They can enrich life or unleash death. But they must be links, not spears; offerings, not swords; tales of bridges to be built, not destroyed. Literature means a beginning, a beginning of faith."[51]

Wiesel's storytelling gift prevents his novels from becoming overtly didactic and even propagandistic. Although he frankly acknowledges his ethical literary agenda, he artistically forwards it in ways that attract his sensitive readers rather than repel them. One way that he keeps this aesthetic balance is by consciously delving deeply into himself for the inspiration and images that he needs in order to communicate his concerns to his readers:

> I write to explore my own self as much as I write in order to help you [a student] explore yourself. I believe that basically, and ontologically, there is only one person in the world. That is the beauty, really, of our teaching: there is only one person. That means the "I" in me and the "I" in you is the same "I." Between our deepest zones there is a bridge.... So in my writing I try to go as deep down as I can in my zone, and I am convinced that if I go deep enough, I will find you.[52]

The images that Wiesel uses to link his "I" with the reader's "I" can only come out of his past experiences which he hopes can be "transformed for me, as a writer, into an act of creativity ... a bridge ... a burning connection. And this connection should not separate me from you — rather, the opposite. It should bring me closer to you, and, so I hope, also you to me."[53] Of course, he specifically wants the *Shoah*'s dead to be memorialized and not forgotten, but he also desires to provide hope for subsequent victims of injustice, like the sexually abused woman quoted above, in order that they, too, may fight against indifference, despair, and the temptation to commit suicide.

For example, Beth and other survivors of sexual abuse may relate to Wiesel's extremely sympathetic treatment of Sarah, the Nazis' "special" twelve-year-old prostitute in *The Accident*: "Whoever listens to Sarah and doesn't change, whoever enters Sarah's world and doesn't invent new gods and new religions, deserves death and destruction. Sarah alone had the right to decide what is good and what is evil, the right to differentiate what is true from what usurps the appearance of truth."[54] Sarah's victimization in the concentration camp has made her a "saint" with no reason for her to feel ashamed: "shame tortures not the executioners but their victims."[55] The abusers should be ashamed, not Sarah and Beth.

Despite his positive ethical agenda, Wiesel is fearless in pouring out his anger at God, another aspect of his writing that keeps it from becoming doctrinaire and that attracts readers also disillusioned with benign platitudes about God after, like Beth, they have experienced unspeakable suffering. The citation below records Eliezer's fury at the God who did nothing to prevent the Nazi officers from annihilating Sarah's innocence:

> The God of chaos and impotence. The God who tortures twelve-year-old children.... The God of impotence made her [Sarah's] eyes flame. Mine too. I thought: I am going to die. Whoever sees God must die ... why should God be allied with death? Why should He want to kill a man who succeeded in seeing Him? Now, everything became clear. God was ashamed. God likes to sleep with twelve-year-old girls. And He doesn't want us to know. Whoever sees it or guesses it must die so as not to divulge the secret. Death is only the guard who protects God, the door-keeper of the immense brothel that we call the universe.[56]

These are some of Wiesel's most condemnatory words against God in all of his novels. In a subsequent text, he moves beyond this condemnation in a positive direction.

Gregor/Gavriel of *The Gates of the Forest* has finally succeeded in persuading the kind hasidic rebbe to admit that God is guilty: "Yes, he [God] is guilty. He has become the ally of evil, of death, of murder, but the problem is still not solved. I ask you a question and dare you answer:

'What is there left for us to do?'"[57] Gregor/Gavriel has no answer but tears. This scene is poignant because it forces the protagonist as well as Wiesel's readers to consider seriously the following question: Even if God is mad, silent, and impotent, is not humankind worse off if they stop believing in Him? Wiesel shows Gregor/Gavriel opting for faith in God. He promises to return to the hasidic gatherings and decides to help his depressed wife, also a *Shoah* survivor, rather than abandon her, as was his original intention, and he accepts a child's invitation to become the tenth man in a *minyan*. Wiesel is careful to demonstrate Gregor/Gavriel's small steps of faith without preaching to his readers that they should do likewise. Thus Wiesel's storytelling gift as well as his personal integrity and respect for his readers prevent his powerful novel from being diverted as a work of art into a religious tract. At the same time, the outcome of the novel provides an image of hope over despair, an encouragement to his readers.

Conclusion

Wiesel as a gifted writer can preserve a Jewish past that the Nazis and their collaborators almost destroyed, can speak prophetically to a tumultuous present whose actors seem to have learned little from that past, and can encourage his readers to work for a better, more humane future. Beyond his storytelling power, however, Wiesel's personal history and integrity add weight to his volumes. Irving Halperin has astutely noted:

> Whoever turns to this writer can expect to have his most basic assumptions questioned. It is not simply that Wiesel asks such age-old questions as, for example, What is the meaning of suffering? Other writers could ask the same question and not at all affect the reader. Rather it is because of *who* he is, a man who has suffered beyond the scope of endurance of most men, that he poses such questions with searing, authoritative force.[58]

Wiesel's *Shoah* past in one sense isolates him from others who have not experienced it and hence cannot fully understand him and it. On the other hand, he has chosen to actualize his storytelling genius to invite others to join him in his ongoing quest for a better world: "Conteur, je fais de la solitude un acte contre la solitude" [Storyteller, I make out of solitude an act against solitude].[59] He has indeed fulfilled this objective when Beth and others can admit that "in some ways, we are on the same journey."

Notes

1. John S. Friedman, "The Art of Fiction LXXIX: Elie Wiesel," in *Elie Wiesel: Conversations,* ed. Robert Franciosi (Jackson: University Press of Mississippi, 2002), 82.

2. Harry James Cargas, *Harry James Cargas in Conversation with Elie Wiesel* (New York: Paulist Press, 1976), 85–86.

3. Elie Wiesel, *The Accident,* trans. Anne Borchardt (New York: Bantam Books, 1982), 21–22.

4. Ibid., 21.

5. Friedman, "The Art of Fiction LXXIX," 90.

6. Curt Schleier, "*Review*: 'The Judges' by Elie Wiesel." *Kansas City Star Tribune*: 25 August 2002: 2–3.

7. Elie Wiesel, interview with author, October 25, 2004, Boston, Massachusetts.

8. Elie Wiesel, interview with author, October 25, 2004, Boston, Massachusetts.

9. Cargas, *Cargas in Conversation,* 34.

10. Irving Abrahamson, ed., *Against Silence: The Voice and Vision of Elie Wiesel,* Vol. 2 (New York: Holocaust Library, 1985), 155.

11. Cargas, *Cargas in Conversation*, 86.

12. Lily Edelman, "A Conversation with Elie Wiesel," in *Elie Wiesel: Conversations,* ed. Robert Franciosi (Jackson: University Press of Mississippi, 2002), 46.

13. Irving Abrahamson, ed., *Against Silence: The Voice and Vision of Elie Wiesel,* Vol. 3 (New York: Holocaust Library, 1985), 116.

14. Anton Laytner, *Arguing with God: A Jewish Tradition* (Northvale, N.J.: Jason Aronson, Inc., 1990), 238.

15. Jacob Jocz, "Israel after Auschwitz," in *The Witness of the Jews to God*, ed. David W. Torrance (Edinburgh: Hansel Press, 1982), 60–61.

16. Friedman, "The Art of Fiction LXXIX," 90.

17. Elie Wiesel, *Memoirs: All Rivers Run to the Sea,* trans. Marion Wiesel (New York: Alfred A. Knopf, 1995), 84.

18. Elie Wiesel, *And the Sea Is Never Full: Memoirs, 1969–,* trans. Marion Wiesel (New York: Alfred A. Knopf, 1999), 70.

19. Abrahamson, *Against Silence,* Vol. 1, 55.

20. Abrahamson, *Against Silence,* Vol. 2, 60.

21. Lily Edelman, "A Conversation with Elie Wiesel," in *Responses to Elie Wiesel,* ed. Harry James Cargas (New York: Persea Books, 1978), 21.

22. Zachary Braiterman, *(God) After Auschwitz: Tradition and Change in Post-Holocaust Jewish Thought* (Princeton: Princeton University Press, 1998), 115.

23. Abrahamson, *Against Silence,* Vol. 3, 71.

24. Ibid., 291.

25. Harold Flender, "Conversation with Elie Wiesel," in *Elie Wiesel: Conversations,* ed. Robert Franciosi (Jackson: University Press of Mississippi, 2002), 19.

26. Elie Wiesel, *A Beggar in Jerusalem,* trans. Lily Edelman and Elie Wiesel (New York: Random House, 1970), 47; 48; 30; 31.

27. Elie Wiesel, *Le Mendiant de Jerusalem* (Paris: Editions du Seuil, 1968), 20.

28. Wiesel, *A Beggar in Jerusalem*, 18; 35.

29. Ibid., 16.

30. Ibid., 18.

31. Elie Wiesel, *Twilight,* trans. Marion Wiesel (New York: Schocken Books, 1988), 114.

32. Ibid., 114–116.

33. Elie Wiesel, *Wise Men and Their Tales: Portraits of Biblical, Talmudic, and Hasidic Masters* (New York: Schocken Books, 2003), 80.

34. Abrahamson, *Against Silence,* Vol. 3, 231–232.

35. Ibid., 253.

36. Abrahamson, *Against Silence,* Vol. 2, 79.

37. Ibid., 79.

38. Elie Wiesel, *The Town Beyond the Wall,* trans. Stephen Becker (New York: Schocken Books, 1982), 9. Italics in text.

39. Wiesel, *Twilight,* 119.

40. Elie Wiesel, interview with author, October 25, 2004, Boston, Massachusetts.

41. Wiesel, *Twilight,* 42. Italics in text.

42. Wiesel, *The Town Beyond the Wall,* 171–172. Italics in text.

43. Wiesel, *Twilight,* 118. Italics in text.

44. Elie Wiesel, interview with author, October 25, 2004, Boston, Massachusetts.

45. Elie Wiesel, *The Judges,* trans. Geoffrey Strachan (New York: Alfred A. Knopf, 2002), 151.

46. Elie Wiesel and Philippe-Michaël de Saint-Cheron, *Evil and Exile,* trans. Jon Rothschild (Notre Dame: University of Notre Dame Press, 1990), 105.

47. Abrahamson, *Against Silence,* Vol. 2, 79.

48. Abrahamson, *Against Silence,* Vol. 3, 229.

49. David R. Blumenthal, *Facing the Abusing God: A Theology of Protest* (Louisville, Kentucky: Westminster John Knox Press, 1993), 232.

50. Ted. L. Estess, "A Conversation with Elie Wiesel," in *Elie Wiesel: Conversations,* ed. Robert Franciosi (Jackson: University Press of Mississippi, 2002), 179.

51. Abrahamson, *Against Silence,* Vol. 2, 107.

52. Abrahamson, *Against Silence,* Vol. 3, 230–231.

53. Ekkehard Schuster and Reinhold Boschert-Kimmig, "Elie Wiesel Speaks," in *Elie Wiesel: Conversations,* ed. Robert Franciosi (Jackson: University Press of Mississippi, 2002), 149.

54. Elie Wiesel, *The Accident,* trans. Anne Borchardt (New York: Bantam Books, 1982), 65.

55. Ibid., 69; 25.

56. Ibid., 66.

57. Elie Wiesel, *The Gates of the Forest,* trans. Frances Frenaye (New York: Schocken Books, 1982), 199.

58. Irving Halperin, "From *Night* to the *Gates of the Forest*: The Novels of Elie Wiesel," in *Messengers from the Dead: Literature of the Holocaust,* ed. Irving Halperin (Philadelphia: Westminster Press, 1970), 83.

59. Elie Wiesel, *Signes d'Exode: Essays, Histories, Dialogues* (Paris: Bernard Grasset, 1985), 241. My translation.

Shaliach Tzibor:
Wiesel as Storyteller of His People

CAREN S. NEILE

Make me worthy to be a storyteller of our Jewish people.—
Schram, "Storyteller's Prayer"[1]

Storyteller is a vexed term. It is commonly used, in academia and in everyday speech, to denote all those employing narrative media, including fiction writers, film directors — and fibbers. For parents, educators, and librarians, moreover, the word primarily implies a children's entertainer. In the emerging field of storytelling studies, storyteller is perhaps best defined by Doug Lipman,[2] who uses it to identify one whose *oeuvre* hinges not only on narrative, but also on four other key elements: nonverbal behavior, imagination, words, and interaction with an audience. That is to say, a storytelling event requires teller and audience to share the same space and time, be they actual or virtual.[3]

Walter Benjamin highlights this link between storytelling and presence when he relates the demise of storytelling to the fact that narrative has been removed from the realm of living speech.[4] He further argues that the rise of the novel, dependent as it was on the development of the printing press, was

> the earliest symptom of a process whose end is the decline of storytelling.... What can be handed on orally, the wealth of the epic, is of a

different kind from what constitutes the stock in trade of the novel. What differentiates the novel from all other forms of prose literature ... is that it neither comes from oral tradition nor goes into it. This distinguishes it from storytelling in particular. The storyteller takes what he tells from experience — his own or that reported by others. And he in turn makes it the experience of those who are listening to his tale.[5]

Benjamin similarly distinguishes between the experiences of reading a novel and a short story. The word storyteller similarly connotes the living oral tradition in Jewish culture.[6] David Roskies describes a world of oral storytelling in noting that: "in the first decade of the nineteenth century, the Jews of central and eastern Europe are a people of storytellers. Men went off to pray three times daily; between afternoon and evening prayers, they swapped a tale or two. On the Sabbath and holidays they returned to the study house or synagogue to hear a *maggid*, an itinerant preacher, weave stories into lengthy singsong sermons."[7] He further notes that although young boys in Yiddish-speaking communities throughout Europe studied the (written) Old Testament, their teachers would then translate the holy book into *khumesh-taytsh*, a Yiddish used solely for this activity and explain obscure points with stories taken from rabbinic lore. "Ultimately," writes Barbara Kirshenblatt-Gimblett, "the oral tradition is an institution in Jewish religious learning as sacred as the written word."[8]

Elie Wiesel also emphasizes the oral tradition in discussing the importance of storytelling in Jewish life,[9] going so far as to claim that the novel *A Beggar in Jerusalem* is a tale because his lips were moving as he wrote it. He clearly places himself within the tradition of the *maggid*,[10] and his published *oeuvre* within the storytelling tradition, as do numerous critics and scholars.[11]

How then to reconcile Elie Wiesel's books as the work of a storyteller for those of us who perform, teach, or analyze our often misunderstood and misrepresented field, who tend to cleave to the notion of the storyteller as a kind of shirt-sleeved-public-intellectual/prophet, balancing on the cusp of the system, alternately buoying and buffeting the community with messages of hope, healing, and justice, and generally using no tools more technologically advanced than the mouths, faces, and bodies with which we were born — with the occasional guitar or harmonica as accompaniment?

For storytellers, the answer may rest in statements by writers such as Mario Vargas Llosa and Peninnah Schram,[12] the latter of whom has described an additional salient quality of the storyteller, that of the "*shaliach tzibor*, the messenger/ prophet of the community who maintains and transmits its traditions, history, values and wisdom."[13] In this essay, I argue that although numerous scholars — including Wiesel himself— have acknowledged his role as a messenger to humanity, it is the importance of his role as a Jewish messenger that ultimately makes Wiesel a storyteller. I first discuss the role of the storyteller as messenger of and to people. Then I examine Wiesel's role as messenger. Finally I shall examine his messages to and on behalf of the Jewish people, ultimately focusing on a dualism that is at the heart of both storytelling and the Jewish response to modernity: tradition versus innovation.

Storyteller as Cultural Messenger

Storytelling has long been understood among folklorists, anthropologists, educators, and others as a highly effective mode of cultural reproduction,[14] transmitting attitudes, beliefs, and values in an indirect and highly pleasurable form. Schram's "Storyteller's Prayer" emphasizes this role:

> *Rebono shel olam*, God of the Universe, listen to my heart
> and my voice as I stand before You, wanting to tell *our* story [italics added].
> Help me to understand and find the right feelings and
> words with which to transmit the tale.
> Make my voice expressive and clear so that the collective
> wisdom of our people can reach the hearts
> of those who *listen* [italics added].
> May I merit to hear well with my ears and heart.
> Keep me from the jealousy of other tellers and from my
> jealousy of them so that we may be able to share and
> hear each other with open hearts.
> Allow me to assume this responsibility as my forebears did
> before me — to continue to retell *our* stories [italics added].
> Help me to choose my stories wisely and let my words live.
> Make me worthy to be a storyteller of our Jewish people.[15]

Unlike the artist who believes that she is making a personal statement, Schram recognizes that as a Jewish storyteller, she is not merely telling her own story, but rather "our" story. The "our" may be read not only as inclusive of the Jewish people, however, but of God, as well. That is to say, "our" story implies the historical covenant between the Jewish people and their God, consisting of observing the Laws on one side (the Jews) and of protecting the people on the other (God). Thus it is that with one heart and one voice, Schram the storyteller attempts to speak for and to all the parties of that covenant.

From the ancient griots of Africa to the seanarchies of Ireland, this mission has traditionally been of critical importance for the continuation of the community. In Vargas Llosa's novel *The Storyteller*, a Jewish agnostic becomes *an hablador*, a storyteller for an indigenous Peruvian tribe on the brink of extinction. Toward the end of the novel, the storyteller recounts the tragic history of the Jews, calling them, in the language of his new tribe, the people of Jehovah-Tasurinchi. The history concludes with the words:

> Could it be that despite everything that happened to it, Jehovah-Tasurinchi's people never was at odds with its destiny? Always fulfilled its obligation; always respected the prohibitions, too. Was it hated because it was different? Was that why, wherever it went, peoples would not accept it? Who knows? People don't like living with people who are different. They don't trust them, perhaps.... People would like everyone to be the same, would like others to forget their own customs, kill their seripigaris, violate their own taboos, and imitate theirs. If I had done that, Jehovah-Tasurinchi's people would have disappeared. Not one storyteller would have survived to tell their story.[16]

Vargas Llosa implies that by reminding the people of their traditions, the storyteller is responsible for their very survival.

Wiesel too has made much of the connection between storyteller and messenger, particularly in his novel *The Oath*. The author of a book of Biblical commentary before the war, afterward, Wiesel "knew that anyone who remained alive had to become a storyteller, a messenger, had to speak up."[17] Like Schram, Wiesel has a Storyteller's Prayer, his own and the one he attributes to the 18th-century master Rebbe Avraham Yehoshua Heschel of Apt, great-grandfather of the philosopher Abraham Joshua Heschel. Revered not only for his saintliness but also for his storytelling, the great Rebbe prays:

Let them say that I am one of the Just, a miracle-maker, one who can revoke misfortune.... Are You jealous of the honor given to Yehoshua Heschel? Do You really think it is he they are honoring? Who is he anyway? What is he? A broken vessel. But since they come to me, since they consider me their *messenger* to You, [italics mine] please, God, do not shame them. Let me be the stick on which they can lean, a stick and not a useless branch.[18]

As is the case with Vargas Llosa's storyteller, Wiesel links the role of the storyteller with that of bulwark against extinction. In the hasidic parable he retells at the beginning of *The Gates of the Forest*, he describes being unable to light the fire, recite the prayer, or locate the place in the forest where his ancestors met to avert misfortune, and that the only thing he can do is to tell the story, which must be sufficient. Wiesel thus makes the point that now, as always, it is the story that preserves and protects the Jewish people by, in part, serving to define their Jewishness.

Wiesel as Messenger

Wiesel has been referred to as "messenger" in print dozens of times. Over the decades, he has been referred to as a messenger from the dead, for the living, to heaven, for the self, and for mankind. He has also been called a messenger to all humanity,[19] and messenger of the departed, and messenger of his people.[20] Wiesel is "obsessed with the messenger aspect of man."[21] Although he states that the single underlying theme in his books is memory,[22] he extends the encomium to remember a step further, asserting that his primary responsibility is to give testimony, to bear witness to these memories. Assailed at times by critics for sacrificing style for substance, Wiesel takes, he attests, the criticism as compliment, asserting that what he expects from literature is a moral dimension. "Art for art's sake is gone," he writes. "We cannot allow it. Just to write a novel, that's why I survived?"[23]

Storytellers often witness the events they describe, and in the Jewish tradition, Wiesel notes, "a witness is a kind of messenger. The witness says, 'That is how things are.' 'Amen,' in Hebrew means, 'That's how it is.' The witnesses that we are make us into messengers."[24]

In the book, *Elie Wiesel: Messenger to All Humanity*, Brown details five steps in becoming a messenger of a catastrophic event, such as the Holocaust:

1. The Event took place: one must speak.
2. The Event defies description: one cannot speak.
3. The Event suggests an alternative: one could choose silence.
4. The Event precludes silence: one must become a messenger.
5. The Event suggests a certain kind of message: one can be a teller of tales.[25]

For Wiesel, the event, is the Holocaust, or, more specifically, his own deportation at age 15 from Sighet, Transylvania, to death camps in Poland, culminating in the murder of most of his family and his own release. Brown's two points about silence are addressed in many of Wiesel's works and interviews, particularly in *The Oath*, which centers on a vow of silence. In *Gates of the Forest*, for example, Gregor tells a story three times, but his comrades still do not believe him. He thinks:

> Do you want my voice? Take it. We'll start again. The human ... voice builds walls, a man knocks his head against them, it hurts; it no longer hurts. Eventually the voice becomes a prison.... It's my voice you need? Take it.... Listening to his own voice, he found it false. This isn't the true story; you're holding that back. The repetition of the truth betrays it. The more I talk the more I empty myself of truth.[26]

The passage is an eloquent disavowal of language due to its potential for betrayal, as well as because of the guilt that can be associated with speech — and prevented with silence. It reflects a central dilemma of Holocaust narrative that has been echoed by numerous writers and critics.[27] In fact, all his books, Wiesel has noted, could be read as one big book, which he would title: *In Pursuit of Silence*.[28] Interestingly, Wiesel actually lost his voice at the completion of *A Beggar in Jerusalem*,[29] perhaps in part due to the fact that, as previously mentioned, he moved his lips as he wrote, or perhaps as a reaction to the enormity of his task.

The point about transmitting a message, Brown's fifth, as justification for survival, is discussed at great length in *The Oath*, which is mainly narrated as a monologue told by a storyteller. "Yes," he says to himself,

> that is the best method; it has been tested and proved. I'll transmit my experience to him and he, in turn, will be compelled to do the same. He in turn will become a messenger. And once a messenger, he has no alternative. He must stay alive until he has transmitted his message. Azriel himself would not still be alive if his father, the chronicler, his friends and

his teacher Moshe the Madman had not made him the repository of their tragic and secret truths. By entrusting the Book to him, his father doomed him to survival.[30]

For half a century, Wiesel's messages have reached people of all faiths, as evidenced by, among other honors, his receipt of the Nobel Peace Prize. Brown, who titled his book *Elie Wiesel: Messenger to All Humanity*, originally intended to focus his book on Wiesel's role as messenger to the Jews. The Christian theologian saw himself as "eavesdropper" to a conversation between Wiesel and his people to which he was invited to listen. Eventually, however, Brown says that he recognized that not only was Wiesel speaking to his fellow Jews, but also to humanists, radicals, theists, and others throughout the world. Wiesel himself has also stated that "in each of my books, I could substitute the word 'human' for 'Jew' and I have done that at times."[31]

Along this universalist vein, Alan Berger details Wiesel's "three-fold message for humanity: the importance of memory, the necessity of accepting moral responsibility, and the imperative of questioning God."[32] He goes on to compare Wiesel, "troubler of an all too frequently complacent humanity" to the biblical "troubler" prophets of Israel.

Wiesel, however, has stated that he is a Jew first, a writer second.[33] I submit that his foremost contribution is as a Jewish storyteller-messenger, not merely as a light among nations, a role that Jews have traditionally been exhorted to fill, but as one who specifically reaffirms and renegotiates the traditions, stories, values, and wisdom that he believes are essential for the continuation of the Jewish people after Auschwitz.

Wiesel as Messenger of the Jews

Brown's description of the role of messenger to humanity also applies to Wiesel as messenger to the Jews: messenger from the dead, messenger for the living, messenger to heaven, and messenger for the self. What follows are some of the storyteller's messages for his fellow Jews:

First, it is incumbent upon Jews to protest against God. Wiesel's protests against God for the atrocities perpetrated during the Holocaust are "firmly within [the] Judaic tradition of protest.[34] Josephine Knopp claims that Wiesel's first five novels, *Night*, *Dawn*, *The Accident* (also known as *Day*), *The Town Beyond the Wall*, and *The Gates of the Forest*, may be read "as a sustained, developing revolt against God from within a Jewish context." Wiesel not only finds precedents for these protests within the Jewish tradition, he even finds legal and moral sanctions.[35]

These protests are borne out repeatedly in Wiesel's fiction, as well as in his interviews. Case in point: In *The Accident*, the protagonist-narrator nearly succeeds in committing suicide. Because the sacredness of life, which God bestowed upon mankind, is among the most basic tenets of Judaism, the attempt may be seen as the most profound act of defiance of God. It is as if now that God has violated the covenant, the Jews are free to do the same.[36] Clearly this message, coming as it does from so deeply within Jewish Law, is meant for Jews above all else.

Second, the covenant with God must be revisioned. Berger discusses Greenberg's conception of "the voluntary covenant" with respect to the children of Holocaust survivors. The covenant between God and the Jews that existed prior to Auschwitz must, according to this view, be "revisioned" to stress the "democratization of access to religious life."[37] This is particularly meaningful, Berger stresses, with respect to two aspects of that covenant: *din Torah* [Jewish law] and *tikkun olam* [the mission to make the world a better place].

The character Michael in *The Town Beyond the Wall* returns to his Hungarian village after the war, only to be asked how it was that the Jews did not fight back against the ten or so policemen who led them to slaughter. The response: Undoubtedly they expected that God would maintain His side of the covenant and come to their aid as He had done in the past; they could not allow themselves to believe that the covenant would be broken. The covenant of our ancestors in Egypt is null and void, Wiesel is saying, because God has not upheld his side. A new document is required to meet the challenges of the post–Holocaust world.

Third, to be a Jew is not only to remember, but also to bear witness. To bear witness, Wiesel tells us, is to uphold the Jewish role in the covenant with God. The storyteller-narrator of *The Oath* asks:

> Was Moshe aware of the prominent role of the witness in Jewish tradition? Even God needs him. The Bible tells us so and the Talmud confirms it: "If you shall be my witness, I shall be your God, if you shall refuse that role, I shall refuse mine."[38]

In novel after novel of Wiesel's, Jews are messengers, witnesses, and storytellers. Wiesel too has taken upon himself these roles. At the outset of *Souls on Fire*, he writes:

> My father, an enlightened spirit, believed
> in man.
> My grandfather, a fervent Hasid, believed
> in God.
> The one taught me to speak, the other to sing.
> Both loved stories.
> And when I tell mine, I hear their voices.
> Whispering from beyond the silenced storm,
> They are what links the survivor to their memory.[39]

Through his tales, Wiesel is able to connect with his memory of his ancestors. By employing the term "their memory," he also implies their knowledge of what it meant to be a Jew, the timeless, oceanic experience of Jewish history to which Wiesel often alludes.[40] In the essay "Whose Messengers Are We?" he further asserts that "to assume one's past — to share in our collective memory — is a privilege."[41] Because Wiesel cannot bring himself to reveal the tragic tales of his own generation, he tells them indirectly through the tales of his ancestors.

Fourth, a Jew must face the problems of others. The narrator of *The Oath*, Azriel, breaks his vow not to tell the story of his village in order to save the life of another man. Moreover in *The Town Beyond the Wall* and *The Gates of the Forest*, the meaning of life is understood as caring, and suffering, for another human being.

Fifth, community is central to Jewish identity. A sense of the community plays a pivotal role in Wiesel's novels, serving alternately as backdrop, foil, teacher, and student. It is a character in and of itself in *The Oath*, taking a vow of silence about a pivotal moment in its history. The town's name, Kolvillag, is Hebrew for "every village," a paraphrase of "everyman." A Jew alone, Wiesel is saying, is weak, ineffectual and, often, in danger. As a group, Jews can assert their mission and fulfill their destiny, which, in part, means serving as a support to each other.

Sixth, a Jew seeks redemption. At the heart of *The Testament* is a Jewish poet's recounting of his life as a Communist to his son prior to his execution. In his last days in prison, Paltiel Kossover laments:

Oh, it is not my death that frightens me, but the impossibility of imparting some meaning to my past.... Tomorrow I shall go on writing the Testament of Paltiel Kossover, filling it with details, turning it into a document of the times — in which the experiences of the past will serve as signs for the future.[42]

When our mistakes help prevent others from making the same, Kossover is saying, perhaps we may be redeemed.

Storytelling is also an act of redemption for Wiesel. A *maggid* in *A Beggar in Jerusalem* states:

"Here is the first question which is put to the soul, in heaven, when it faces the celestial tribunal: 'Have you lived in expectation of the Messiah?' As for me, I shall answer: 'I was not content merely to wait for him, I went looking for him everywhere, even within myself.'"[43]

Messages Not Received

Wiesel readily admits that he has far more questions than answers. In his writing, he frequently refers to questions.[44] "In general," Wiesel has said, "all of my work is a question mark. My work does not contain one single answer. It's always questions, questions I try to make deeper as in a concentric circle."[45] The answers that Wiesel has not yet received have to do with "the content, with the soul of writing." They also have to do with life, death, and solitude. "What does man do to break out of his own self and attain a kind of presence in the world?" he writes. "Why does one write, if it's not to break out of this solitude."[46] And that may be the most important message of all that Wiesel brings to his fellow Jews. For Wiesel, every Jew is a messenger without answers, a difficult, but crucial, role. In so doing, each Jew exhorts others to find their own answers, which is a far deeper learning experience.

Innovation and Tradition

In *Souls on Fire*, Wiesel's identification of the Maggid of Mezeritch as a "vessel of communication, of executor rather than innovator" could serve as self-description as well."[47] Indeed, Wiesel asserts:

Repetition, in Judaism, can assume a creative role.... To transmit is more important than to innovate.... In Hebrew, the word *massora*, tradition, comes from the verb *limsor*, to transmit. In our history, this need to communicate, to share, comes close to being an obsession.[48]

Along these lines, Freedman quotes an anonymous author who supports this view of Wiesel as executor:

we have turned the messenger into the message. Many people who have not sat down with a Jewish history don't have any context for what Wiesel says, for the Holocaust itself. They don't know what happened. So there's this amorphous desire to lament, to romanticize, and it seizes on a person. Into the vacuum comes a type of idol making.[49]

By viewing Wiesel as a personality, a famous writer like any other, the author suggests, we miss the point of his life and his work. We miss his message.

Despite this apparent emphasis on tradition, an emphasis on innovation also exists in Wiesel's work. On one hand, for example, Wiesel calls himself a student of Kabbalah, Jewish mysticism.[50] Yet, Hyams notes, that after the Holocaust, "[w]ithin Wiesel warred the rationalism of his father with the mysticism of his mother."[51] Similarly, he reflects the desire expressed in the introduction to *Legends of Our Time*, not to be attached to the name of his grandfather — at the same time that he says he wrote *Souls on Fire*, a collection of hasidic tales that he first heard from his grandfather, to feel closer to him.

Perhaps this interplay of innovation and tradition is due to the fact that Wiesel sees rationalism as "a failure and a betrayal"[52] based on his experience in the Holocaust. Whatever the overt reason for its presence, the duality resides at the very foundation of Wiesel's identity as a Jewish storyteller. This is because one of the primary qualities of folklore is the tension between tradition and innovation. The storyteller at once relates a tale that has been transmitted across hundreds of generations and puts his or her own personal stamp on the telling. In addition, each storytelling event, by its nature, constitutes a slightly new variant, based on audience response, the mood of the teller, and countless other factors, including length of performance and even quality of the sound system.

All these factors contribute to innovations on, if not always improvements to, the tale. Throughout, the responsible storyteller ideally strives to remains true to the spirit of the variant on which she chooses to model her work. The messenger-storyteller must find his or her own way to relay the message. For his part, Wiesel uses the hasidic tales, as well as his fictional characters, to impart the stories he can tell and the stories he believes must forever be shrouded in silence. The messages that he transmits likewise balance between the demands of tradition and the opportunities of innovation. The idea that the covenant with God must be revisioned falls into the category of innovation, but so does the idea that to be a Jew is not only to remember but also to bear witness. The remembering represents adherence to tradition, while the bearing witness differs with every teller.

Not coincidentally, the same explanation of variants may be used to describe the way that many modern Jews fashion their religious observance. They put their personal spin on the *mitzvot* [commandments], participating in some, while eschewing others. One by one, they refashion their personal covenant with God, as has Wiesel himself, who no longer leads the hasidic life to which he was born.

Summary

Elie Wiesel's remarkable *ouevre* spans six decades and more then forty works, including autobiography, memoir, and drama; the vast majority are fiction. Despite his recognition that storytelling is based on the oral tradition, Wiesel considers himself primarily a storyteller. The story that he attempts to tell is "first of all, a story of night which the Kabbalah calls *shvirat hakelim*— the breaking of the vessels —... a cosmic cataclysm."[53] Wiesel employs his art as a howl in the darkness of the post–Auschwitz night. At the same time, it serves as a silken thread to connect him with the past, present, and future of Jewish experience. It is this quality that aligns his narratives with those of the wandering *maggid,* with whom he identifies. It is these messages, of a continual negotiation between Jewish rebellion and tradition that make him not only a Jewish novelist, but also a Jewish storyteller, a messenger of and to his people.

In the epigraph to *The Gates of the Forest,* Wiesel writes, "God made man because he loves stories." For his part, Wiesel makes stories because he loves man. And that — as he writes in the parable at the beginning of the book — must be sufficient.

Notes

1. Peninnah Schram, "Storyteller's Prayer," in *Jewish Stories One Generation Tells Another* (Northvale, N.J.: Jason Aronson, Inc., 1987), xxxv.

2. Doug Lipman, "Story Dynamics, What Is Storytelling?" *Storytelling Workshop in a Box(tm),* 12, Story Dynamics, P.O. Box 541165, Tulsa, Oklahoma 74152. <www.storydynamics.com/swb>, September 2005, accessed October 2005.

3. See Brenda Laurel, *Computers as Theatre*, 2nd edition (Reading, Massachusetts: Addison-Wesley Longman, 1993); Anne Pellowski, *The World of Storytelling: A Practical Guide to the Origins, Development, and Applications of Storytelling*, expanded and rev. ed. (Bronx, N.Y.: H.W. Wilson, 1990); Norma J. Livo and Sandra A. Rietz, *Storytelling: Process & Practice* (Littleton, Colo.: Libraries Unlimited, 1986).

4. Walter Benjamin, *Illuminations: Essays and Reflections*, ed. Hannah Arendt and trans. H. Zohn (New York: Schocken Books, 1968), 87.

5. Ibid., 87.

6. See Peninnah Schram, "Jewish Models: Adapting Folktales for Telling Aloud," in *Who Says? Essays on Pivotal Issues in Contemporary Storytelling*, ed. Carol L. Birch and Melissa A. Heckler (Little Rock: August House, 1996), 64–90.

7. David G. Roskies, *A Bridge of Longing: The Lost Art of Yiddish Storytelling* (Cambridge: Harvard University Press, 1995), 1.

8. Steven J. Zeitlin, ed., *Because God Loves Stories: An Anthology of Jewish Storytelling* (New York: Simon & Schuster, 1997), 18.

9. See Irving Abrahamson, *Against Silence: The Voice and Vision of Elie Wiesel*, Vol. 2 (New York: Holocaust Library, 1985).

10. See Irving Abrahamson, *Against Silence: The Voice and Vision of Elie Wiesel*, Vol. 1 (New York: Holocaust Library, 1985).

11. See Harry James Cargas, "In Conversation with Elie Wiesel," in Elie *Wiesel, Conversations*, ed. Robert Franciosi (Jackson: University Press of Mississippi, 2002), 58–68; Irving Abrahamson, *Against Silence: The Voice and Vision of Elie Wiesel*, Vol. 1–3 (New York: Holocaust Library, 1985).

12. See Mario Llosa Vargas, *The Storyteller*, trans. Helen Lane (New York: Farrar Straus Giroux, 1989); see Peninnah Schram, *Jewish Stories One Generation Tells Another* (Northvale, N.J.: Jason Aronson, Inc., 1987).

13. Caren S. Neile, personal communication, December, 2000.

14. See Joseph D. Sobel, *The Storyteller's Journey: An American Revival* (Urbana: University of Illinois, 1999); Barre Toelken, "The Icebergs of Folktale: Misconception, Misuse, Abuse," in *Who Says? Essays on Pivotal Issues in Contemporary Storytelling,* ed. Carol L. Birch and Melissa A. Heckler (Little Rock: August House, 1996), 35–63; Alasdair MacIntyre, *After Virtue*, 2nd edition (Notre Dame, Ind.: University of Notre Dame Press, 1984); Linda Degh, *Folktales and Society: Story-telling in a Hungarian Peasant Community*, trans. Emily M. Schoosberger (Bloomington: Indiana University Press, 1969).

15. Schram, "Storyteller's Prayer," xxxv.

16. Mario Vargas Llosa, *The Storyteller*, trans. Helen Lane (New York: Farrar Straus Giroux, 1989), 219–220.

17. Cargas, "In Conversation with Elie Wiesel," 61.

18. Irving Abrahamson, *Against Silence: The Voice and Vision of Elie Wiesel*, Vol. 1 (New York: Holocaust Library, 1985), 55.

19. Robert McAfee Brown, *Elie Wiesel: Messenger to All Humanity*, rev. ed. (Notre Dame: University of Notre Dame Press, 1989).

20. Barry Hyams, "Witness and Messenger," in *Elie Wiesel: Conversations*, ed. Robert Franciosi (Jackson: University Press of Mississippi), 9–15.

21. Brown, *Elie Wiesel: Messenger to All Humanity*, 19.

22. See Elie Wiesel, *From the Kingdom of Memory: Reminiscences* (New York: Schocken Books, 1990).

23. Samuel G. Freedman, "Bearing Witness: The Life and Work of Elie Wiesel," in *Elie Wiesel: Conversations*, ed. Robert Franciosi (Jackson: University Press of Mississippi, 2002), 108.

24. Cargas, "Conversation with Elie Wiesel," 58.

25. Brown, *Elie Wiesel: Messenger to All Humanity*, 20.

26. Elie Wiesel, *Gates of the Forest*, trans. Frances Frenaye (New York: Schocken Books, 1966), 163.

27. See Caren S. Neile, "Poetry after Auschwitz: Emotion and Culture in Fictional Representations of the Holocaust," *Innovation*, Vol. 10, No. 4. (1997): 405–417.

28. Robert Franciosi and Brian Shaffer, "An Interview with Elie Wiesel," in *Elie Wiesel: Conversations*, ed. Robert Franciosi (Jackson: University Press of Mississippi, 2002), 127.

29. See Irving Abrahamson, *Against Silence: The Voice and Vision of Elie Wiesel*, Vol. 1–3 (New York: Holocaust Library, 1985).

30. Elie Wiesel, *The Oath*, trans. Marion Wiesel (New York: Random House, 1973), 33.

31. Jacques de Ricaumont, "The Prix Medicis to Elie Wiesel: Overcoming Adversity," in *Elie Wiesel: Conversations*, ed. Robert Franciosi (Jackson: University Press of Mississippi, 2002), 16.

32. Alan Berger, "The Judges: Book Review," *Shofar*, Vol. 21 No. 3, 151 (Spring 2003): 3.

33. See Irving Abrahamson, *Against Silence: The Voice and Vision of Elie Wiesel*, Vol. 1–3 (New York: Holocaust Library, 1985).

34. Josephine Knopp, "Wiesel and the Absurd," *Contemporary Literature*, XV (1974): 212–220.

35. Elie Wiesel, "Jewish Values in the Post-Holocaust Future: A Symposium," *Judaism*, 16 (1967): 281.

36. Byron L. Sherwin, "Elie Wiesel and Jewish Theology," *Judaism*, XVII (1969): 39–52.

37. Alan Berger, "The Holocaust, Second-Generation Witness, and the Voluntary Covenant in American Judaism," *Religion and American Culture: A Journal of Interpretation*, Vol. 5, No. 1 (Winter 1995): 27.

38. Wiesel, *The Oath*, 188.

39. Elie Wiesel, *Souls on Fire: Portraits and Legends of Hasidic Masters*, trans. Marion Wiesel (New York: Random House, 1972), 1.

40. See Jacques De Ricaumont, "The Prix Medicis to Elie Wiesel: Overcoming Adversity," in *Elie Wiesel: Conversations*, ed. Robert Franciosi (Jackson: University Press of Mississippi, 2002), 16–18.

41. Irving Abrahamson, *Against Silence: The Voice and Vision of Elie Wiesel*, Vol. 3 (New York: Holocaust Library, 1985), 102–103.

42. Elie Wiesel, *The Testament*, trans. Marion Wiesel (New York: Summit Books, 1981), 335–336.

43. Elie Wiesel, *A Beggar in Jerusalem*, trans. Lily Edelman and Elie Wiesel (New York: Random House, 1970), 85.

44. See Michiko Kakutani, "Wiesel: No Answers, Only Questions," in *Elie Wiesel: Conversations*, ed. Robert Franciosi (Jackson: University Press of Mississippi, 2002), 99–102; See Elie Wiesel, *From the Kingdom of Memory: Reminiscences* (New York: Schocken Books, 1990).

45. Harold Flender, "Conversation with Elie Wiesel," in *Elie Wiesel: Conversations*, ed. Robert Franciosi (Jackson: University Press of Mississippi, 2002), 19.

46. Ibid., 19.

47. Freedman, "Bearing Witness: The Life and Work of Elie Wiesel," 111.

48. Wiesel, *Souls on Fire*, 257.

49. Freedman, "Bearing Witness: The Life and Work of Elie Wiesel," 111.

50. See Ekkehard Schuster and Reinhold Boschert-Kimmig, "Elie Wiesel Speaks," in *Elie Wiesel: Conversations*, ed. Robert Franciosi (Jackson: University Press of Mississippi, 2002), 146–159.

51. Hyams, "Witness and Messenger," 11.

52. Lily Edelman, "A Conversation with Elie Wiesel," in *Elie Wiesel: Conversations*, ed. Robert Franciosi (Jackson: University Press of Mississippi, 2002), 50.

53. Cargas, "Conversation with Elie Wiesel," 59.

Teaching Beyond the Text: Examining and Acting On the Moral Aspects of *Night*

ELAINE O'QUINN

In Hebrew there is a word for the face and what it reveals. It is *panim*, which takes the plural form because it indicates a record of what is thought and known as well as what is felt.[1] Faces speak of experiences and emotions that cannot be masked. Both joy and sorrow leave an indelible mark. The only way, however, to see our own face is as a reflection, and often we are surprised, even startled by the truths the mirror exposes. For while faces tell personal stories, they also tell the stories of those we have known. Here is the crease deepened by a brother's death; there the line etched by a mother's long illness; lingering yet, the wrinkles brought on by the laughter and quick smiles of friendship and enduring love. The face, like the heart, is a keeper of all things past.

And in April of 1945 when, weeks after the liberation of Buchenwald, Elie Wiesel looks at his reflection for the first time since leaving the Jewish ghetto in 1944 and sees "[f]rom the depth of the mirror a corpse gaz[ing] back."[2] It is not surprising that he recognizes in his own face the collective face of six million Jews. "The look in his eyes, as they stared into mine, has never left me,"[3] declares the young Elie. Though it would take this adolescent boy with an old man's face over ten years to tell the story leading to this one revealing moment, he would tell it with undeniable insights of character, authenticity, and courage. He would tell a story so disturbing and raw that the moral and existential questions it raises continue to reverberate. He would tell a story meant to connect people across many differences through the memory of events made knowable, even though the circumstances and incredible loss surrounding the story remain almost unfathomable. "Your choice transcends me," Wiesel states to his audience in the opening remarks of his 1986 Nobel Peace Prize acceptance speech. So too does his unforgettable story.

Many consider the "official" beginning of the Holocaust to be November 9, 1938. Kristallnacht, as it has been called for many years, or the November Pogrom, as it is sometimes referred to now, is the day in history when Nazi cruelty started its rise. It was on this fateful day that the Nazis began in earnest to obscure the memory of the Jewish people. With little opposition from those who watched, they broke out store fronts of Jewish proprietors, destroyed synagogues, beat and killed dozens of innocents, and arrested then sent thousands of men, women, and children to concentration camps.[4] Yet, as the sound of breaking glass echoed through the streets of Germany and Austria, the world remained eerily silent. The consequence of that silence lingers even today. It resounds in every act of injustice and inhumanity that goes unnoticed and untold.

For Elie Wiesel and for those whose story he tells, Kristallnacht was only one of a long series of catastrophic events that would become the litany of Holocaust tragedy. Life was to be shattered over and over again, and no less so on that grim day in April when, in a single glance, a young boy knew with certainty that his nightmare existence of the last few years could not be denied. At some level, he must have recognized that it also should not be erased. Perhaps it was at this defining moment that Wiesel, who learned in one instant and then another that one's destiny cannot always be known, became a guardian spirit of the Holocaust and its literature. Perhaps in the instant when what mirrored image stood horrified by its own reflection, the need to give public voice to personal atrocity gave way to a genius muse, a muse all the more profound because it pits itself against a genius of evil, turning the despair and suffering born of darkness into a redemptive act of remembrance honoring violated lives. Through the colorless shroud of persecution, slavery, starvation, and murder, Wiesel was bound to weave the illuminating fiber of personal dignity, social conscience, cultural understanding, and moral accountability.

In doing so, he made it possible for all of us to understand what it means to live a worthwhile life.

My own small world also broke into unrecognizable pieces the first time I read Wiesel's *Night* as a girl of fifteen. I recall sitting in my English class after finishing the text, sickened and shocked by the story I just finished. As the horror of the writer's words stabbed at me, I sensed that I, like Elie, would never again feel my own innocence. The incomprehensible acts of hatred and slaughter that I was forced to imagine weighed heavily on my teenage soul. That someone could watch his own father die and possibly feel relief when the end came was a concept that stunned and disoriented me; that a human being could even survive such an assault on the spirit seemed impossible. For days I had terrible dreams that woke me from my sleep, leaving me scared and confused about the brutality I suddenly understood existed in the world. Never before had I been face to face with such unthinkable pain and senseless suffering. It was a difficult and exhausting juncture, and the questions the reading raised were profound and pressing.

In expectation, I waited for the in-class discussion that would somehow help me sort out the moral consequences of the acts I had witnessed. I wanted to know how such transgression against others could possibly be amended and why such immoral behavior had been tolerated. I wanted to know how Eliezer could have one shred of faith left in God or in humanity or why he should; more so, I wanted to know why I should. I was young, just learning how to live, how was I expected to understand so much death that came not at the random hand of nature, but at the calculated command of vicious murderers. My head pulsed with such questions, and I needed the reassurance of discussions that would allow me to work through my thoughts and feelings. I was fifteen. Elie Wiesel was fifteen. What were our common lives? "I was fifteen years old,"[5] he says as he sees father and son die over a crust of bread. "Fifteen," he declares, as he exists on water made of snow and soup that "taste[s] of corpses."[6] I was fifteen, and I could not comprehend how such things could happen; yet I knew they had. I was fifteen, and I needed to match what my mind was fighting to understand with what my heart refused to acknowledge, to explore how anyone could treat others so terribly and not feel the shame of the defiled meaning, made of collective lives. But the conversations never came, and the questions about hatred and bigotry, leadership and responsibility, society and the individual were left unspoken and unanswered.

Instead, the teacher had us took at Wiesel's autobiographical narrative as a piece of literary art and a telling of history. He praised the stark language that fit the bleak landscape. He pointed out the significance of dates and places. He made much of the bare bones structure of the text, comparing it to the skeletal images of the characters throughout. We looked at the symbolic nature of father figures, contrasted Eliezer's journey with Odysseus's, and pondered the appropriateness of the title. We acknowledged the ugliness of war and agreed no people deserved to be treated so unfairly. But we took on none of the moral, religious, spiritual, or existential challenges and made only superficial connections to societal and political issues. Instead, we objectified the text as a terrible historical event that happened in another place and another time; the end result was a story well told with inherent lessons we would do well to consider.

In retrospect it is clear that what we did in that classroom was "fix" the evil presented to us by simply resolving our own good and determining that what had happened in Europe could never happen in America. But as we spoke, we were a nation at war, people of color experienced daily discrimination, women continued their fight for equal rights, gays and lesbians lived in persistent fear, children went hungry, the elderly were alone, and around the world apartheid, ethnic cleansing, and political persecution were a matter of course. At some level, I knew even then that what we had done was not enough, but it would have to do. It was clear it was all I was going to get. While the historical and aesthetic approaches to the text were carefully examined, the place of compassion and affinity deep inside of me that suffered Eli's pain was left an open wound. I was on my own to close it. Instead of being taught to trust and act on the great emotion I felt, I was educated in how to divorce my feelings from my intellect, though I was certain the two were inexplicitly intertwined. I knew what all the symbols in the story meant; I understood the power of autobiography to make the reader look through a different set of eyes; I had a grasp on the events of the war. In essence, I knew what fifteen year olds are charged to know in school and that was supposed to be enough. I willed my teacher to see it was not.

The thoughts and feelings I experienced throughout that one unit of study never left me. When I became an English teacher myself, the associations I had with *Night* remained so strong that I refused to teach the text. I was afraid my students would want answers and direction, and all I would be able to offer them would be my lingering doubts. There was a moral thread to unravel in Eliezer's story that could prove as unknowable as the Holocaust itself, and I refused to take the chance of leaving my own students to suffer the same hopelessness I had felt when I came to his last line. I did not want them to struggle like I had with fracturing narrative that left me feeling as powerless as I knew young Elie had felt, with a disruption of faith that still had not mended. To accept the story Eliezer told was to contemplate that evil might be perfect and goodness flawed, a complete turnaround of everything youth is taught to believe. How could I possibly make sense of such a notion with my students? It barely made sense to me.

It took years of trying to understand why I was so opposed to teaching Wiesel's text to finally comprehend what had happened to me: there had been so little dialogue about the moral implications of the subject matter itself when I had been assigned the story, that I had no model I could refer to in my own teaching. Aside from history and aesthetics, our discussions had all been about our skilled ability to interpret and dissect a text. We had not talked about what it means to endure so much pain that even the desire to be alive is extinguished. We did not discuss how a person could possibly determine life is still worth living, despite the senseless loss of a mother, a sister, a father, and friends at the hand of unprecedented depravity and viciousness. I had no guidelines for raising issues of bias and prejudice or race and power other than to simply state: "it's wrong to oppress others" and "everyone should be treated equally." As an adolescent, those words had proved superficial and insufficient to me; as a new teacher, I knew such arguments would not be substantial enough to answer the weighty questions the story was sure to yield.

Night was more than just a good narrative account, of that I was certain; but I had no sense of where to begin a discussion about the personal and societal attitudes that prefaced it or how to assign activities that explored the ethical terrain it exposed. I knew it was important for students to come away from the text with changed perceptions not just about war but about the conditions that herald it, with new understandings that questioned not just how others should be treated and accepted, but why it is they are not valued in the first place. However, the road was rocky and I had been given no indicators of how to navigate it. I wanted to take what my former teachers and current colleagues considered a literary masterpiece and temper it with what it means to quit believing in God, in life, in other people, and possibly even in oneself. I wanted to talk not only about the indomitable spirit of human beings, but about the social manifestation of oppression that causes unimaginable suffering and inconsolable grief. I wanted to know what society could and should do to prevent such atrocities from ever again happening and why it must. It was moral and existential meaning that I saw at the heart of *Night*, not compelling plot and surreal settings; it was how each of us is connected to humanity at large that concerned me, not word choice and imagery. It was Elie and the story he told of others like him that moved me, not discussion about artistic invention and narrative detail. Some say we live in times that caution teachers against asking students to unpack and examine moral systems of belief, but my experience convinces me that these warnings are not new. Opening classroom discussion to such issues has always been a step onto dangerous ground, and it is not surprising that some teachers hesitate at the edge. However, those who claim it is not the teacher's role to lead students through the complex matters of social codes and values fail to see that teachers are always already moral agents and not just practitioners of subject matter. Because teaching is about the discovery and building of relationships, it is by its nature a moral enterprise; and like all moral enterprises, the way one proceeds influences more than just aesthetic sensibilities and gains in skill, intended or not. The affective lives and future intellectual choices of students are shaped in a classroom by the teacher's pedagogical choices, and the significance of how each arena of learning is approached is critical and real. While this can be an exciting consideration, some might also consider it a daunting one.

Teachers cannot evade the fact that their perceptions about what students should attend to in the classroom are under constant scrutiny. Students put together everything they hear and see and sense in a classroom and connect it to the world outside the classroom door. As they grapple with personal questions and understandings in public spaces, they begin to define what it means to be educated. They begin to discern their expected relation and responsibility to others and look to the teacher as a source of direction. What they encounter there has immediate and long-term effects. If all they get are minimal indicators of the connection between subject matter and self, what they learn to take away from their learning is equally minimal. If, for example, they observe that the main significance of story seems to lie only in its literary merit, they may miss it as a transformative touchstone of their lives. When Wiesel asks "[h]ow could it be possible for them to burn people, children, and for the world to keep silent,"[7] he is not merely presenting a protagonist's struggle with a dire situation. He is asking a world of readers how such a thing could happen. The teacher, as moral agent, is obligated to ask the same question and struggle with the answer or, possibly, even the lack of one.

At this point, it is significant to remember that Wiesel is also a teacher. It may be important to ask why someone who so effectively communicates in writing, someone who has the choice to only write would chose to engage in this other, equally demanding profession. I suggest that in part it is because while writing about the Holocaust assures a witnessing of past events, actually leading students to consider the impact of such events on humanity is a gateway to engaging future generations in the ongoing obligation to eliminate conditions that made the Holocaust possible. It allows what might be heard only as the voice of despair to become the language of hope and change. It is the teacher, not the writer, who has the opportunity to connect subject matter to a personal and public ethics of care. The writer may pose the questions, but it is the teacher who must insist that students consider what those questions mean. What happens to a society when it finds worth only in certain cultural groups and then privileges those groups over others? How do people maintain any sense of dignity, continue to show kindness, or retain a spiritual core when all self-worth has been stripped from them, kindness comes in the form of a thin piece of cardboard slipped in a worn shoe, and children's ashes rise from a distant chimney? It is the teacher who can help students consider the far-reaching significance of such questions, for writers cannot know if the reader will follow their words to new depths. The amplification of Wiesel's genius is dependent not only on his message, but on how that message is received, taught, and expanded, giving the teacher the precarious, but necessary job of allowing for the hard questions and then moving those questions into community where they can change the direction not only of how we live but also of why we live. In avoiding this responsibility, teachers allow for the unintended consequence that students too may look away.

If we expect students to explicate Wiesel's story but not feel it or act on it, we solicit only minimal awareness and reaction rather than thoughtful consideration of possible long-term response. In walling a text off from feeling, we disparage the humanity of those whose story is told, the individual reading the story, and the community that would benefit from possible action called for in the story. We tell students that narrative is a powerful tool of the imagination, but fail to teach them it is also a mirror returning life as art and requiring careful deliberation and critique. It is not ironic, but just, that a story that takes place under circumstances allowing little opportunity for moral consideration on the part of its protagonist has the power to call into question the existential values that precede it. While a passive, technical reading of *Night* might elicit pity, an active, moral teaching of it has the power to evoke the empathy and discovery necessary for change. It gives readers the courage to ask what it is in a person that finds a need to shame, harm, or dehumanize others. If we desire to get to the transactive part of story that recreates and ameliorates, there is a need to bridge the gap between subject and action. We may note that the moral markers of humanity are invariable, but it is an empty observation if we fail to connect unacceptable events of the past to those equally unacceptable in the present. When we make these connections, students learn that upholding a basic moral code is an ongoing endeavor and a charge that all people of all times share. This is what teaching beyond the text can do, and, I suggest, what it should do.

There are other things to be done in the classroom to ensure students understand how inextricably their futures are linked to the lives and fates of others. Instead of relegating literature that deals with particular groups of people and historical issues of social injustice to a special unit or single week or month on the calendar, we must work with regularity to infuse our curriculum with like-minded texts that expose issues of intolerance, class, race, gender, and ethnic, sexual, or cultural differences. We must challenge the status quo that holds canonical curricula in place to recognize the enormous public benefit that comes from including more writers of color, stories depicting varying spiritual and religious beliefs, the thoughts of those who live and think differently, and the recounting of lives that have been routinely oppressed. We must also acknowledge the prejudices inherent in schooling and in our own classrooms that we as teachers help hold in place and that we have the power to topple, if only we are willing to take the chance. For Wiesel's message to be heard, felt, and actuated, it must be taught not in isolation but in concert with other literatures that force a voice of consciousness and require a moral uncovering. While none of this may be easy, it is necessary. "You must never lose faith, even when the sword hangs over your head," cries one of the doomed prisoners of *Night*.[8] For teachers, complacency is the figurative sword that threatens everything they profess to believe in: a better world, the right to think critically, wise choices, and a life of meaning for those entrusted to their care. Indifference is a perilous choice.

As I learned when I finally understood my own resistance to teaching *Night*, making the journey from merely exposing students to disturbing narrative to a pedagogy that asks them to examine and act on the moral issues that it reveals is risky at worst and difficult at best. When we ask students to move beyond the basic cognitive meaning and aesthetic value of a text to its moral implications, we must be prepared for the chaos of emotion, spirit, and self that follows. This is especially true of texts like *Night* that have the power to bring worlds crashing down. Teachers must think carefully about the attitude and approach they will take, making time to fully consider how to teach stories with acts so horrific that even as adults we cannot fully grasp the reality of them, while recognizing the equally important task of preventing students from plunging into hopelessness when such things are revealed. It is not easy to consider how narrative that raises issues of humanity by telling stories of unthinkable atrocities can be presented in a way that allows for the possibilities for good that may still arise from despair; but if this is not done, it becomes too easy for students and teacher alike to determine that the problems presented are beyond their ability to change, and inertia rather than moral discussion and action wins.

Complicating the choice to teach in a way that encourages moral scrutiny is the fact that students become vulnerable in new and troublesome ways. There exists the possibility of alienating family and friends whose belief systems may stand in opposition to the ones students begin to consider; issues of identity may be toppled, causing discomfort and even serious doubts about the self and others; and the familiar understandings of life might suddenly appear empty, leaving students open to depression and feelings of helplessness. To examine community, personal, and cultural beliefs is to challenge established values, and to challenge those values is to challenge the assumptions and intentions of the people who put the values in place. Such confrontation, as we know, is difficult for us even as adults; for a young person, it can feel overwhelming. There is no way around it: The road to moral awareness winds over rough ground. Those who choose this path will find it at turns both difficult and uncertain.

Teachers too are susceptible. They may be targets of students or parents who resist looking at texts and school as mediums of change.

Institutions that employ them, as well as the communities of which they are a part, might not feel it is appropriate for teachers to address matters of personal, societal, and political morality. While such an attitude is not as much of a problem for those who teach at the university, it can be quite a difficult position for those who teach in public schools; although I will suggest that in the current climate, even university professors feel the pressure of parents and watch groups that oppose classrooms as sites of moral questioning and social justice. Suggesting that existing attitudes toward ethnicity, class, faith, and other issues of the individual might propagate conditions that make an event like the Holocaust possible is heresy among the American public who prides itself on matters of character, righteousness, and free will. Exploring such delicate positioning leaves teachers open to attacks on many sides, an uncomfortable and unpleasant situation. Yet it is crucial to understand that if the big questions about life and the individual's as well as the community's moral responsibilities to it do not get asked in the classroom, they may never get asked at all.

In addition to accepting the risk and vulnerability inherent to students and teachers in classrooms that engage moral issues, we must also must acknowledge that teachers have a responsibility to understanding issues raised by texts like *Night* the best they can. They owe it to students to be well informed about pertinent historical and/or social matters that surround the text. They need to consider in advance aspects that will be unknown to students that will require explanation. They might need to be familiar with at least some of the available scholarship, whether it is particular to the text being studied or to the subject matter overall, in order to help students develop more meaningful and deeper understandings. Teachers must know how to lead students to and through materials that may be necessary for further deliberation, but this will not happen if they believe the focus on the text should remain outside the context from which it builds. In order to connect text that disrupts to a collective awareness of the issues it discloses, teachers must be prepared to see it not in isolation but in relation to the larger world from which it is drawn. Most of all, they owe it to students to have struggled with the very questions they want to consider.

Delving into the moral concerns evoked by a text means the teacher must also be willing to take a public stand. It is not sufficient to simply voice an opinion. This goes against so much of what we are told is wise to do in our current political climate, that many teachers have come to see it as an impossible option. However, it cannot be avoided if the teacher is to model citizens' rights to question and their obligation to act. This does not mean that students are punished or treated poorly for their views. However, it does mean recognizing that it is impossible to create morally aware communities without challenging the arrangements that oppress, subordinate, and undermine them. If we believe it is everyone's moral responsibility to stand with those who may be complete strangers so they may have the same human rights that we do, we must do more than simply tell; we must show. We instruct students that it is wrong to harm others, and with the recent attention to bullying we even insist they not allow others to harm them. Yet, if we are to convince them that to change the wrongs done to others they must stand at the side of those who are intimidated and persecuted, it is imperative they see we too are willing to stand. The same courage students are asked to have to alter the way they live in the world is also required of teachers, if the desire is to move from mere awareness of injustice to action that transforms such inequity.

Discovering that world changes only when communities of people are willing to take up the burden of others is not a particularly easy revelation to attend to or to accept. For many students, this idea is nothing more than a vague, abstract concept reported on the nightly news. While they may have already acted on the principles of being neither prey nor bully, the notion of taking responsibility for those who suffer but are unknown is a distant one. Such commitment moves beyond rejecting acts of aggression by not participating in them; it consists of evaluating whole value systems of belief and then determining if those systems are as equitable and caring as they claim to be. Confronting the denigration of other human beings means deciding how to act on what is revealed, and often that means having to give up something of ourselves in order that others may have something. The creation of a more humane world is difficult and not even particularly desirable when pitted against standards of happiness measured in terms of superiority and pleasure rather than altruism and sacrifice, which is why it becomes even more important to explore those standards when they present themselves.

To teach only to the aesthetic and cognitive aspects of a text like *Night* is to objectify it. In doing so we simply protect students and ourselves from actually having to do anything about the problems it presents. It is not sufficient to exclaim the quality of the narrative and then give only a nod to the issues it raises, no matter how worthy it is as a work of literature. We also must be prepared to explore difficult questions, feel the weight of the sorrow and anguish experienced by other human beings, and demand changes that prevent any further inhumanity to others, realizing full well that such action does not come easily or even clearly. If we want on-going, humane responses to the horrors that exist in the world, rather than temporary reactions that appear productive, but dissipate when the last word is read or the last terrorist has come to trial, then we must risk teaching in a way that encourages moral discussion, moral attention, and moral deeds. We must ally the devastating experiences of a Jewish boy named Eliezer with the private and public experiences of similarly dehumanizing situations that we can know and explore the limits and possibilities of each. It may not be the thing itself, but it is something tangible from which we can work.

Students may not be able to fully imagine the world Eliezer exists in when around him "everything [is] dancing a dance of death," but they will be able to relate to what he suffers when "[i]n the depth of [his] heart, [he feels] a great void," for they too have felt the pull of emptiness that lies always in wait. They may not be able to experience with him the incredible agony of "[s]ons [who] abandoned their fathers' remains without a tear," but they will recognize beyond a doubt what it means when he cries out "I was alone — terribly alone,"[9] for they have felt the sharp stab of loneliness and understand how it aches. By giving the students' own experiences of misery and anguish voice, we make them a part of the community that seeks to right the terrible wrongs done to others. By honoring the emotional pain of their own histories, we flex the intellectual muscles needed to assure that they do something to prevent further injury to others. Students have faced difficult events in their lives, in private and in public. Getting them to think and talk and write about these experiences helps them realize that release from the past comes only when we name the things we fear and then act on them. In naming, we dissolve the power fear has to define us; in acting, we work to ensure certain events do not happen again. Students learn, not only from Eliezer, but also from their own life histories, that while certain experiences may require us to move differently through life than we once imagined that difference does not have to mean defeat. By giving students ownership of morally charged texts through what they know of the moral situations of their own lives, we enable them to take part in public moral action and to understand the necessity and consequences of doing so.

In *Man's Search for Meaning*, Viktor Frankl reminds us that: "'Life' does not mean something vague, but something very real and concrete, just as life's tasks are also very real and concrete."[10] We make moral meaning more than just academic abstraction by recognizing that it is not just some "thing" that randomly happens and over which we have no control. People either take up or lay down moral burdens. By encouraging public discussion and critique, engaging feelings, and promoting research, study projects, and activities that move beyond the classroom door, we teach how to respond to prejudice and bias beyond vague awareness. Ironically, Frankl actually gives us a model for thinking about this when he describes the three stages prisoners appeared to go through if they survived the concentration camps: shock, apathy (blunted feelings, lack of emotion), and a way to live after liberation. Encountering a text like *Night* is shocking, and it should be. All caring readers go through stage one. It is the chance that a reader might become mired in stage two that should profoundly concern us; for in doing nothing, either for lack of understanding of what can be done or because we have separated our emotions so far from our intellect that we no longer feel anything, we ignore the possibilities of stage three. Like Eliezer, the reader must move beyond stage two and decide what can be done with such unimaginable pain. To choose otherwise is to perpetuate the silence Wiesel's words intend to break.

My first encounter with Eli Wiesel's *Night* happened many years ago, but it feels like only yesterday. At the time, two of my best friends were Jewish, and it just so happened that my favorite teacher that year also was. Yet somehow I made no association between them and the injustices I later came to realize people in their families must have suffered. Because *Night* had been presented to me mostly as a symbol of extraordinary literary feat and a shameful stain on history, rather than as a confrontation to the inhumanity of which we are all capable, it never occurred to me that my friends and my favorite teacher were probably experiencing their own moments of darkness. I had no idea of the burden I am now certain they carried. All around me, I heard occasional whispers of "Jew," but I made no connection between what those whispers meant and what these people I loved so well were enduring. I did not know that the code I had in friendship was a moral one that needed to be extended to the life I was living, and that I owed it to myself, to my friends, and to my community to speak against those whispers. How could I know? I was fifteen, and I was in need of those who could show me. And so I write now for these long-ago friends and a teacher who mattered so much to me. I write with the hope that their children's friends are not nearly so unaware as I was, and in faith that their grandchildren's friends will as a matter of course stand and speak out. In putting these words to paper, I honor the intent and genius of Eli Wiesel to bear witness, to end the indifference, and to invoke the memory.

Notes

1. Jean Chevalier and Alain Gheerbrant, ed. and John Buchanan-Brown, trans., *The Penguin Dictionary of Symbols* (New York: Penguin Books, 1996), 367.

2. Elie Wiesel, *The Night Trilogy* (New York: Hill & Wang, 1985), 119.

3. Ibid., 119.

4. See Michael Berenbaum and Abraham J. Peck, ed. *The Holocaust and History: The Known, The Unknown, The Disputed, and The Reexamined* (Bloomington: Indiana University Press, 1998).

5. Wiesel, *The Night Trilogy*, 106.

6. Ibid., 105; 72.

7. Ibid., 41.

8. Ibid., 40.

9. Ibid., 95; 76; 97; 75.

10. Viktor Frankl, *Man's Search for Meaning* (New York: Pocket Books, 1984), 98.

Afterword:
Night— the Memoir —
a Promise Fulfilled

Miriam Klein Kassenoff

It was May 5, 2005, and I was standing in the drizzling rain under grey skies with 18,000 other people in commemoration of the 60th year of the liberation of the infamous death camp, Auschwitz-Birkenau. We were listening to Elie Wiesel as he told the story of a young Talmudic student who last saw his little sister Tzippora and his mother in 1944, during the infamous selections of who goes to the "left" and who goes to the "right." He told how they slowly walked away from him, sent to the "right," while he and his father, Shlomo, were selected to go to the "left" by the SS Nazi officer. At that moment though, Elie did not know that his mother and sister were destined for the crematoria and that he would not ever see them again.

I looked around at the others who stood near me on that day in May in Birkenau as Wiesel told this story and watched their faces, riveted, as Wiesel's memories unfolded. I knew their transformations had begun, just as mine had the very first time I read Wiesel's memoir *Night*. I always knew I had come from Europe, and that our family, the Klein family, had escaped the horror of the Holocaust. I knew we were Hungarian by language and culture as I relished the favorite Hungarian dishes my mother made. I knew we were born in Czechoslovakia, and I knew there were nightmares and dreams I had of running and hiding and being fearful. But that is all I knew. I rarely heard my parents talking of the experience except in Yiddish, behind the closed door of their bedroom, and I certainly didn't learn about it in the history books in school in the 1950s and 1960s. Not until I found and read Elie Wiesel's memoir *Night* in the late 1960s did I finally know. The book and his story transformed me, for I was finally discovering my own history. There on page 21, describing the horrible train ride on the way to Auschwitz after the deportation from his town of Sighet, Wiesel writes, "The train stopped at Kaschau, a little town on the Czechoslovak frontier. We realized we were not going to stay in Hungary. Our eyes were opened but too late."

What Wiesel did not know at that moment was that the entire town of Kaschau (Kassa) was being liquidated of its population of 15,000 Jews, and that they were all immediately annihilated upon their arrival in Birkenau in May of 1944. I know this because I was born in Kassa and have spent most of my life since 1960, when I first read this passage in *Night*, devoted to not only researching my own past, but also becoming a Holocaust educator in public schools and universities throughout the United States. Yes, I had made this commitment after reading *Night*, after I finally understood that it could have been me on that train when the Jews of Kassa were boarded and taken to Birkenau. I believe this transition was part of my destiny. Since I was already a certified and degreed literature teacher, I began the journey by researching and developing lesson plan ideas for the memoir *Night*, never dreaming that one day I would actually have the unique experience of introducing Elie Wiesel to my university class! Let me explain this turn of events.

It was March, 2005, and I was in the midst of teaching a class at the University of Miami under the auspices of the Sue & Leonard Miller Judaic Studies Department and the School of Education. The course, Studying the Holocaust Through Film and Literature, is based on a resource/curriculum book I co-authored. Enrolled in this particular class were 20 students, representing a mix of ethnicities. Half of them had already read *Night* by Wiesel either during high school or through their religious upbringing in Hebrew School or Sunday School. I usually assign the book during the first class and ask that it be finished and ready for discussion by the midterm. Due to usual class delays and some unexpected visits from Holocaust survivors, we finally were going to have a thorough discussion on *Night* on Tuesday, March 29, 2005. To facilitate their reading, I prepared a detailed study guide that they used as they read Wiesel's memoir.

What followed next is any instructor's dream. I had a call the weekend previous to the proposed class discussion, from Dr. Sherri Porcelain, a professor of the Global Public Health Policy and Ethics Seminar. She had been contacted by the staff of MTV and advised of a pending visit to the University of Miami by Elie Wiesel who wanted to speak to university students about the present world situation of genocide in Darfur. This was to be part of a project MTV project called Stand-In, where a noted celebrity visits a university, surprises the class, and "stands-in" for the professor. The conditions are that no one knows of this impending visit except the professors and university officials for the purpose of keeping it a surprise for the students. Knowing of my course, Dr. Porcelain called me and asked that we join classes for this event; I, of course, agreed with much joy and anticipation.

During the appointed class time when Wiesel was due to come and surprise the class, my students had just asked me the question, "What does Elie Wiesel do with his life today?" Suddenly, as planned, there was a knock on the classroom door. I answered, "Come in," and as Elie Wiesel walked into the room, I said, "Ask him yourself!!!" Wiesel's visit to my classroom just at the moment we were reading and discussing his memoir *Night* had a most transformative effect on my students. This evident on their faces at that particular moment, and in the following class when we sat for two hours in a circle and discussed his visit, past life, present life, and effect on their lives.

Earlier, as mentioned, I had prepared a study guide for the students to help them read *Night*. This guide was very personal and included questions and comments that came deeply from inside me as I read Wiesel's haunting and unforgettable memoir. As I looked for threads of commonalities expressed by Wiesel, I came up with the following themes for students to explore and discuss: Silence (since the original title of the memoir in Yiddish was *Un di Velt Hot Geshvign* [*And the World Remained Silent*]); A Journey from Darkness to Light; The Loss of Innocence; Fathers and Sons: Sustaining Religious Faith During the Holocaust (Where was G-d?); and of course, the symbolism of the title, *Night*.

The discussion in the class the week after Wiesel's visit centered around these themes, and it was then that I began to hear the transformative effect the memoir had on my students. Was it a coincidence that this discussion occurred on April 5, 2005, and that the first day of the stages of liberation for Wiesel from the Buchenwald Concentration Camp occurred on April 5, 1945?

Soon after this once-in a lifetime experience, I had the opportunity to work with 25 public school teachers in the Miami area during a week's intensive summer institute at the University of Miami on the topic of teaching the Holocaust in the public school classroom. I assigned *Night,* just as I had done with the university students and the transformative effect of the book on them was equally evident. The following comments express how *Night* so deeply affected participants from each group:

> The reading of *Night* pulled me into the bottom of myself— it made me feel dead and alive at the same time. Now I breathe deeper and feel more than I ever did before. Elie Wiesel expressed to me what my own father could not say.— Rebecca Meeks, daughter of a Holocaust survivor.

> After reading *Night* and meeting Wiesel, it compels me to be even more involved in responsible social activism...,— Alissa Stein, seminar assistant.

> Reading *Night* gave me personal strength to face my own problems today. — Jay Jensen, seminar participant.

> Although the title "Night" is used to denote darkness and death, it also holds the possibility of life and redemption. The existence of night after all requires the existence of day; Wiesel's immersion in the darkness of "night" during the Holocaust necessarily promises the eventual dawn of day.— Jamie Adler, age 20, university student.

> I am not Jewish — nor am I a Judaic Studies major — I am a biology major studying to be a veterinarian.... I was given permission to take this course by Dr. Klein Kassenoff because I want to better understand humanity.... Although my main focus is animals, I am extremely concerned about the improper treatment of all God's creatures. Yesterday (when you spoke to our class) I felt as though you were speaking directly to me, as if you and I were the only ones in the room. Lately I have come across such racism ... that I began to feel there was no "good" in this world, making me feel helpless. You proved me wrong and enlightened me ... for YOU are good — and have motivated me to keep trying to make a difference...." — Yvette Witte, university student, age 19.

We often wonder when we teach if the students listening or just ingesting information for the credit and the grade? To read Jamie Adler's and

Yvette Witte's comments (and I purposely added their ages) is to give me hope that indeed not only is Wiesel transforming the lives of students through his powerful storytelling memoir efforts, but that we, as educators who have been already transformed by his work, are carrying on his messages and thereby affecting the lives of many learners of the future who then will go on to transform others.

In his recent memoir, *And the Sea Is Never Full*, Eli Wiesel includes a quote that inspired the title of this essay, *Night*— the Memoir — A Promise Fulfilled:

> Long ago, over there, far from the living, we told ourselves over and over that if we were to come out alive, we would devote every moment of our lives to denouncing by word and deed the cynicism and silence of mankind toward victims past and future. Convinced that the free world knew nothing of the cursed and evil kingdom where death reigned, we encouraged one another. The one among us who would survive would testify for all of us. He would speak and demand justice on our behalf; as our spokesman he would make certain that our memory would penetrate that of humanity. He would Do Nothing else. His days and nights would be devoted to telling the story. He would turn his entire life into a weapon for our collective memory; Thanks to Him, it would not be lost [From *And the Sea Is Never Full*].

I believe that through the power of his storytelling, in his memoir *Night,* Eli Wiesel has fulfilled his promise to his fellow Holocaust survivors and to those who perished. May they rest in peace.

About the Contributors

Deborah Lee Ames is an assistant professor of English at Palm Beach Atlantic University. Her scholarship focuses on Holocaust autobiographies. She wrote the entry on Wiesel, as well as the entry on the theme of survival, for the *Encyclopedia of Life Writing*. Her other publications concerning *Shoah* memoirs include *Women's Life Writing and Imagined Communities*, *Prose Studies*, and *a/b: Auto/Biography Studies*.

Alan L. Berger holds the Raddock Eminent Scholar Chair of Holocaust Studies and directs the Center for the Study of Values and Violence After Auschwitz at Florida Atlantic University. Among his books are *Children of Job* (SUNY, 1997) and *Second Generation Voices* (Syracuse University Press, 2001), which he and his wife Naomi co-edited.

Jacqueline Bussie is an assistant professor at Capital University, where she teaches courses in theology, ethics, religion and the arts, problem of evil studies, and Holocaust studies. Her dissertation is entitled "Laughter, Language, and Hope: Risibility as Resistance in Elie Wiesel's *Gates of the Forest*, Shusaku Endo's *Silence*, and Toni Morrison's *Beloved*." Her current research includes the book-length project *Laughter of the Oppressed*.

Rosemary Horowitz, an associate professor of English at Appalachian State University, is interested in Jewish literature and literacy and has written extensively about *yizker* books, memorial books published by Holocaust survivors. Her book-length work on the subject is *Literacy and Cultural Transmission in the Reading, Writing, and Rewriting of Jewish Memorial Books* (Austin & Winfield Press, 1998).

Miriam Klein Kassenoff is the education director at the Holocaust Memorial in Miami Beach, the director of the Teacher Institute on Holocaust Studies at the University of Miami, and the education specialist for Holocaust studies for Miami–Dade County Public Schools. With Anita Meyer Meinbach, she authored *Memories of the Night: A Study of the Holocaust* (Christopher-Gordon Publishers, 2004); *A Guide to the Holocaust* (Grolier Educational, 1997); and *Studying the Holocaust Through Film and Literature* (Christopher-Gordon Publishers, 2004).

Katherine Lagrandeur works as an archivist at the Library and Archives of Canada. Her dissertation, "Poétique de la perte dans l'oeuvre autobiographique d'Élie Wiesel," examines the poetics of loss in the autobiographical writings of Wiesel. Her ongoing research looks at the ways in which Wiesel articulates the relationship between God and Jews in a post–Holocaust context. Currently, she is rereading Wiesel's non-fiction to explore loss as it pertains to children and family.

Carole J. Lambert is a professor of English and the director of research at Azusa Pacific University. She is the author of *The Empty Cross: Medieval Hopes, Modern Futility in the Theater of Maurice Maeterlinck, Paul Claudel, August Strindberg, and George Kaiser* (Garland, 1990) and co-editor with William D. Brewer of *Essays on the Modern Identity* (Peter Lang, 2000). Her latest book, *Is God Man's Friend? Theodicy and Friendship in Elie Wiesel's Novels*, appeared in 2006 (Peter Lang). In addition, she has published articles in several journals.

Caren S. Neile is founding director of the South Florida Storytelling Project at Florida Atlantic University and a founding managing editor of *Storytelling, Self, Society: An Interdisciplinary Journal of Storytelling Studies*. She is the co-author of *Hidden: A Sister and Brother in Nazi Poland* (University of Wisconsin Press, 2002). She has chapters in *A Beginner's Guide to Storytelling* (National Storytelling Press, 2003), *Entremundos: New Perspectives on the Life and Work of Gloria Anzaldua* (2005), and *The Storytelling Classroom* (Teachers Ideas Press, forthcoming).

Elaine O'Quinn is an associate professor of English at Appalachian State University. She teaches courses in adolescent literature, issues in English studies, and the teaching of composition. Her research interests include identity development and its place in the English classroom and moral imagination as it applies to the teaching of literature and writing. Her work has appeared in numerous journals, including the *ALAN Review*, *Education and Culture*, and the *Journal of Adolescent and Adult Literacy*.

David Patterson holds the Bornblum Chair in Judaic Studies at the University of Memphis and is director of the University's Bornblum Judaic Studies Program. A winner of the Koret Jewish Book Award, he has published more than a hundred articles and book chapters on philosophy, literature, Judaism, and Holocaust studies, as well as more than two dozen books. His most recent book is *Hebrew Language and Jewish Thought* (Routledge Curzon, 2005).

Zoe Trodd teaches in the history and literature department at Harvard University. She published *Meteor of War: The John Brown Story,* with John Stauffer (Brandywine, 2004), and her book *American Protest Literature* is forthcoming with Harvard University Press. She has published numerous articles on American literature, history, and visual culture and is currently working on a book about contemporary slavery, with Kevin Bales, for Cornell University Press.

Graham B. Walker, Jr. is the associate dean for the Master of Divinity Degree Program and associate professor of theology at Mercer University. He has published numerous articles in various religious journals and has authored *Form, Style, and Qualitative Research for Graduate Theological Education in Asia, A Deep Rooted Faith*, and *Elie Weisel: A Challenge to Theology* (McFarland, 1988).

Index

Abraham (patriarch) 78–79, 93–96, 99, 115, 135–136, 185
The Accident 42, 47, 53–54, 77, 183–184, 193, 203–204
Adorno, Theodor 132, 146
Against Silence 110
Aggadah 4, 6, 11, 71, 76, 102, 104, 107, 109, 113, 115–118
Akeda 11, 74, 93–98
All Rivers Run to the Sea 73, 84
Ambiguity 10, 39, 55
And the Sea Is Never Full 73, 84, 93, 230
Ani Ma'amin 11, 73, 78, 80, 82–83, 85, 95, 96
Ariel (character) 42–43, 176
Azriel (character) 168–173, 202, 205

Baal Shem Tov 102–103, 119, 125, 127
Bakhtin, Mikhail 15, 18, 20, 30, 32
A Beggar in Jerusalem 29, 41, 46, 112, 115–116, 131, 186–187, 202
Benjamin, Walter 3, 18, 68, 197–198
Berenbaum, Michael 8, 80
Berish (character) 81–85
Bontchek (character) 174–175
Booth, David 9
Brown, Robert McAfee 6, 8, 80, 82, 201–203
Buber, Martin 30, 106–107, 116, 149
Buxbaum, Yitzhak 4–5, 125

Cargas, Harry James 8, 72
Characters *see under* individual character names

David (character) 41–42, 46–47
Davis, Colin 8, 38, 54, 86
Dawn 40, 53–54, 203
Dawson (character) 40–41

Derrida, Jacques 65
Des Pres, Terrence 164

Elhanan (character) 50, 108, 115
Eliach, Yaffa 129
Elisha (character) 40–41, 54–55
Ethics and Memory 17

Fackenheim, Emil 91, 117–118, 147
family 58
The Fifth Son 42, 109–110, 173, 176–170
Fine, Ellen 8
The Forgotten 50, 108, 115, 128
Four Hasidic Masters 9, 125
Frankl, Viktor 224

The Gates of the Forest 11, 51–52, 71, 102, 111, 124, 131, 136, 139, 142, 145, 152, 193, 201–204, 208
Gavriel (character) 52–53, 111, 124, 136–138, 140–151, 193–194
Golem 109
Greenberg, Irving Rabbi 10, 67, 69, 147, 204
Gregor (character) 51–53, 136–137, 141–142, 145–146, 148–150, 193–194, 202

Haggadah 109–110, 173
Hasidism 5, 102, 116, 124–129, 139, 141, 149
Hayim (character) 49

Indifference 44, 78–79, 85, 118, 126, 185, 192–193, 220, 225
Isaac (patriarch) 11, 23, 74, 78–80, 93–99, 112, 135–137

Jacob (patriarch) 78–80, 99, 119, 185
A Jew Today 57, 67, 108

Job 71, 77–82, 143–144, 185
The Judges 43, 115, 184, 189, 190

The Kabbalah 11, 80, 85, 102, 103, 116, 125, 163, 207–208
Kabbalastic 104, 116, 114
Kathleen (character) 42
Katriel (character) 86, 116, 131
Kirshenblatt-Gimlett, Barbara 4, 198
Kolbert, Jack 8, 38, 52

Langer, Lawrence 10, 60, 62, 69
Laughter 124–125, 130, 135–138, 140, 143, 148–152

Madness 48–49, 52, 108, 118, 138, 189, 191
Maggid: of Mezeritch 57, 103, 117; role of 71, 198; Wiesel as 71, 102, 107, 112, 116, 118–119, 206, 208
Malkiel (character) 50–51, 115
Mauriac, François 8, 17, 38, 157, 163
Memory 4, 9, 12, 32, 41, 48–50, 54, 90, 108–109, 115, 131, 160, 164, 168, 170–172, 176–179, 184, 201, 203, 205; as theme 12, 115, 201
Messengers of God 8–9, 23, 93–94, 104
Messiah 78, 111–114, 119, 130, 141, 148, 170, 187, 189, 206
Michael (character) 44, 110, 183, 189–190, 204
The Midrash 4, 6, 11, 71–72, 90–91, 102, 104–107, 109, 111, 114–115, 118–119
Midrashic 11, 59, 72, 86, 90–91, 95–97, 99, 104, 109, 114, 118
Moshe the Beadle (character) 19, 23, 26, 30, 73–74, 150
Moshe the Mystic (character) 168–173, 203–204

Nahman (Nachman), Rebbe 7, 11, 71, 111–112, 114, 125–135, 137–146, 148–151, 191
Night 7, 11, 15, 16, 17, 18, 23, 25–27, 72–77, 84, 94–98, 108, 139, 156–157, 162–167, 173, 178, 217
Night Trilogy 53–54
Nobel Prize 1, 71, 77, 123, 182, 184, 203, 213

The Oath 12, 44, 112–113, 168, 171–173, 200, 202, 204–205

Paltiel (character) 45, 113, 205–206
Pedro (character) 49, 110, 189–190

Raphael (character) 48–49, 55, 114–115, 190
Razziel (character) 43, 115–116, 184, 190–191
Roskies, David 5, 9, 198
Rubenstein, Richard 71

Sarah (character) 193, 47–48, 77, 93
Schneerson, Menachem Mendel 106
Schram, Peninnah 4–5, 198–200
Sholem Aleichem 8–9
Sibelman, Simon 8
Sighet 17, 19, 71, 74, 107, 117–119, 161, 165, 202, 227
Silence 27, 29–30, 64, 69, 71, 73, 75, 84, 97–102, 108, 113, 119, 132–134, 143, 148, 161–179, 186, 202, 208, 224, 230
Somewhere a Master 9, 102
Souls on Fire 8–9, 126, 138, 205–207
Storytelling: African American 21; Jewish 4–5, 9, 11, 109; literary 8–9, 99, 102, 116, 157–158; Native American 18, 20–24, 28, 31–32
Suffering 57

The Talmud 6, 81, 102, 107, 111, 116, 141, 189, 204
Talmudic 4, 9
The Testament 12, 45, 113, 205
Testimony 11, 29, 53, 83–84, 98–99, 118, 145, 157, 169–172, 201
Torah 4–6, 76, 96, 102, 104–106, 111, 116–119, 125, 151, 161
The Town Beyond the Wall 44, 110, 183–184, 189–190, 200, 204–205
Trauma 25, 62–63, 96–97, 182
Trial of God 78, 81, 83, 85
Twilight 48, 114, 118, 187–190

Un di Velt Hot Geshvign 7, 16–17, 30, 54, 157, 228

Wiesel, Elie: childhood 19; education 4, 6–8, 162; father (Shlomo) 73; influences on writing 6–8, 38, 52, 102; as maggid 71, 102, 107, 112, 116, 118–119, 206, 208; mother (Sarah) 73, 226; sister (Tzippora) 73, 226; works *see under* individual titles

Yiddish: literature and language 6–8, 198; Wiesel's memoir 16, 54, 98, 154, 157, 228

Zalman or The Madness of God 117
Zohar 4, 85, 105–106, 108–109